The Long Shadow of the Past

The process of coming to terms with its National Socialist past has been a long and difficult one in Austria. It is only over the past thirty years that the country's view of its role during the Third Reich has shifted decisively from that of victimhood to complicity, prompted by the Waldheim affair of 1986–1988. Austria's writers, filmmakers, and artists have been at the center of this process, holding up a mirror to the country's present and drawing attention to a still disturbing past.

    This book undertakes close readings of key contemporary Austrian literary texts, films, and memorials that treat the legacy of Nazism and the Holocaust. The analysis focuses on texts by Robert Schindel, Elfriede Jelinek, and Anna Mitgutsch, documentary films by Ruth Beckermann and by Margareta Heinrich and Eduard Erne, as well as recent memorial projects in Vienna, examining what these reveal about the evolving memory culture in contemporary Austria. Aimed at a broad readership, the book will be a key reference point for university teachers, undergraduates, and postgraduates engaged in scholarship on contemporary Austrian literature, film, and visual culture, and for general readers interested in confrontations with the National Socialist past in the Austrian context.

Studies in German Literature, Linguistics, and Culture

The Long Shadow of the Past

Contemporary Austrian Literature, Film, and Culture

Katya Krylova

Rochester, New York

Copyright © 2017 Katja Krylova

All Rights Reserved. Except as permitted under current legislation, no part of this work may be photocopied, stored in a retrieval system, published, performed in public, adapted, broadcast, transmitted, recorded, or reproduced in any form or by any means, without the prior permission of the copyright owner.

First published 2017 by Camden House
Reprinted in paperback 2020

Camden House is an imprint of Boydell & Brewer Inc.
668 Mt. Hope Avenue, Rochester, NY 14620, USA
www.camden-house.com
and of Boydell & Brewer Limited
PO Box 9, Woodbridge, Suffolk IP12 3DF, UK
www.boydellandbrewer.com

Paperback ISBN-13: 978-1-64014-073-8
Paperback ISBN-10: 1-64014-073-5
Hardcover ISBN-13: 978-1-57113-591-9
Hardcover ISBN-10: 1-57113-591-X

Library of Congress Cataloging-in-Publication Data

Names: Krylova, Katya.
Title: The long shadow of the past : contemporary Austrian literature, film, and culture / Katya Krylova.
Description: Rochester, New York : Camden House, 2017. | Series: Studies in German literature, linguistics, and culture | Includes bibliographical references and index.
Identifiers: LCCN 2017008224 | ISBN 9781571139399 (hardcover : alk. paper) | ISBN 1571139397 (hardcover : alk. paper)
Subjects: LCSH: Holocaust, Jewish (1939–1945), in literature. | Holocaust, Jewish (1939–1945), in motion pictures. | Holocaust, Jewish (1939–1945)—Austria. | Waldheim, Kurt—Influence.
Classification: LCC PN56.H55 K76 2017 | DDC 830.9/3584360522—dc23 LC record available at https://lccn.loc.gov/2017008224

For my parents, Elena and Victor

Contents

List of Illustrations	ix
Acknowledgments	xi
List of Abbreviations	xv
Introduction: Confrontations with the Past	1
1: Melancholy Journeys to the Past: The Films of Ruth Beckermann	25
2: Reconstructing a Home: Nostalgia in Anna Mitgutsch's *Haus der Kindheit*	49
3: Silencing the Past: Margarete Heinrich's and Eduard Erne's *Totschweigen* and Elfriede Jelinek's *Rechnitz (Der Würgeengel)*	63
4: Historicizing the Waldheim Affair: Robert Schindel's *Der Kalte*	79
5: Missing Images: Memorials and Memorial Projects in Contemporary Vienna	96
Conclusion: Living with Shadows	135
Notes	143
Bibliography	173
Index	191

Illustrations

Fig. 1. Ulrike Lienbacher, *Idylle*, 2002.   103

Fig. 2. Ulrike Lienbacher, *Idylle*, 2002, on the wall of Brandmayergasse 27, Vienna.   104

Fig. 3. Maria Theresia Litschauer, *transcription*, 2010.   106

Fig. 4. Maria Theresia Litschauer, *transcription*, 2010, on the wall of the Thury-Hof, Marktgasse 3–7, Vienna.   107

Fig. 5. *The Vienna Project* stencil spray.   111

Fig. 6. Vienna Regional Court building.   114

Fig. 7. Detail from Catrin Bolt's *Alltagsskulptur* in the Hermann-Gmeiner-Park in Vienna's first district.   119

Fig. 8. Further detail from Catrin Bolt's *Alltagsskulptur* in the Hermann-Gmeiner-Park.   119

Fig. 9. Platform five on the Vienna West Station, with one of Catrin Bolt's *Alltagsskupturen* (everyday sculptures) visible on the platform.   121

Fig. 10. Detail from Catrin Bolt's *Alltagsskuptur* (everyday sculpture) on platform five of the Vienna West station.   121

Fig. 11. Ruth Beckermann, *The Missing Image* installation positioned in front of Alfred Hrdlicka's figure of the "street-washing Jew."   125

Fig. 12. An explanatory plaque, attached to the side of Ruth Beckermann's *The Missing Image* installation.   128

Fig. 13. Iris Andraschek and Hubert Lobnig, *Turnertempel Erinnerungsort*, 2011.   130

Fig. 14. Detail from Olaf Nicolai, *Denkmal für die Verfolgten der NS-Militärjustiz*, 2014.   141

Fig. 15. Olaf Nicolai, *Denkmal für die Verfolgten der NS-Militärjustiz*, 2014.   142

Photographs by author.

Acknowledgments

THIS BOOK WOULD NOT HAVE BEEN POSSIBLE without the generous support of the Leverhulme Trust, through their Early Career Fellowship scheme. I was very fortunate to be awarded this fellowship for a research project that would result in this monograph. The research fellowship was held in the Department of German Studies at the University of Nottingham between 2012 and 2015, which provided a stimulating environment within which to work on this project. I am grateful to colleagues in the Department of German Studies at Nottingham, in particular Dirk Göttsche, Nicola McLelland, Franziska Meyer, Rachel Palfreyman, Matthias Uecker, and Roger Woods, for their support and engagement with my project. Membership of the Memory Studies and the Politics of Memory research cluster, based in the Department of German at Nottingham, allowed me to workshop ideas that would eventually find their way into this book, and the German Studies Research Seminar provided a great forum for giving papers and soliciting valuable feedback from colleagues. Developing and teaching a final-year undergraduate course at Nottingham on "Confronting the Past in Contemporary Austrian Literature and Film" and supervising dissertations arising from the same, allowed me to clarify my thinking on issues of Austrian contemporary culture with groups of enthusiastic students, eager to learn more about a country most associated in the Anglophone world with *The Sound of Music*.

Two research visits to Vienna, Austria, undertaken in the summers of 2014 and 2015, made possible with the generous support of the Leverhulme Trust, allowed me to carry out vital research in libraries and archives and also to meet some of the writers and artists who are the focus of my monograph. I am most grateful to the staff in the Documentation Center for Modern Austrian Literature Vienna (where I worked extensively with the Newspaper Cuttings Collection) and at the Austrian National Library for their helpful assistance. Working on living writers and filmmakers offers a wonderful opportunity to interact with the "subjects" of one's research. I am greatly indebted to Ruth Beckermann for being such a generous correspondent and conversation partner, for her hospitality in Vienna, and for being a wonderful special guest at the "Contemporary Austrian Literature, Film, and Culture" international conference that I organized at the University of Nottingham with the generous sponsorship of the Leverhulme Trust and the Austrian Cultural

Forum London in 2015. Thank you very much also to Frederick Baker for the generous supply of his books and for sharing his memories as an eyewitness in the 2000 anti-Haider protests in the context of a screening of his film *Widerstand in Haiderland* (Resistance in Haider Country) at the same conference in Nottingham. I would like to thank the conference committee, the keynote speakers, special guests, and all delegates, for their participation in the conference and for the warm exchanges that have extended beyond the confines of the three-day conference to form a veritable community of contemporary Austrian studies scholars around the world. Thanks are also due to Robert Schindel for taking the time to meet and talk about his most recent novel with me at his *Stammcafe* in Vienna in August 2015. I am grateful to Karen Frostig for the conversation we had at a performance connected to her *Vienna Project* in the summer of 2014. Thank you to Eduard Erne for patiently answering my questions and for his interest in my work. Thanks are also due to Nora Höglinger at Kunst im öffentlichen Raum Wien (Art in Public Space Vienna), who kindly met with me and provided me with all manner of leaflets and publications about recent memorial projects sponsored by the organization.

I am fortunate to have been able to present my research at numerous conferences in the United Kingdom and abroad, including the Modern Language Association Annual Convention held in Boston, Massachusetts, in 2013; the German Studies Association conference in Washington, DC, in 2015; the Association for German Studies in Great Britain and Ireland conference, held in Manchester in 2014; the Women in German Studies conferences in Sheffield in 2013 and Cambridge in 2014; and the European Cinema Forum, held in Edinburgh in 2013. National and international networks provided further opportunities, through their annual symposia, to gain valuable new perspectives on my research from scholars working both in related and diverging disciplines. These included the German Screen Studies Network, based at King's College London; the Picturing Austrian Cinema research symposium, based at St. John's College, University of Cambridge; the Domestic Imaginaries Network; the AHRC-funded research group Reverberations of War in Germany and Europe since 1945 at University College London; the Transnational Holocaust Memory network at the University of Leeds; the Genre Studies network at the University of Birmingham; the Embodiments Research Group based at the University of Liverpool.

I am grateful also to Sarah Bowden, Martin Brady, Erica Carter, Ben Schofield, and Catherine Smale in the Department of German at King's College London, where I held a Teaching Fellowship in 2016. Their collegiality and support provided a welcome diversion as I approached the final stages of work on this study. I would like to thank Andrew Webber of Churchill College, Cambridge, who kindly commented on the earliest drafts of research proposals that would eventually develop into the Leverhulme-funded project and result in this book. I would also like to thank Jim Walker at Camden House for expertly seeing this monograph through to its completion and for his patience in answering my many queries. I am grateful to the Leverhulme Trust and to the University of Nottingham for supporting the publication of this book through their generous contributions to the publishing subvention.

Finally, my debt of gratitude to my parents, Elena and Victor, is one that I can never repay. I am deeply grateful for their unconditional love and support and for creating an environment in which this study could be completed. It is to them that this book is dedicated.

Earlier versions of material in this volume have appeared elsewhere. Parts of chapter 1 appeared in "Melancholy Journeys in the Films of Ruth Beckermann," *Leo Baeck Institute Year Book* 59, no. 1 (2014): 249–66; parts of chapter 3 in "Genre and Memory in Margareta Heinrich's and Eduard Erne's *Totschweigen* and Elfriede Jelinek's *Rechnitz (Der Würgeengel)*," in *Genre Trajectories: Identifying, Mapping, Projecting*, edited by Garin Dowd and Natalia Rulyova (Basingstoke: Palgrave Macmillan, 2015), 66–85; and parts of chapter 4 in "Disturbing the Past: The Representation of the Waldheim Affair in Robert Schindel's *Der Kalte*," in *Reverberations of Nazi Violence in Germany and Beyond: Disturbing Pasts*, edited by Stephanie Bird, Mary Fulbrook, Julia Wagner, and Christiane Wienand (London: Bloomsbury Academic, 2016), 107–23. I wish to thank Oxford University Press, Palgrave Macmillan, Bloomsbury Academic, as well as the editors of these works, for their kind permission to reprint.

Katya Krylova
West Bridgford, Nottinghamshire
March 2017

Abbreviations

DK   *Der Kalte* (The Cold One, 2013)

H   *Homemad(e)* (2001)

HdK   *Haus der Kindheit* (House of Childhood, 2000)

HoC   *House of Childhood* (2006, translation by David Dollenmayer of *Haus der Kindheit*)

PB   *Die papierene Brücke* (The Paper Bridge, 1987)

R   *Rechnitz (Der Würgeengel)* (Rechnitz: The Exterminating Angel, 2009)

T   *Totschweigen* (Deathly Silence; in English as *A Wall of Silence*, 1994)

WR   *Wien retour* (Return to Vienna, 1983)

Translations are mine, unless otherwise indicated.

Introduction: Confrontations with the Past

What happens when we forget to remember?
—Karen Frostig, *The Vienna Project* (2013–14)

On May 24, 2016, something extraordinary happened. Austria was on the front pages of several British national newspapers, including the *Times* and the *Guardian*.[1] The reason was the narrow victory of Alexander Van der Bellen, an independent candidate and former leader of *Die Grünen* (Austrian Green Party), against the *Freiheitliche Partei Österreich* (FPÖ, Austrian Freedom Party) candidate, Norbert Hofer, in the second round of the Austrian presidential election, held on May 22, 2016. Van der Bellen had won the election by the narrowest of margins, by only 30,863 votes, getting 50.3 percent of the total vote, with Hofer polling at 49.7 percent.[2] The election was effectively decided by the 759.968 postal voters,[3] making up almost 14 percent of the electorate,[4] whose votes were counted on the day after the Sunday, May 22, election. For an Austrian presidential election to be decided by postal votes in this way was a highly unusual occurrence. Ordinarily, the winning candidate is able to gain enough of a majority for the postal vote count on the following day to be largely a formality, with the winner announced already on the Sunday evening. On this occasion, the end of the election day saw Hofer lead at 51.9 percent (with Van der Bellen at 48.1 percent),[5] while pollsters from the SORA Institute for Social Research and Consulting predicted the final result (including postal votes), to stand at circa 50 percent and 50 percent for the respective candidates, with everything still to play for.[6] The presidential election saw the candidates of the ruling political parties, the Social Democratic Party of Austria and the Austrian People's Party, eliminated in the first round, with Norbert Hofer, the far-right Austrian Freedom Party candidate, winning this first heat with 35,1 percent of the votes.[7] It was an election that polarized the country, rural against urban areas, male voters against female voters, young against old, and divided those communities where the vote reflected the national picture of a near fifty-fifty split of votes for the two candidates.[8]

Van der Bellen's narrow victory left liberals in Austria, and in Europe more generally, breathing a sigh of relief that the election of the first far-right head of state in contemporary Western Europe had been averted, "edged out in knife-edge Austrian poll,"[9] and that Austria had "pulled back from the far-right abyss."[10] However, the relief was very short-lived. No sooner had Van der Bellen made his first speech as president-elect on May 23, 2016, than accusations were being raised in the Austrian Freedom Party about possible electoral malpractice, with a formal suit submitted to the *Verfassungsgerichtshof* (Constitutional Court) on June 8, 2016.[11] While, initially, it did not seem that these allegations could gain much traction, on July 1, 2016, Austria's Constitutional Court announced that the final round of the presidential election would be rerun, largely due to early counting of postal votes in a number of municipalities, affecting 77,926 votes in total.[12] Considering the narrow margin by which Van der Bellen had won, it was decided that this could have altered the outcome of the election. The Constitutional Court also criticized the premature announcement of results via social media.[13] The date for the rerun of the presidential election was later set by the Austrian Council of Ministers as October 2, 2016.[14] The saga did not end there, however, as the already postponed rerun of the final election round was further delayed in September 2016 due to faulty glue on postal ballot envelopes, a case that became known as "Klebergate" (glue gate).[15] The final election round was thereby once again postponed, to December 4, 2016. During this time, the election campaign continued to polarize the country, with Norbert Hofer coming under fire for using the words "So wahr mir Gott helfe" (So help me God; a religious affirmation, which may be spoken as part of the presidential inaugural oath)[16] on his election posters, thereby drawing criticism both for his assumption of electoral victory and, from church leaders, for misusing religion for political gain.[17] A video, originally posted on Alexander Van der Bellen's Facebook page, in which an 89-year-old Austrian Holocaust survivor, identified only as "Gertrude," criticized the divisive rhetoric of the Austrian Freedom Party and urged voters "vernünftig [zu] wählen" (to vote sensibly), was viewed over three million times by the December election.[18] Moreover, endorsements from leading politicians, such as the outgoing Socialist president, Heinz Fischer, as well as the leader of the conservative Österreichische Volkspartei (ÖVP, Austrian People's Party), Reinhold Mitterlehner, arguably turned the tide in Van der Bellen's favor.[19] In this final round of a yearlong election process, the independent candidate Alexander Van der Bellen substantially increased his majority, defeating Hofer by 348,231 votes with a 7 percent margin (in contrast to 30,863 votes in the May election), to gain 53.8 percent of the total vote, with Norbert Hofer polling 46.2 percent of the vote.[20] Many political observers, both in Austria and abroad, once again breathed "a sigh of relief" following Van der Bellen's election win.[21] As a number of commentators noted, the far-right threat had once again been "staved off"[22]—the question is for how long.

"The Waldheim Affair Changed Austria from the Ground Up"[23]

The 2016 Austrian presidential election reopened the familiar fault lines, between left and right, between cosmopolitan attitudes versus "Österreich zuerst" (Austria first),[24] that had emerged in Austrian society since another Austrian presidential election took place almost exactly thirty years ago, namely the presidential election that saw Dr. Kurt Waldheim, the Austrian People's Party candidate, elected president on June 8, 1986. The 1986 presidential election gave rise to what became known as the Waldheim affair of 1986–88, during the course of which it emerged that the former UN Secretary General (1972–81) had lied about the extent of his involvement in the Nazi war machine, which did not stop him becoming president. The Waldheim affair marked a turning point in Austrian society, sparking the beginning of a belated process of coming to terms with the country's National Socialist past. The Waldheim affair saw a young generation of artists and intellectuals (among them many of the writers and filmmakers who are the focus of this study) lead a protest movement against the presidential candidate, who had first tried to whitewash his Nazi past in his autobiography and then, when it was eventually brought to light, denied any wrongdoing, asserting that he, like hundreds of thousands of Austrians in the Second World War, had "only done his duty" as a soldier.[25] Many of those dismayed by Waldheim's election campaign were involved in the formation of the *Republikanischer Club–Neues Österreich* (Republican Club–New Austria) in 1986, which aimed to shed light on and prompt an engagement with Austria's Nazi past:

> Der "Republikanischer Club–Neues Österreich" wurde gegründet. Sein erstes Ziel: Wir—in Österreich—hätten die Aufgabe, die Vergangenheit aufzuhellen, wir selbst, wir in Österreich, unsere Vergangenheit, von der wir kaum mehr zu wissen hatten, dass es einen gewissen Hitler (auch Österreicher) und eine Befreiung gegeben hatte, 1945 durch die Alliierten, 1955 von den Alliierten . . . Nazi? KZ? Pogrom? Vernichtung? Eichmann? Kaltenbrunner? (beide auch Österreicher) . . . na ja.[26]

> [The "Republican Club–New Austria" was founded. Its primary aim: We—in Austria—had the task, of shedding light on the past, we ourselves, we Austrians, on our past, where we hardly remembered anymore that there had been a certain Hitler (also an Austrian) and a liberation in 1945 *by* the Allies, in 1955 *from* the Allies . . . Nazi? Concentration camp? Pogrom? Annihilation? Eichmann? Kaltenbrunner? (both of them also Austrians) . . . indeed.]

The club's mascot became a wooden horse (designed by architect Alfred Hrdlicka), clothed in an SA cap (added to the design by caricaturist Manfred Deix), which served to draw attention to the "Trojan horse" of Waldheim's Nazi past, "ein Holzpferd, ein trojanisches, aus seinem Bauch sollten die Gespenster der Vergangenheit kriechen" (a wooden horse, a Trojan one, the ghosts of the past should creep out of its stomach).[27] Waldheim, who had repeatedly denied having been a member of the SA, was found, during the course of the 1986 election campaign, to have been part of the *SA-Reiterstandarte* (SA riding unit) between 1937–39, while a student at the Consular Academy in Vienna.[28] This was parodied by then Austrian Chancellor Fred Sinowatz as follows: "Wir nehmen zur Kenntnis, daß Waldheim nicht bei der SA war, sondern sein Pferd bei der SA gewesen ist" (Let us then register the fact that Waldheim was not in the SA, but his horse was).[29] Hrdlicka's wooden horse became a key fixture of the Republican Club's demonstrations against Kurt Waldheim, both during the election campaign and during the course of Waldheim's presidency, "accompanying" the president, for example, on visits to the Salzburg Festival and to the Vatican.[30] Subsequently, the symbolic value of the mascot has repeatedly been acknowledged in public exhibitions in Austria.[31] It was most recently exhibited in the Wien Museum (Vienna Museum) between March and May 2016, in conjunction with a series of events marking the thirtieth anniversary of the Waldheim affair.[32]

The so-called Waldheim affair lasted from the 1986 election campaign until February 1988 when an International Historians' Commission, set up to investigate Waldheim's wartime record, had concluded that Waldheim could not be deemed a war criminal as such, but that he "clearly must have known" about crimes perpetrated in *Wehrmacht* units in the Balkans and in Thessaloniki, where he had served as an aide-de-camp.[33] However, the Waldheim affair was less about Waldheim himself than about the processes that his candidacy and presidency unleashed. For some Austrians, as Barbara Tóth and Hubertus Czernin argue,[34] Waldheim was a proxy "father figure" through which to confront one's own family history: "Viele von ihnen setzten sich mit ihm anstelle ihrer Großväter oder Väter auseinander, weil auch in ihren Familien über die eigene Kriegsvergangenheit nicht gesprochen wurde." (Many of them grappled with him rather than with their own fathers or grandfathers, as the war past was not spoken about in their families.)[35] For the first time in the history of the Austrian Second Republic, "ein geradezu verstörender Generationenkonflikt" (a well-nigh disturbing generational conflict) broke out.[36] The so-called *Wehrmachtsgeneration* (Wehrmacht generation) was defensive about what it saw as the "defamation" of their generation (who, like Waldheim, had "only done their duty"), both by young liberals and intellectuals in Austria and by foreign powers, euphemistically referred to as the "Ostküste" (East Coast). For Waldheim's supporters, this was anti-Semitic code for "gewissen Kreisen in Amerika aus dem jüdischen Element" (certain circles in America from the Jewish element), as the nascent Austrian Freedom Party politician Jörg Haider put it in an interview conducted during Waldheim's election campaign.[37] Nevertheless, the Waldheim affair was of profound significance for the Second Republic, with commentators subsequently calling the events of 1986–88 "einen Epochenbruch in der Geschichte Österreichs nach 1945" (an epochal break in Austria's history after 1945),[38] "der Beginn einer vergangenheitspolitischen Zäsur in Österreich, die . . . bis heute noch nicht abgeschlossen ist" (the beginning of a historical-political caesura in Austria . . . that has not been completed to this day),[39] and "das Ende der Nachkriegszeit" (the end of the postwar era), as the writer Robert Schindel has asserted.[40]

The Waldheim affair destroyed the Second Republic's founding myth of having been "Hitler's first victim," as stated in the Moscow Declaration of 1943.[41] Waldheim's assertion of having done his duty raised questions regarding to whom this duty was performed. One had to conclude that this duty was to the Wehrmacht, the same army that, according to the Austrian postwar *Lebenslüge* (life-sustaining lie), had "invaded" Austria in 1938. As the historian Walter Manoschek has asserted "Waldheim war insofern wichtig, als er durch sein Verhalten und seine Aussagen ungewollt den österreichischen Opferstatus in Frage gestellt hat." (Waldheim was important insofar as that, through his behavior and his statements, he unintentionally called Austria's victim status into question.)[42] Thirty years on from the beginning of Waldheim affair, the news weekly *profil*, which, through the work of its investigative journalist Hubertus Czernin, was instrumental in bringing Waldheim's past to light thirty years earlier, recalled the role it had played in the Waldheim affair with a title story entitled "Als Österreich erwachsen wurde" (When Austria grew up).[43] Here, the Waldheim affair is presented as a shift away from the false naiveté of a nation seeing itself as a victim of National Socialism, rather than as an active accomplice and perpetrator. While Austrian historians differ in their analysis of the effects that Waldheim's candidacy and presidency had on Austria,[44] eyewitnesses and artists are often effusive in their assessment, viewing the Waldheim affair as "transformative," as can be gleaned from the titles of edited volumes and cover stories.[45] For the documentary filmmaker Ruth Beckermann, the fallout from the Waldheim affair constituted nothing less than the second foundation of the Republic of Austria.[46]

What most incensed intellectuals and liberals about Waldheim was not his Nazi past per se (which, as Waldheim rightly pointed out, was not dissimilar to that of hundreds of thousands of Austrians of his generation), but rather Waldheim's continued inability to see any wrong-doing in his actions more than forty years earlier. In Waldheim, the eyewitness and journalist Christa Zöchling saw the hyperbolic embodiment of the first-victim myth: "Trieb hier doch jemand auf die Spitze, was Millionen Kriegsteilnehmer, was Väter und Großväter, Mütter und Großmütter als Lebenslüge in sich trugen" (Someone was carrying to extremes the life-sustaining lie that millions of those who had participated in the war, fathers and grandfathers, mothers and grandmothers, contained within themselves).[47] The protest movement that sprung up in opposition to Waldheim became known as "das andere Österreich" (the other Austria), a protest movement that, according to leading commentators and eyewitnesses, would not have been possible without Waldheim.[48] In her film, *Die papierene Brücke* (The Paper Bridge, 1987), which will be discussed further in chapter 1 of this study, Ruth Beckermann documents the vehement protests that took place for and against Waldheim at the height of the election campaign in Vienna in 1986. The generation of Austrian intellectuals, liberals, and artists, which protested Waldheim's candidacy and election, was instrumental in the formation of a civil society and oppositional culture in Austria, as Dagmar Lorenz has highlighted, asserting that "the political activism instigated by the Waldheim affair was the first step toward an Austrian civil society."[49] The formation of this civil society allowed a formidable protest culture to develop in Austria, which notably came into its own during the *Lichtermeer* (sea of lights) demonstration of 1993 against the *Ausländervolksbegehren* (anti-immigration referendum) instigated by the Austrian Freedom Party in 1992, and subsequently, in the protests against the Austrian Freedom Party's entry into the coalition government in 2000.[50] The latter demonstrations are treated in Ruth Beckermann's film *Homemad(e)* (2001), which will be discussed in chapter 1 of this book.

The significance of the events of 1986–88 in Austria for writers and artists, who were in the formative stage of their creative careers and at a relatively young age at the time, should not be underestimated. The lasting impression that those years made on a number of Austrian writers and filmmakers can be gleaned, for example, by Robert Schindel's fictionalization of the Waldheim affair in his novel *Der Kalte* (The Cold One, 2013), published nearly three decades after the Waldheim affair. The twenty-year-long gestation period of the novel, the interval between the publication of *Der Kalte* and his previous novel *Gebürtig* (Born-Where, 1992), is indicative of a long-standing preoccupation with the topic. The award-winning filmmaker Ruth Beckermann is also returning to the Waldheim affair in her new documentary film project *Waldheim oder THE ART OF FORGETTING* (Waldheim or The Art of Forgetting), which is due to be completed in 2017.[51]

Waldheim's persistent denial of any wrongdoing in the Second World War, throughout the course of his presidential campaign, resonated with many Austrians belonging to the war generation. Moreover, as a number of historians have observed, the Waldheim affair served to pave the way for the rehabilitation of National Socialist ideology undertaken by the Austrian Freedom Party under the Jörg Haider leadership (1986–2000), which continues to inform the party's policies.[52] During Austria's most recent presidential election, the long shadow of the country's National Socialist past was never far from the surface, with Norbert Hofer, the Austrian Freedom Party candidate, coming under fire for wearing the *Kornblume* (cornflower), a symbol originating in a nineteenth-century *Alldeutsche* (pan-German) movement (which was deeply anti-Semitic in its nature) led by Georg von Schönerer, who wanted Austria to join Bismarck's Germany.[53] The movement's symbol was chosen as a means of paying tribute to Bismarck, whose favorite flower was the cornflower.[54] Up until Austria's *Anschluss* (annexation) with Nazi Germany in 1938, the cornflower had been the symbol of the illegal Austrian Nazi Party.[55] Hofer's nonchalant approach to the wearing of political symbols associated with far-right organizations, and his membership in the notorious German-nationalist Marko Germania fraternity, did not stop him almost winning a presidential election that came in the wake of the 2015 refugee crisis, which saw an estimated 500,000 refugees travel through Austria's borders.[56] The ruling *Sozialdemokratische Partei Österreichs* (SPÖ, Social Democratic Party of Austria) and *Österreichische Volkspartei* (ÖVP, Austrian People's Party) coalition government lost credibility, having first adopted an attitude of welcoming refugees and then calling for a strengthening of the country's borders, which left the presidential candidates of the two ruling parties unable to gain enough votes to take them through to the second election round. Rudolf Hundstorfer (SPÖ) won only 11.3 percent of the vote and Dr. Andreas Khol (ÖVP) 11.1 percent of the vote in the first election round, in contrast to Norbert Hofer's 35.1 percent (making him the winner of the first election round).[57] The recent success of the Austrian Freedom Party in the presidential elections has been viewed as symptomatic for the ever-growing *Salonfähigkeit* (social acceptability) of right-wing populism in Austria,[58] and the inexorable rise of the party since the late 1980s. This trajectory was punctuated by the Austrian Freedom Party entering the coalition government with the Austrian People's Party in 2000, following the 1999 general election. This coalition remained in government until 2005 and triggered a wave of protests in Austria.

Nevertheless, the 1990s and 2000s were marked by notable steps forward with regard to Austria addressing its Nazi past. On July 8, 1991, Austrian chancellor Franz Vranitzky finally acknowledged Austrian *Mitschuld* (complicity) in the crimes of the Third Reich in a speech to the Austrian parliament. A law introduced in 1993 simplified the process of regaining Austrian citizenship for Holocaust survivors originating from Austria, who had been stripped of their citizenship during the

Nazi era.⁵⁹ In 1995 a *Nationalfonds der Republik Österreich für Opfer des Nationalsozialismus* (National Fund of the Republic of Austria for Victims of National Socialism) was established, marking the beginning of restitution.⁶⁰ Additionally, a *Gedenktag gegen Gewalt und Rassismus im Gedenken an die Opfer des Nationalsozialismus* (a Memorial Day against Violence and Fascism in Memory of the Victims of National Socialism) on May 5 (the date of the liberation of Mauthausen concentration camp by the US Army in 1945), was instigated in 1997.⁶¹ In addition to the commitment to maintain graves and monuments to Allied soldiers who perished on Austrian soil, which is enshrined in Article 19 of the *Staatsvertrag* (Austrian State Treaty) of 1955,⁶² the *Washingtoner Abkommen* (Washington Agreement) of 2001 committed Austria to "provide additional support for the restoration and maintenance of Jewish cemeteries, known or unknown, in Austria."⁶³ A Jewish Museum was reestablished in Vienna in 1993, and a Holocaust memorial to commemorate the 65,000 Austrian Jews killed in the Shoah was commissioned in 1996. The design of the internationally renowned architect Rachel Whiteread was selected, with the memorial, constructed on Vienna's Judenplatz, finally unveiled in 2000. However, commemoration of victim groups persecuted in the Holocaust has not only taken place through centralized memorials. As will be explored in chapter 5 of this study, since the beginning of the new millennium there has been a veritable explosion of decentralized memorial projects in Austria, and in Vienna in particular. This is testament to what the historian Heidemarie Uhl has termed "die Wiederentdeckung der Orte" (the rediscovery of place), the refocusing of attention on the ordinary places and spaces where Nazi persecution took place, thereby drawing attention to the complicity of ordinary men and women in the Holocaust.⁶⁴

From the 1990s onward, a number of high-profile art restitution cases, most notably the restitution in 2006 of five Klimt paintings to Maria Altmann, niece of Adele Bloch-Bauer (whose famous portrait was one of the paintings restituted), drew further attention, both within and outside Austria, to Austrian complicity in and profit from the Nazi policy of "Aryanization." This high-profile art restitution case was recently dramatized in the Hollywood film *Woman in Gold*, directed by Simon Curtis and starring Helen Mirren as Maria Altmann.⁶⁵ The film received a lukewarm reception both in Austria and abroad. Austrian critics drew attention to the historical inaccuracies of the fictionalized portrayal,⁶⁶ and in the Anglophone sphere it was criticized for what was perceived as an overly simplistic and "emotionally manipulative" treatment of a complex issue.⁶⁷ The issue of property restitution will be explored in more depth in chapter 2 of this study through Anna Mitgutsch's novel *Haus der Kindheit* (House of Childhood, 2000), where the protagonist regains a childhood home, which was expropriated from his Jewish family by the Nazis, only to become thoroughly disillusioned with his longed-for return to the country of his birth.

Another significant moment in recent history in Austria's long journey in coming to terms with its National Socialist past was the *Wehrmachtsausstellung* (German Army exhibition). The exhibition, the full title of which was *Vernichtungskrieg: Verbrechen der Wehrmacht 1941–1944* (War of Annihilation: Crimes of the Wehrmacht 1941–1944) was mounted by the *Hamburger Institut für Sozialforschung* (Hamburg Institute for Social Research) and toured thirty-four German and Austrian cities altogether, beginning with Hamburg in March 1995.[68] It was shown in all major cities in Austria, including Vienna, Innsbruck, Klagenfurt, Linz, Graz, and Salzburg, between 1995 and 1999.[69] A revised exhibition was later mounted and shown in eleven cities, including Vienna, between 2001 and 2004.[70] It is estimated that the two exhibitions were viewed by approximately 1.5 million people altogether.[71] The exhibition documented the war crimes perpetrated on the Eastern Front against Jews, Soviet prisoners of war, and the civilian population, and served to further erode the *Wehrmachtslegende* (Wehrmacht myth), or the persistent idea post-1945 in German and Austrian culture of the so-called *saubere Wehrmacht* (clean army), the myth that the Wehrmacht was "*unpolitisch*" (unpolitical) and not responsible for perpetrating atrocities, in contrast to the SS.[72] This idea had long been discredited by historians, beginning in the late 1960s in Germany, but it is only through the exhibition that "das Thema 'Verbrechen der Wehrmacht' zu einem gesellschaftlichen geworden [ist]" (the issue of "Wehrmacht crimes" became a topic for public discussion) in Austria.[73] It was a discussion that the Waldheim affair had triggered ten years earlier, but which only really gained traction with the *Wehrmachtsausstellung* nearly a decade later. Manoschek describes the effect of the *Wehrmachtsausstellung* as prompting a "kathartische Reaktion" (cathartic reaction) among fathers belonging to the *Wehrmachtsgeneration*, shortly before their deaths, leading to long-overdue discussions in the family sphere.[74] By contrast, Ruth Beckermann's documentary *Jenseits des Krieges* (Beyond War, 1996; in English as *East of War*, 1996), shows the reactions of former Wehrmacht soldiers and their descendants, visiting the first *Wehrmachtsausstellung* in Vienna in 1995, to be dominated by silencing rather than speaking openly about the past.[75] In the film and in the diary that Beckermann kept during filming, the reactions of visitors, with only a few exceptions, fall into the category of various self-exculpatory strategies, including denial of personal and collective responsibility and relativization of Nazi crimes.[76] While many of the individuals Beckermann filmed are now no longer alive, the question that Beckermann poses regarding the lasting effect of the *Wehrmachtsgeneration* on subsequent generations remains pertinent: "Aber was haben diese Väter ihren Kindern mitgegeben? Und was kommt aus diesen Kindern erst so richtig raus, wenn die Väter tot sind?" (What have these fathers passed on to their children? And what will really seep out of these children, once their fathers are dead?)[77]

In addition to re-examining the legacy of its National Socialist past during this period, the changes that swept across Europe in the late 1980s and early 1990s could not fail to leave their mark on a country at the heart of Europe, which shares its border with eight nations. The fall of the Iron Curtain has made Vienna into a reborn crossroads of Central European culture, with Austria benefiting both economically and culturally from the opening up of Eastern and Central Europe, regaining the ability to easily travel to and cooperate with countries with which Austria has a shared history, not least through the common heritage of the Habsburg Empire. Yet the changes sweeping the continent were also a subject of political exploitation inside Austria. The breakup of former Yugoslavia meant that hundreds of thousands of refugees from the conflict fled to neighboring Austria. Austria welcomed some 108,000 refugees between 1991 and 1999, with most of these coming from Bosnia (of whom approximately 60,000 remained in Austria).[78] The influx of refugees was taken advantage of by Haider's Austrian Freedom Party, which exploited rising xenophobia among voters.[79] The Austrian Freedom Party launched a petition in November 1992, with the title of "Österreich zuerst" (Austria first), calling for restrictions on immigrants living in Austria and for the assertion that Austria is not a land of immigration, to be written into the Austrian constitution.[80] The petition failed, gaining only 417,278 signatures,[81] far short of the one million that the Austrian Freedom Party had hoped for,[82] and prompted the hitherto largest public demonstration (in protest against the petition) in the history of the Second Republic. Between 250,000 and 300,000 gathered on January 23, 1993, on Vienna's Heldenplatz to demand "Anständigkeit zuerst" (decency first) in contrast to the Austrian Freedom Party's "Österreich zuerst" (Austria first).[83] The demonstration, coordinated by the organization *SOS Mitmensch* (SOS Fellow Human Being), which was founded in December 1992 as a direct result of the Austrian Freedom Party's petition, saw demonstrators hold up candles creating a *Lichtermeer* (sea of lights), a word that has since become synonymous with the demonstration. It was the most prominent display of the civil society that had come into being in the wake of the Waldheim affair several years earlier.

Despite the defeat of the Austrian Freedom Party's "Österreich zuerst" initiative, the party, under the leadership of Jörg Haider, continued to make gains in local and national elections throughout the 1990s, before gaining 27.2 percent of the vote in the general election of 1999, making the Austrian Freedom Party the second largest party in terms of vote share.[84] Following the election, coalition talks between the SPÖ and ÖVP, the political parties that had dominated the postwar era of "grand coalitions" in Austria, broke down, and the hitherto unthinkable happened. On February 4, 2000, Haider's FPÖ entered the coalition government with the ÖVP, under Wolfgang Schüssel as chancellor. The entry of a far-right party into the government of a Western European country sparked protests both in Austria and abroad. The remaining fourteen European Union member states (pre-EU enlargement) introduced diplomatic sanctions against Austria. These were, however, lifted six months later, following an independent report that asserted that these could start to become "counterproductive" and increase "nationalist sentiment" in the country.[85]

In Austria, the civil society that had come into being during the Waldheim years mobilized against the entry of Haider's party into the Austrian government. The continuities between the protest movements of 1986 and 2000 have repeatedly been stressed both by scholars and by the leading actors of the protests themselves.[86] Robert Misik highlights this most emblematically in his 2006 article "Kein Heldenplatz ohne Waldheim" (No Heldenplatz without Waldheim), asserting that "1986 wurde das 'andere Österreich' geboren, im Februar 2000 erlebte es seine grosse Weihestunde" (the "other Austria" was born in 1986, it was consecrated in February 2000).[87] On February 19, 2000, the historically freighted Heldenplatz (most commonly associated in the twentieth century with March 15, 1938, when thousands gathered on the square to support Hitler's annexation of Austria[88]) was, once again, similar to the *Lichtermeer* seven years earlier, the scene of mass protests against the Austrian Freedom Party, with 300,000 people gathering to protest against the new government.[89] Prior to this, demonstrations had taken place every day in February, beginning with the occupation of the Austrian People's Party headquarters in Vienna on February 1, 2000, which drew 25,000 protesters.[90] The symbolic significance of the Heldenplatz as former site for the celebration of fascism and now site of resistance to the same was noted by the writer and son of Holocaust survivors, Doron Rabinovici, reflecting a decade later on speaking at the February 19, 2000, demonstration:

> Es war die ganze Zeit aber an diesem Tag die Vergangenheit präsent, und ich stand dort auf dieser Buhne, und es war ein sehr merkwürdiges Gefühl. Auch ein sehr merkwürdiges Gefühl, muss ich sagen, für den Sohn von Leuten, die verfolgt waren. Meine Mutter, meine Großmutter im Lager, der andere Teil der mütterlichen Familie ermordet. Ich kenne die Geschichte dieses Platzes und das Merkwürdige ist, dass, wie ich die Rede gehalten habe, dieses Bewußtsein in meiner Stimme geriet, ohne dass ich das gesteuert habe. Ich wurde heiser und ich war sehr aufgeregt. Es war so, als spreche ich dagegen an.[91]

[The past was very present on this day, and I stood there on this stage, and it was a very strange feeling. Strange also because I am the son of people who were persecuted. My mother and grandmother were in concentration camps, the rest of the family on my mother's side was killed. I know the history of this place and the strange thing was that, when I gave my speech, the consciousness of this history entered my voice, without my controlling this in any way. I became hoarse and very agitated. It was as if I was speaking against it.]

The Austrian-British filmmaker Frederick Baker has echoed Rabinovici's statements regarding the historical significance of staging the biggest demonstration in the history of the Second Republic on Heldenplatz: "Es war eine Art Gruppentherapie, in der der Geist jenes Mannes verbannt werden sollte, der 62 Jahre zuvor von diesem Balkon sprach" (It was a kind of group therapy, which aimed to banish the ghost of that man who had spoken from that balcony sixty-two years earlier)[92] The momentum of the February 19 demonstration continued. Beginning on February 24, 2000, and ending with new elections on November 24, 2000, protestors gathered every Thursday at different locations in the capital to march against the Haider/Schüssel coalition.[93] The demonstrations became known as the *Donnerstagsdemonstrationen* (Thursday demonstrations) or the *Wiener Wandertage* (Viennese outings) and continued to draw high numbers of protesters, although naturally the numbers able to commit to participating in demonstrations every week were far fewer than the number of those who had gathered on Heldenplatz on February 19, 2000. The number of demonstrators for the *Donnerstagsdemos* peaked at 15,000 on March 2, 2000.[94] While many prominent intellectuals and artists who had come of age during the Waldheim affair (notably Doron Rabinovici, Isolde Charim, Elfriede Jelinek) became similarly mobilized in the protest movement against the ÖVP/FPÖ coalition, the movement was characterized by a far broader membership than the protest movement that had sprung up against Waldheim in the late 1980s. The protesters came from different sides of the political spectrum, united in their condemnation of Haider's FPÖ and dismayed by the fact that the ÖVP (many ÖVP supporters were among the protesters) had gone into a coalition with Haider's party.[95] Another reason that this protest movement was far broader than the one against Waldheim, was because many Austrians saw the entry of an extreme right-wing party into the government as more significant than the election of Waldheim to the ceremonial post of Austrian president more than a decade earlier.[96] The unifying motto of the movement was "Wir gehen bis ihr geht" (We'll march until you go).[97] The movement was also characterized by a lively publishing and performance culture, with essay collections and literary texts, published at the time and subsequently, testifying to the vibrancy of the *Demonstrationskultur* (demonstration culture) that developed during this period.⁹⁸ The enduring legacy of the protest culture that formed in the wake of the 1999 elections has been the subject of a documentary entitled *Widerstand in Haiderland* (Resistance in Haider Country, 2010) by Frederick Baker, as well as of a keynote lecture given by Allyson Fiddler, at a 2015 conference on Contemporary Austrian Literature, Film, and Culture at the University of Nottingham.⁹⁹

The effect of the FPÖ's membership in the coalition government was ultimately limited due to the party's inexperience of government and infighting within the party. Moreover, Schüssel's ÖVP could use the threat of further international isolation "to exert control" over the FPÖ.¹⁰⁰ Haider himself never entered the government, remaining governor of Carinthia, instead making his deputy in the party, Susanne Riess-Passer, vice-chancellor.¹⁰¹ The infighting within the FPÖ led Schüssel to dissolve the coalition and call new elections for November 2002. In these elections the FPÖ's vote share fell by 17 percent to just 10 percent of the vote, while the ÖVP climbed by 15 percent to 42.3 percent.¹⁰² Again Schüssel's party decided to form a coalition with the FPÖ. However, as Steven Beller asserts, the "tamed FPÖ" was much weaker in this second coalition government,¹⁰³ which lasted until the 2006 national elections, when there was a return back to the "grand coalition" of an SPÖ-ÖVP government. In the interim, the Austrian Freedom Party had split in 2005, with Haider leading the breakaway *Bündnis Zukunft Österreich* (BZÖ, Alliance for the Future of Austria), a party that has failed to draw significant vote share following Haider's death in 2008. By contrast, the Austrian Freedom Party has continued to make gains under the leadership of Heinz-Christian Strache since 2005, as evidenced by the near 50 percent vote share in the second round of the 2016 presidential election.

Austrian writers, filmmakers, and cultural practitioners have occupied and continue to occupy a significant role in Austrian public life, and their work is often political, reflecting on the changes and events exercising the country. This could be observed even in the course of the most recent presidential election campaign, with the Nobel literature laureate Elfriede Jelinek publishing a text entitled "Das Kommen" (The Arrival) on her website on April 26, 2016, satirizing Hofer's and the FPÖ's ascent in the polls.¹⁰⁴ This text is, as Jelinek explains, a "gekürzt und leicht geändert" (shortened and slightly altered) extract from her 2000 dramolet *Das Lebewohl* (Les Adieux), which was, in its turn, written in response to the ÖVP-FPÖ coalition government in 2000.¹⁰⁵ *Das Lebewohl* premiered in central Vienna at the makeshift *Botschaft Besorgter BürgerInnen* (Embassy of Concerned Citizens) as part of a *Donnerstagsdemonstration* on June 22, 2000, for which, as for other political initiatives, Jelinek made an exception on the performance ban on her works, which she had introduced in protest to the ÖVP-FPÖ coalition.¹⁰⁶ While broad references to the FPÖ are preserved in the 2016 text, the subject of the lampooning is now Hofer rather than Haider. To ensure that the subject of her satire is absolutely unambiguous, "Das Kommen" is prefaced with a large image of a cornflower, while an image of Hofer (albeit with his head cut out of the picture), wearing the controversial symbol on his lapel, is placed immediately below the text. Underneath the Hofer "portrait," further symbols of Nazi and German nationalist organizations that used or continue to use the cornflower in their symbols are displayed together with an excerpt from a Wikipedia article about the flower.

In addition to Nobel laureate Elfriede Jelinek using her celebrity to voice her criticism of Hofer, by adapting one of her earlier texts, the cabaret artist Christoph Grissemann also drew on an earlier dramatic monologue, *Der Herr Karl* (Mr Karl, 1961), written by Carl Merz and Helmut Qualtinger (who, as the eponymous Herr Karl, immortalized the character), to draw attention to the dangerous charismatic appeal of Hofer and the Austrian Freedom Party.[107] *Der Herr Karl* (1961), in its presentation of an "average" Austrian, speaking in Viennese dialect, and describing his opportunistic outlook on life and accommodation with both the National Socialists and, in the postwar era, the four Allied Powers, sparked outrage when the monologue was first aired on the Austrian state broadcaster ORF on November 15, 1961.[108] The drama has since become a classic. Among the various episodes that Herr Karl recalls throughout the course of his reminiscences (which make up the bulk of the drama) is the Anschluss in 1938, and the time when he met Adolf Hitler during a *Blockwartentreffen* (Meeting of NSDAP Block Wardens) at the Vienna City Hall. The encounter is described in an almost erotic manner: "Er hat mi ang'schaut . . . mit seine blauen Augen . . . i hab eahm angeschaut. . . . hat er g'sagt 'Jaja.' Da hab i alles g'wußt. Wir haben uns verstanden." (He looked at me . . . with his blue eyes . . . and I looked at him. . . . "Yes, yes," he said. I understood everything then. . . . We understood each other.)[109]

In a sketch for the satirical weekly entertainment program *Willkommen Österreich* (Welcome Austria, 2007–) broadcast on May 3, 2016, which Christoph Grissemann hosts in conjunction with co-host Dirk Stermann, Grissemann repeated the passage (albeit in slightly shortened form) from *Der Herr Karl* where the protagonist describes the *Jubel* (jubilation) accompanying the Anschluss in 1938 and his meeting with Adolf Hitler. The sketch is introduced by Stermann asking Grissemann to report on an evening at an FPÖ election party where Grissemann is supposed to have met Norbert Hofer. Following this, Christoph Grissemann dons a black wide-brimmed hat, as famously worn by Helmut Qualtinger in his performance of Herr Karl, while a black-and-white camera filter is used to replicate the original 1961 black-and-white broadcast as Grissemann, shown in close-up (as in the 1961 production of *Der Herr Karl*), recalls "meeting" Hofer in the words used by Herr Karl to describe his meeting with Hitler. The words "seine blauen Augen" (his blue eyes) are, however, substituted by the words "seine schönen braunen Augen" (beautiful brown eyes) in Grissemann's performance, which prompts laughter from the audience. Given that Norbert Hofer's eye color is green,[110] this modification of Merz's and Qualtinger's original script can only have occurred due to the fact that in Austrian-German *braun* (brown) is a colloquial term for *nationalsozialistisch geprägt* (National Socialist in character), deriving from the color of the SA *Braunhemden* (brownshirts) uniform that became synonymous with the Nazi Party's paramilitary organization.[111] The parallels between the fascination that far-right parties exert in contemporary Austria, and the Austria of the 1930s, is further emphasized at the end of Grissemann's monologue by co-host Stermann, who remarks ironically: "Schön wenn sich Geschichte so wiederholen kann." (How nice when history can repeat itself like that.)[112]

Of particular focus throughout this study will be the long shadow that Austria's past continues to exert on the country's present. The term "long shadow" is a common phrase to describe the persisting legacy of something and, as the memory-studies scholar Aleida Assmann has noted, it has been a favored phrase for titles of historical studies in particular.[113] In her own 2006 book *Der lange Schatten der Vergangenheit: Erinnerungskultur und Geschichtspolitik* (The Long Shadow of the Past: Remembrance Culture and the Politics of History), Assmann describes the shadow as "das universale Bild für diesen Bann einer Vergangenheit, 'die nicht vergeht'" (the universal image for the spell cast by a past "that will not go away").[114] In her study, Assmann reflects on the evolving process of remembering the Second World War and the Holocaust, both in the German context and internationally, at the beginning of the twenty-first century. Assmann understands the "negative Erinnerung" (negative memory) of National Socialism and the Holocaust to be constitutive of postwar German identity, "in das Fundament des deutschen Staats eingebrannt" (branded into the foundation of the German state).[115] Her answer to the rhetorical question she poses in the conclusion to her study, regarding when we will be able to "heraustreten" (step out) of the shadow of the National Socialist period and the Holocaust, is as follows: "Verstehen wir unter 'Schatten' die nachwirkende Präsenz der traumatischen Vergangenheit, so werden wir mit ihm leben müssen." (If, by "shadow," we understand the lasting presence of the traumatic past, we will have to live with it.)[116] Further, Assmann characterizes the shadow as not only defined by a "nachhallende Präsenz" (reverberating presence), but also by "Verdunklung und Verdüsterung" (darkening and clouding over).[117] The crimes of National Socialism are such, Assmann argues, that they continue to darken and besmirch our present. It must be noted here that Assmann, as a German scholar, is operating in a very different remembrance tradition vis-à-vis the Second World War and the Holocaust than that in Austria. Beginning in the 1960s, the "negative memory" of the crimes of National Socialism has been inscribed, as Assmann traces, into the German national identity, and, certainly, Germany (and the two German states preceding reunification in 1990) was never allowed to regard itself as a "victim" of fascism by the Allies, in the same way that Austria was through the Moscow Declaration. The move from the self-perception of victimhood to one of acknowledging *Mitschuld* (complicity) in the crimes of National Socialism has been a slow journey in Austria. Yet, this does not make the concept of the past's long shadow any less relevant in the Austrian context. Indeed, it is perhaps more so. For, a shadow is cast involuntarily, regardless of whether a nation wishes to acknowledge its past or sweep it under the carpet, the past's traumatic legacy, symbolized by the shadow, as Assmann elucidates, continues to haunt us.

As William Faulkner wrote: "The past is never dead. It's not even past."[118] The Second World War and the Holocaust are a past that is not past in Austrian culture, as writer and historian Doron Rabinovici has described:

> Es gibt einen Unterschied in der Sprache zwischen Geschichte und Vergangenheit. Geschichte ist das was abgeschlossen ist, und Vergangenheit ist das, was in Wirklichkeit nicht vergangen ist. . . . Vergangenheit meint, etwas ist offen, und deswegen sprechen wir von österreichischer Geschichte und meinen dann eher den Kaiser, und von österreichischer Vergangenheit und da meinen wir die dreißiger, vierziger Jahre."[119]
>
> [There is a difference between the words "history" and "past." History is something that is finished, and the past is something that, in reality, has not passed. . . . "Past" means that something is left open, and for that reason we speak of Austrian history and tend to mean the Kaiser, and we speak of the Austrian past and mean the 1930s and 1940s.]

In their works, the writers and filmmakers who are the subjects of this study persistently draw attention to a past that "has not passed," a past that is not able to pass in a different manner to that diagnosed by Assmann in the case of Germany.[120] The analysis in the following chapters is informed by trauma theory, which posits that, as Sigmund Freud wrote in his landmark study *Der Mann Moses und die monotheistische Religion* (The Man Moses and Monotheistic Religion, 1939; in English as *Moses and Monotheism*, 1939), a repressed and unconfronted trauma will eventually manifest itself in the form of belated symptoms and haunt the subject in displaced and distorted forms.¹²¹ The word "trauma" literally means wound¹²² and characterizes "lebensbedrohende und die Seele tief verwundende Erfahrungen von extremer Gewalt . . ., deren Wucht den Reizschutz der Wahrnehmung zerschlägt und die aufgrund ihrer fremdartigen und identitätsbedrohenden Qualität psychisch nicht verarbeitet werden können" (experiences that are life-threatening and deeply wounding to the soul, the violence of which breaks the protective barrier of perception, and which, because of their unfamiliar quality and the threat they pose to one's identity, cannot be psychically worked through).¹²³ In his essay on *Aufarbeitung der Vergangenheit* (working through the past), Theodor W. Adorno characterized the German attitude to the past as testifying to something "psychisch Nichtbewältigten, eine[r] Wunde" (psychically unmastered, a wound).¹²⁴ Austria's past too has often been compared to an "open wound," as in a speech given on March 12, 2013, the seventy-fifth anniversary of the Anschluss, by then Austrian president Heinz Fischer: "Nur gereinigte und sauber gemachte Wunden können ohne Entzündungsgefahr heilen. Und dieses Saubermachen der Wunden, das hat sehr lange Zeit auf sich warten lassen." (Only wounds that have been cleaned and tidied up can heal without inflammation. And this process of cleaning up the wounds has been a very long time coming.)¹²⁵ In his writing, as in the above-mentioned *Der Mann Moses*, Freud frequently wrote about repression and belatedness manifesting themselves not just in the individual but also among groups or nations. As the preceding discussion of the Waldheim affair has shown, Austria is a nation that in the postwar era has very much been characterized by belatedness vis-à-vis coming to terms with its own past, a belatedness that many of the works that will be considered in this study explicitly draw attention to. As such, psychoanalytic theories of repression and belatedness particularly lend themselves to analyzing the works under consideration.

This introduction is subtitled "Confrontations with the Past," but this is a term that also cannot be taken for granted and requires glossing in the context of postwar engagements with the Nazi past in the German-language context. In the German context, *Vergangenheitsbewältigung* (dealing with/mastering the past) is a term that has been in use in the Federal Republic of Germany since the mid-1950s to denote "die ausstehende Auseinandersetzung mit der jeweiligen individuellen Beteiligung am Nationalsozialismus" (the outstanding confrontation with one's individual involvement in National Socialism).¹²⁶ It is a term that has, however, frequently been criticized for the implication that the past can be mastered or overcome, which the verb *bewältigen* (to master/overcome) in the composite noun implies, with the enormity of the crimes of National Socialism rendering such a mastery of the past impossible. The philosopher Adorno famously criticized existing efforts at *Aufarbeitung der Vergangenheit* (working through the past) in the Federal Republic of Germany in his 1959 radio essay "Was bedeutet: Aufarbeitung der Vergangenheit" (What Does It Mean: Working through the Past, 1959; first translated into English as "What Does 'Digesting the Past' Mean?," 1961).[127] He argued that such efforts are often dominated by a desire to forget the past and to draw a line under it: "man will einen Schlussstrich darunter ziehen und womöglich es selbst aus der Erinnerung wegwischen" (one wants to draw a line under it and, if possible, wipe it away from memory).[128] In contrast to this, Adorno called for an "Aufarbeitung der Vergangenheit als Aufklärung" (working through the past as enlightenment), a deeper, psychoanalytically informed attention to the legacy of National Socialism in the present.[129] Here Adorno follows the Freudian principle of *durcharbeiten* (working through) the past, as elucidated in Freud's essay "Erinnern, Wiederholen, Durcharbeiten."[130] Writing in 1959, Adorno's fears about memorial efforts being informed by a desire to forget rather than remember are prescient and are even more of a concern today when more than seventy years have elapsed since the end of the Second World War, and when our living connection to that time diminishes year by year. This study presents a number of different confrontations with the past, and I use the word "confrontations" deliberately here because the book includes a range of responses to the Austrian legacy of National Socialism. The primary definition of "confrontation" is "face-to-face meeting," the nature or end point of this meeting is left open,[131] thereby encompassing a range of responses to the country's Nazi past.

The writers, filmmakers, and artists that are the focus of this study can be ascribed to the so-called second postwar generation of writers, artists, and filmmakers, who came of age in the 1980s and who continue to dominate the Austrian cultural landscape. As such they did not live through the Second World War—or, in some cases, survive the Holocaust—as their parents did, but instead are socialized with the memories and stories of their parents to such an extent that their lives have become, as Marianne Hirsch describes, "dominated by narratives that preceded their birth."[132] Hirsch has termed this particular form of memory "postmemory," which is particularly powerful precisely "because its connection to its object or source is mediated not through recollection but through an imaginative investment and creation."[133] While Hirsch developed the concept to describe the experience of the children of Holocaust survivors, she stresses that the term can also be applied to "other second-generation memories of cultural or collective traumatic events and experiences."[134] Nevertheless, in the following chapters, postmemory will, in fact, be seen to be particularly operative in the case of subjects (in documentary films) or protagonists (in works of fiction) with familial experience of the Holocaust, precisely because of the annihilation that underpinned the Shoah. It will be seen that a lack of material traces calls for precisely the kind of "imaginative investment," that Hirsch describes,[135] to reconstruct and forge a connection to an irretrievable family past, and that the search for a lost place and time is often, as will be seen in the following chapters, colored by the operations of melancholy and nostalgia. In his essay "Trauer und Melancholie" (Mourning and Melancholia, 1917), Freud defines melancholy as a coping mechanism characterized by cathexis (investing emotion or feeling in) of a lost object's characteristics in one's own ego in order to better endure its loss.[136] Examples of melancholic cathexis (be this for a person or people, for a specific place or time) abound in the works of Ruth Beckermann and Anna Mitgutsch in their representation of the search for the remnants of a pre-Anschluss Austrian Jewish culture, as will be explored in chapters 1 and 2 of this study.

While melancholy, defined by Freud as a psychopathological condition, is largely associated with the individual fixated on loss, the concept of nostalgia, which draws on traditional conceptions of melancholy, is additionally concerned with a desire to make good this loss by returning to a vanished past, real or imagined. Nostalgia is derived from the Greek *nostos* ("return home") and *algia* ("longing").[137] Nostalgia is therefore characterized by the longing to return home, whatever the subject understands by this. In her groundbreaking 2001 study *The Future of Nostalgia,* Svetlana Boym coined the terms "restorative nostalgia" and "reflective nostalgia" to distinguish between two distinct types of nostalgia. Boym characterizes "restorative nostalgia" as concerned with a return to origins, where the focus is on the *nostos,* "rebuild[ing] the lost home."[138] "Reflective nostalgia," meanwhile, is characterized by the *algia* aspect of nostalgia, a longing for the past or to return home, but with the acceptance that the past cannot be restored or the lost home returned to. In contrast to restorative nostalgia, reflective nostalgia is not concerned with a return to or restoration of a "prelapsarian moment,"[139] but rather with reflection on "the past the way it could have been,"[140] (instead of an idealized image of how it was), from which one then strives to salvage something for the future.

Nostalgia, both restorative and reflective, should also be understood in relational terms. Linda Hutcheon frames nostalgia as a temporal phenomenon, arguing that the power of nostalgia lies in "its structural doubling up of two different times, an inadequate present and an idealized past."[141] Examples of both restorative and reflective forms of nostalgia, arising from the subject's dissatisfaction with the present, abound in the works of Anna Mitgutsch and Ruth Beckermann, which will be the focus of chapters 1 and 2 of this study. Often, a very Austrian form of nostalgia is at play, which is Habsburg nostalgia, a longing for a perceived golden age of the multiethnic Austro-Hungarian Empire, submerged in 1918. As will be seen in the analysis of Ruth Beckermann's *Die papierene Brücke*, Habsburg nostalgia is Janus faced. Against the background of renascent anti-Semitism in Waldheim's Vienna, Habsburg nostalgia is shown to constitute a return to an idyllic multicultural realm of a protagonist's childhood. On the other hand, we see in the same film how nostalgia for the golden era of the Habsburg Empire and, in particular, for Vienna's fin-de-siècle Jewish heritage, is exploited for commercial gain by the country's tourism and culture industries.

In the field of memory studies, there has recently been a shift away from focusing on the nation "as the master unit of analysis," to study the operations of memory from a "transcultural" perspective.[142] This privileges an attention to the operations of "multi-directional memory" across national borders, in an age of globalization and global media.[143] While it is undoubtedly true that historians and memory-studies scholars operate within this "transcultural" frame, as the preceding discussion has illustrated, there is still much to be said for considering the operations of memory and remembering within "closed groups" such as that of the Austrian nation,[144] a nation that differs markedly from its neighbor Germany with regard to facing up to their collective experience in the Third Reich. Historical discourse is often ahead of the curve here; the *Opfermythos* (myth of Austrian victimhood) has been unanimously discredited by Austrian historians, yet a survey conducted in Austria in 2014 by the SORA Institute for Social Research and Consulting found that 42 percent of respondents still adhere to the view that Austria was the first victim of fascism.[145] In this context, it is writers, filmmakers, and other cultural practitioners who are able to reflect the real—rather than ideal—experience of groups or individuals in their work and capture the *Zeitgeist* or mood of a nation at a specific moment in its historical development. This can be observed both in works of fiction, such as novels and dramatic works, and in documentary films, in which hitherto unseen images and unheard voices are able to illuminate and add new perspectives to our understanding of contemporary Austria.

This study builds on scholarship hitherto undertaken on the individual writers and filmmakers considered in this monograph. Several of the writers, such as Elfriede Jelinek, which will be discussed in the following chapters, have been the subject of numerous monographs and countless articles. Scholarship on the specific texts under consideration will be engaged with throughout; a selective approach has been taken with regard to studies considering aspects of the writers' work not directly related to the texts under consideration. While the authors and films that I will focus on have certainly been the subject of scholarly attention in German studies, the particular constellation of authors, filmmakers, and artists that is treated here has not been examined together, nor has it been analyzed concurrently through the specific lens of coming to terms with the past in the context of the last three decades in Austrian culture. Some comparative studies dealing with the same period that is the focus of my investigation, which should be mentioned here, are: Matthias Beilein's

86 und die Folgen,[146] and Andrea Reiter's *Contemporary Jewish Writing: Austria after Waldheim*.[147] Beilein's 2008 study of the writers and intellectuals Robert Schindel, Robert Menasse, and Doron Rabinovici focuses on how the Waldheim affair shaped all three of the writers, and examines the political dimension in their essayistic and fictional work. While Beilein provides an interesting examination of three very significant writers on the contemporary Austrian literary scene, and, indeed, it would have been difficult to include other writers in his study given the close focus on a large number of works by Schindel, Menasse, and Rabinovici specifically, the exclusive focus on male authors neglects these writers' female colleagues in the shape of writers and filmmakers such as Elfriede Jelinek and Ruth Beckermann, whose work is also intensely political.

Andrea Reiter's 2013 study *Contemporary Jewish Writing* is an exploration of Austrian Jewish identity after the Waldheim affair through the work of contemporary Austrian Jewish writers and filmmakers. Informed by human geographers, such as Doreen Massey, Reiter's analysis is primarily concerned with how contemporary Austrian Jewish writers and filmmakers have constructed a "Jewish space,"[148] both physical and virtual, in today's Austria, and the new self-confident "visibility" of Jews in Austrian culture following the Waldheim affair.[149] A notable further study that should be mentioned here in this regard is Hillary Hope Herzog's 2011 monograph on Jewish writers in Austria from the fin de siècle to the present, which devotes a chapter to "Viennese Jews from Waldheim to Haider and Beyond."[150] While a significant proportion of the writers, filmmakers, and artists analyzed in the following chapters are Austrian Jewish or of Austrian Jewish heritage (which raises interesting questions about who is carrying out the task of working through Austria's past in contemporary Austria), articulations of Austrian Jewish identity/identities are not the primary focus of this study, and indeed this book considers works by both Jewish and non-Jewish Austrian writers, filmmakers, and artists. The studies mentioned above also neglect to discuss visual culture in their analysis of cultural production following the Waldheim affair, an incredibly dynamic area of cultural activity to which a substantial section of this book is dedicated. My analysis of memorial projects in Vienna also includes examples from as recently as 2014 and 2015, which have not been written about extensively, or—in some cases—at all, before.

Chapter Outline

This book is composed of five chapters, which undertake close readings of key literary texts, films, and memorials in order to examine the diverse ways in which the legacy of Nazism and the Holocaust is treated in contemporary Austrian literature, film, and culture. While there are other authors, filmmakers, and cultural practitioners who could have been included to extend the study, the focus on a delimited number of case studies allows for in-depth analysis of these various texts that may be said to exemplify a range of critical responses to the country's historical legacies and their resonances in the present. My analysis examines the treatment of the past and Austrian identity in contemporary Austrian literature, film, and culture through case studies in literature, film, and visual culture taken from approximately the last three decades. The majority of the works under consideration here were published after the Waldheim affair of 1986–88, with the earliest work considered being Ruth Beckermann's *Wien retour* (Return to Vienna, 1983) and the latest being a memorial project by the same artist from 2015. The study proceeds broadly chronologically, thereby showing the thematic development in authors', filmmakers', and artists' aesthetic treatment of the Austrian past. At the same time, several of the chapters, notably chapter 3 and chapter 5, engage in comparative analysis of texts and artworks produced at different points in time, thereby allowing for interesting comparison of works treating the same topic.

Chapter 1 examines three films by the Austrian documentary filmmaker Ruth Beckermann (1952–), *Wien retour*, *Die papierene Brücke*, and *Homemad(e)*, and shows how the films trace the melancholy and nostalgic search for the remnants of a pre-Anschluss Austrian Jewish culture, destroyed in the Holocaust, as well as documenting an unsatisfactory present. All three films are concerned with returns to origins of various kinds as Beckermann, as an Austrian Jewish woman, attempts to forge a link to an Austrian and central European Jewish cultural tradition from which the second generation, growing up in postwar Vienna, was severed. The chapter examines how the melancholy mood that permeates Beckermann's work constitutes an attempt to preserve remnants of the past and counter forgetting of the Holocaust in the face of growing xenophobia and right-wing populism in Austrian politics at the turn of the millennium.

Chapter 2 focuses on the novel *Haus der Kindheit*, by the writer Anna Mitgutsch (1948–), a text that, in a similar manner to the early films of Ruth Beckermann, is concerned with the search for the remnants of a pre-Holocaust Austrian Jewish culture, and the attempt to "restore" (quite literally in the form of the reclamation and restoration of a family property) a lost home. The chapter examines this very problematic quest of the novel's central protagonist to make good or return to the past, and the inevitable failure of this endeavor, due to the fact there is no point of origin or "prelapsarian moment" to return to.[151] My analysis highlights how the protagonist's growing understanding of the country's troubled past and imperfect present is reflected in the move from restorative nostalgia, in his attempt to restore a regained family property, to reflective nostalgia, in his writing of a chronicle documenting the town's submerged Jewish history.

In contrast to the melancholy and nostalgia characterizing the texts and films examined in chapters 1 and 2, chapter 3 explores two aesthetic treatments of a massacre carried out in Rechnitz, a small Austrian village close to the Hungarian border, where two hundred Jewish slave-laborers were murdered on the night of March 24–25, 1945. The perpetrators have not been brought to justice, and the mass grave has not been found to this day. Instead, Rechnitz has become a model case for the repression and silencing surrounding the Nazi past in postwar Austria. *Rechnitz (Der Würgeengel)* (Rechnitz: The Exterminating Angel, 2009), a controversial play by Nobel literature laureate Elfriede Jelinek (1946–), is examined in conjunction with the documentary *Totschweigen* (Deathly Silence, 1994, in English as *A Wall of Silence*), by filmmakers Margareta Heinrich (1951–94) and Eduard Erne (1958–). The chapter investigates how both Jelinek and Heinrich and Erne utilize the possibilities of their respective genres to explore the repercussions and legacy of the Rechnitz massacre in the present day. It will be shown that, while *Totschweigen* is able to find a powerful visual language for the repression and denial of the past, Jelinek confronts her audience with ongoing strategies of self-exculpation, denial, and relativizing of the past, drawing attention to the empty rituals of token *Vergangenheitsbewältigung*.

Chapter 4 focuses on the most sustained literary treatment of the Waldheim affair to date, the novel *Der Kalte* by Robert Schindel (1944–). In this panoramic novel, Schindel highlights the extent to which the political scandal came to dominate every sphere of Austrian life. The chapter examines how, through fictionalizing Austria's recent past and staging his own interventions in it, Schindel evaluates the Waldheim affair from the perspective of today, disturbs narratives of Austrian victimhood, and highlights missed opportunities for reflecting on Austria's National Socialist legacy. My analysis draws attention to Schindel's performative reinscriptions of aspects of the Waldheim affair, reinscriptions that serve to draw attention to the work that remains to be done in order for Austria to fully confront its past.

Chapter 5 examines recent memorial projects in Vienna, and what these reveal about the politics of memory in contemporary Austria. My analysis centers on the surge in decentralized memorials and memorial projects commemorating Holocaust victims in Austria and the refocusing of attention on the concrete places where Nazi persecution took place. Concentrating on a number of memorials and memorial projects that have been undertaken in Vienna in recent years by the artists Ulrike Lienbacher (1963–), Julia Schulz (1979–), Maria Theresia Litschauer (1950–), Iris Andraschek (1963–), Hubert Lobnig (1962–), Karen Frostig (1948–), Ruth Beckermann (1952–), and Catrin Bolt (1979), the chapter analyzes the specific strategies that the memorials use. These range from contextualization of existing problematic memorials to engaging the public in a communal process of remembrance through a range of participation initiatives. My analysis highlights how, in the twenty-first century, Austria's memory culture has shifted from one of repression to active remembrance of the nation's complicity in the Holocaust.

The analysis of the different case studies presented here will be grounded in a cultural-historical framework, as well as drawing on memory-studies scholarship and theories of melancholy and nostalgia outlined above. The discussions that follow will show how Austrian writers, filmmakers, and artists attempt to make sense of the legacy of Austria's traumatic history in their works and explore the various aesthetic strategies that they use to do so. In examining works covering a three-decade time span, shifts and progressions in Austria's relationship to its past will be highlighted. Moreover, while the focus will be on cultural production that is uniquely shaped by and could only have arisen in the Austrian context, the phenomena that Austrian cultural practitioners diagnose and identify will be shown to have resonance for postconflict contexts around the world.

1: Melancholy Journeys to the Past: The Films of Ruth Beckermann

> *Es hat mich einfach dazu gedrängt, das nicht untergehen zu lassen.*
> [I felt the strong urge not to let this become lost.]
> —Franz West (1909–85)

IN HIS SEMINAL ESSAY "Trauer und Melancholie" (Mourning and Melancholia, 1917), Freud defines melancholy as a coping mechanism of cathecting (incorporating and investing emotional energy in) a lost object's characteristics in one's own ego in order to cope with its loss.[1] We find many such examples of melancholic cathexis in the work of the Austrian documentary filmmaker Ruth Beckermann, be they for a person or people, for a particular place, or correspondingly for a particular time. Beckermann (1952–), who started making documentary films in 1977, has been described as "obsessed with the past, with finding out the truth about the Shoah, victims and perpetrators."[2] Most of her films deal in some way with Austrian Jewish culture following the Holocaust, beginning with the film trilogy on Jewish identity *Wien retour*, *Die papierene Brücke*, and *Nach Jerusalem* (Toward Jerusalem, 1990),[3] and continuing with *Ein flüchtiger Zug nach dem Orient* (A Fleeting Train to the Orient; in English as *A Fleeting Passage to the Orient*, 1999), *Homemad(e)*, and *Zorros Bar Mizwa* (Zorro's Bar Mitzva, 2006). While Beckermann's work has been examined in the context of the predominant issue of memory in her films,[4] the particular status of the city of Vienna,[5] and re-emerging Jewish culture in Austria at the turn of the millennium,[6] there has been no sustained discussion of the function of melancholy and nostalgia with relation to space and place in her work. This chapter will focus on three films in particular, *Wien retour*, *Die papierene Brücke*, and *Homemad(e)*, and explore how all three deeply personal documentaries constitute an attempt to recoup, in some small way, the loss caused to Austrian Jewish culture by the destruction wrought by the Holocaust, and how the journeys that Beckermann undertakes to the places and spaces that were previously home to Jewish culture are consequently inflected with varying degrees of melancholy and nostalgia.

In my choice of focus on the first two films of Beckermann's trilogy on Jewish identity and on *Homemad*(e), I follow Christina Guenther who has described *Wien retour*, *Die papierene Brücke*, and *Homemad(e)* as Beckermann's "Vienna films," testifying to the fact that, despite the filmmaker's deeply ambivalent attitude to the city of her birth "Vienna nevertheless remains for Beckermann, in both her writing and her films, the center of her artistic engagement."[7] Moreover, there are a number of thematic continuities between *Die papierene Brücke* and *Homemad(e)* in particular, which render a comparative analysis of *Wien retour*, *Die papierene Brücke*, and *Homemad(e)* more germane than an analysis of the earlier two films and *Nach Jerusalem*. All three films are insistently concerned with journeys to or from Vienna and with returns to origins of various kinds, whether this is, as in *Wien retour*, to the time of interwar Red Vienna, to the ancestral land of Beckermann's father in *Die papierene Brücke* or, in *Homemad(e)*, to a community within the city of Vienna where one can feel secure. We find many examples of what Svetlana Boym has termed "reflective nostalgia," a nostalgia "for the past the way it could have been,"[8] in Beckermann's work, as she, as an Austrian Jewish woman, attempts to forge a link to an Austrian and central European Jewish cultural tradition from which the second generation, growing up in postwar Vienna, was severed. It is this focus on an Austrian and central European Jewish cultural tradition that unites all three films discussed here and allows for interesting points of comparison. As she goes in search of a lost time, the visual images that Beckermann creates constitute a reflective meditation on what might have been, had history taken a different course. My chapter will examine how the films treat the painful history of Austrian and central European Jewry in the twentieth century, and how the melancholy mood that permeates Beckermann's work constitutes an attempt to preserve the remnants of the past and counter forgetting of the Holocaust in the face of growing xenophobia and right-wing populism in Austrian politics at the turn of the millennium.

Wien retour

Wien retour is a film unyieldingly concerned with melancholy journeys of various kinds. Yet in this film, co-directed with Josef Aichholzer, Beckermann ventures no farther than her own home city of Vienna, specifically the second district, the center of Jewish life in the capital prior to the Holocaust. The viewer's guide on this journey is the retired journalist Franz West (1909–85), a secular Viennese Jew who grew up in the second district, and who, as a young man, was involved in the Austrian socialist movement of the interwar years. His narrative charts the growing anti-Semitism in Austria even before the Anschluss, his arrest and flight to England in 1938 (where, due to his involvement in a refugee aid organization, he changed his name from Weintraub to West for security reasons), his return to Austria in 1945, the offices he held in the

Kommunistische Partei Österreichs (Communist Party of Austria), and his disillusionment with communism following the crushing of the Prague Spring. Yet in this life span it is the years leading up to the Anschluss, West's youth in Vienna, that are afforded the most screen time (seventy-eight minutes of the eighty-nine-minute film). Indeed, the temporal focus of the documentary is specified in the film's subtitle "Franz West (Weintraub) 1924–1934."

In Beckermann's project of forging a link to an Austrian Jewish culture and tradition destroyed in the Holocaust, of establishing what Christina Guenther has termed a "counter-memory" to "the dominant narrative of Austrian history and national identity,"[9] the present time as well as the postwar years in Austria are virtually elided in favor of a concentration on the interwar years. This is reinforced by the fact that West's narration is underpinned by contemporary black-and-white photographs and archive films from the 1920s and 1930s. Through the film's handling of space, specifically the almost total exclusion of spatial images of contemporary Vienna, *Wien retour* fosters feelings of melancholy and nostalgia for a bygone Vienna. The only present-day images of Vienna that we see, at the beginning and end, respectively, are from the window of a train, traveling to and then away from the city. The opening sequence is, additionally, followed by a sequence in Vienna's *Prater* park, where we are first introduced to West. *Wien retour* offers a return ticket to a submerged past, which is re-created and brought to life in Beckermann's film primarily through West's masterful narration and through the near exclusion of images of present-day Vienna. Apart from the aforementioned sequences in the train and in the Prater, in a primary sense the action remains firmly within the confines of West's living room. There are a couple of establishing shots within the apartment, showing West writing at his desk and a medium shot where we see West sitting opposite Beckermann and co-director Josef Aichholzer. Otherwise, West is only filmed from two angles (left and right) for the whole duration of the film. This facilitates the return to the past that *Wien retour* undertakes; with little to distract the viewer, the aural is privileged as much, if not more, than the visual realm, as West's narration facilitates an imaginary return to the time of his youth.

Through West's narrative the viewer of *Wien retour* is transported to the spaces and places of Jewish Vienna of the 1920s and early 1930s. At times West's narration provides a voice-over for the contemporary photographs shown on-screen (we see black-and-white images of cafés and sports clubs); at others the short archive films (twelve in total) accentuate West's narrative. For example, when West is recalling the Workers' Movement in Austria and his impressions of the May Day demonstration of 1925, there is an archive clip of the demonstration with a rousing accompaniment of the Austrian socialist song *Die Arbeiter von Wien* (Workers of Vienna, 1927).[10] Another sequence of black-and-white photographs of the Leopoldstadt is accompanied with the specially composed *Leopoldstadt* by the composer Georg Herrnstadt, a piece that is very melancholic in tone. West's description of his youthful romantic experiences, on the other hand, is punctuated by a further archive sequence of the Prater park, which is accompanied by Hermann Leopoldi's playful duet *Überlandpartie* (Country Outing, 1931). An excursus on the challenges West faced in his part-time job selling stationery in the late 1920s, owing to the difficult economic circumstances of the time, is followed by a film clip taken from Walter Reisch's film *Episode* (Episode, 1935), set in 1920s Vienna. The clip shows a jolly cabaret performance of Frank Silver's and Irving Cohn's song "Yes! We Have No Bananas" (1922), while in the next sequence there is a close-up of a newspaper headline reporting that a Viennese banker has committed suicide as a result of the collapse of the *Boden-Creditanstalt* (Land Credit Bank) in the financial crash of October 1929. The combination of up-tempo and melancholic music, accompanying the images and archive clips on screen, projects Vienna of the interwar period as a golden age, one that was, however, threatened from the outset.

The history of the second district, where prior to the Second World War every second inhabitant was Jewish,[11] belongs to a vanished past, which members of Beckermann's generation can hardly imagine, so distant is it from their own experience, and yet simultaneously cannot help but be nostalgic for. In Boym's formulation, nostalgia "is a longing for a home that no longer exists or has never existed."[12] Here West provides a link to the vibrant Jewish culture of Beckermann's grandparents' generation, from which her own generation has been severed.[13] As mentioned above, following the journey into Vienna on the train, during which we hear the opening movement of the mournful *Concerto for Alto Saxophone and String Orchestra* (1959) by Pierre-Max Dubois, we first encounter West speaking to Beckermann and Josef Aichholzer in the Prater park. Before West enters the frame we see a series of high-angle panoramic shots of Vienna's second district, and the narrator introduces the *Prater Riesenrad* (giant Ferris wheel) to the audience as having been "für viele Tausende Juden, der erste Eindruck von Wien, wenn sie mit der Nordbahn aus allen Teilen der Monarchie, in die Residenzstadt kamen" (*WR*; for many thousands of Jews, their first impression of Vienna, when they arrived in the imperial capital from all the different parts of the Austro-Hungarian Empire on the North Railway).

Following West's opening words we are shown a black-and-white archive sequence of the Prater and *Nordbahnhof* (North Station), before the camera spans several photographs of streets in the second district, shop fronts with the names of their German-Jewish owners emblazoned on them, synagogues, and cafés. Many of these photographs are reproduced in Beckermann's edited volume about the second district *Die*

Mazzesinsel (The Matzos Island, 1984), published a year after the release of *Wien retour*.[14] These photos, static images from over seventy years ago, many of them showing buildings that do not exist anymore (synagogues, destroyed in the November pogroms of 1938, being a case in point) or in the form depicted, reinforce the idea of a Viennese Jewish culture vanished forever. Marianne Hirsch, drawing on Roland Barthes's theories of photography and death, has described the specific experience of viewing the "Holocaust photograph" (she includes in her definition both pre-Holocaust family photographs and images of shtetl life, as well as pictures from concentration camps),[15] as being characterized by "the viewer fill[ing] in what the picture leaves out: the horror of looking is not necessarily *in* the image but in the story the viewer provides to fill in what has been omitted."[16] The photographs included in *Wien retour* are therefore doubly melancholic, firstly through the perennial association of photographs with mortality (we photograph because we wish to preserve transient life), and secondly, due to the uncomfortable knowledge that we, as contemporary viewers, have about those depicted in them, namely that many of the photographed will have been subject to persecution, degradation, and murder in the Holocaust.

West's narrative begins where that of the film narrator Paola Löw (1934–99, an Austrian film and radio actor) ends. His introductory statements on the Prater and Vienna's second district establish the other side of the coin of the district, an area that, due to the large number of Jews who lived there, was a perennial target for the National Socialists. He describes how groups of SS and SA would congregate in a nearby Nazi pub, and afterward traverse the main avenue of the Prater, shouting anti-Semitic slogans and attacking Jewish youths. West's opening statements introduce the underlying climate of anti-Semitism that plagued the lives of Viennese Jews, and they undermine the idyllic and nostalgic image of the second district as a haven for Jewish migrants from all over the Austro-Hungarian Empire that has been introduced by the narrator. A dialectic is established of a vanished cultural center on the one hand, and a district that was always threatened by violence and anti-Semitism on the other. There is, in other words, no vanished ideal or home to return to, and this is brought out potently in the film through the sheer number of anti-Semitic incidents that West recounts. Although on an aesthetic level *Wien retour* allows a nostalgic image of the second district to emerge, on a thematic level such uncritical forms of nostalgia are constantly undermined. *Wien retour* thereby constitutes a melancholy reflection on the vanishing of Viennese Jewish culture in its pre-1938 form, and on the demise of the Social Democratic movement in the interwar years, with the two shown to be intertwined.

West's narrative, and the filmic focus on West's childhood and youth in the 1920s and 1930s, constitutes a melancholic lament to the downfall of Red Vienna and the subsequent rise of Austrofascism. Key achievements of Hugo Breitner (councillor for finance in the Social Democrat-ruled Vienna of the interwar years), such as the municipal housing program, and system of progressive taxation, are lauded by West. As the historian Steven Beller has asserted, the constitutional reforms of 1920 made Vienna into "a socialist island in a sea that was 'bourgeois,' or worse."[17] The inevitable attacks to which the vulnerable bastion of Red Vienna was subjected are detailed in West's account from the middle of the film onward: the murder of a man and child by a *Frontkämpfer* (front fighter, right-wing combat organization 1920–35), subsequently acquitted; the demonstration by the Social Democrats that followed, and the fire of the Palace of Justice on July 15, 1927, leading to the deaths of some eighty-nine demonstrators; the elections of 1930, in which the right-radical *Heimwehr* (home guard, Austrian right-wing paramilitary organization, active 1918–38) got into parliament for the first time, and, finally, the February revolts of 1934, where the *Sozialdemokraten* (Social Democrats) were defeated by the Dollfuss Christian Social *Ständestaat* (corporate state) together with the Heimwehr (home guard). West's narrative of the interwar years terminates in October 1934, as the narrator of the film Paola Löw describes how Franz Weintraub was arrested and sentenced to six months in prison for socialist activities. This reinforces the progressive historical view that it was the civil war of February 1934, and the ascendancy of Austrofascism that this signaled, and not the Anschluss of 1938, that marked the definitive turning point in Austria's path to National Socialism, thus undermining Austria's dominant postwar self-image as "Hitler's first victim."[18] As Renate Posthofen has emphasized, Beckermann "demonstrates with Franz West's testimony that . . . anti-Semitism was not simply a German import."[19]

West's narration of the events of the 1920s and 1930s in Austria constitutes a melancholy reflection on this time period, and leads the viewer to contemplate how events may have turned out differently. At the same time, West's tracing of the rise of the Heimwehr and its implications for himself as a Jew undermines any notion of the "first victim" thesis, with brutal anti-Semitism shown to have been prevalent since the early thirties. In one of the most poignant sequences of the film, West describes an incident in May 1932 after the Heimwehr was elected into Vienna's *Gemeinderat* (district council) in April of that year. West had been attending a compulsory afternoon seminar at the University of Vienna. Upon walking out of the main entrance of the university he was subjected to a beating, with shouts of "Haut den Juden" (*WR*; Beat the Jew), instigated by twenty to thirty students attending a National Socialist demonstration, during which he was thrown down the ramp of the university entrance. Following this, West managed to escape and climb on a nearby tram, whereupon he was torn off it and beaten again. Upon escaping a second time, he ran down a nearby street but was caught again and beaten until he became unconscious. Two workers in the vicinity took care of him and reported the incident to the police. Three days later he was summoned to the police headquarters on charges of *öffentliche Ruhestörung* (*WR*; disturbance of the peace), as the police took the view that West must have provoked his abusers. The police subsequently informed the university administration about the incident, and a disciplinary investigation was launched during which West's studies were suspended.

While the story of Franz West's life after 1934 is given by the narrator in brief (which the viewer assumes to be the end of the film), this does not constitute the final words of the documentary. Instead, it is West's playing of a tape to Beckermann and Aichholzer, an addendum to the interview of the day before, that forms the epilogue to the documentary. It is a monologue that, as Dagmar Lorenz has suggested, is evocative of a Kaddish for all of West's relatives who did not survive the war (including West's mother, and seven uncles and aunts and their families).[20] As Beckermann has described in an interview, for West, who had never spoken publicly about being Jewish, and who had only ever seen himself as having been persecuted for his political beliefs, this was the first time that he had spoken publically about the fate of his Jewish family.[21] Introducing the recording, West describes his sudden wish to speak about his family's experience in the Holocaust as a compulsion to preserve memory: "Es hat mich einfach dazu gedrängt, das nicht untergehen zu lassen" (*WR*; I felt the strong urge not to let this become lost). Toward the beginning of the monologue, there is a static shot of the Vienna Riesenrad by night, in contrast to the daytime image of the Riesenrad at the beginning of the film, signaling that we are now leaving Vienna on our return journey out of the city. As at the beginning of the film, there is a long take of the view from the window of a train, now traveling out of Vienna at dusk. The Nordbahnhof, buildings, and warehouses, and the Danube all come into view, before the images are reduced to lampposts against a pitch-black sky, seen from the train compartment window. In this manner, the narrative curve of the film mirrors the journey that Jews from all corners of the Austro-Hungarian Empire made to the imperial capital at the turn of the twentieth century, before being driven out of the city, which they had made their home, during the Holocaust. The shot of the nighttime Riesenrad is held by the camera for several seconds, as if to imprint the image on the retina of the viewer, in a similar way that those driven east to ghettos and concentration camps by the Nazis would perhaps imprint such picture-postcard images of Vienna in their minds, not knowing whether they would ever see the city again. The images from the window of the train, departing the city with its manifold lights, giving way to a landscape where only the lights of passing trains or lampposts may be seen, evoke the desolate journey into literal and figurative darkness that West's relatives and thousands of other Viennese and Austrian Jews took.

The title of the film, "Return to Vienna," evokes the precariousness of Jewish assimilation in Austria prior to the Anschluss. Despite decades of assimilation, Viennese Jews were still regarded as not belonging to the Austrian *Heimat*, something Beckermann has written about poignantly in her 1989 book *Unzugehörig: Österreicher und Juden nach 1945* (Not Belonging: Austrians and Jews after 1945).[22] Assimilation is revealed to have been in vain, with the home of Austrian Jews in Vienna manifesting itself as transitory, precarious. This is underlined by the use of window imagery in the film, which evokes spatial separation and the idea of the outsider looking in. Windows feature prominently both here and in *Die papierene Brücke* (there will be more to say about this in the next section), in both cases serving to underline literal and figurative distance from the objects depicted. West's final words, meanwhile, uphold an imperative to remember the Holocaust:

> Schon lange her, viel Zeit ist vergangen, man weiß nicht mehr viel davon. Es gibt viele, die nichts mehr davon wissen wollen. Deshalb ist es doch gut, wenn man ab und zu davon spricht, daran erinnert, was das für eine Zeit war, in der man damals gelebt hat. (*WR*)
>
> [It was long ago, a lot of time has passed, one does not know a lot about it anymore. There are many who no longer want to know anything about it. Therefore, it is good to speak about it now and then, and remember what kind of time it was, in which one lived.]

Here West, for the first time during the whole interview, alludes to the political climate in contemporary Austria, implying that there are many who would prefer to forget that the Holocaust ever happened. Indeed, this attitude was adopted as official government policy in the postwar era, a stance notoriously epitomized by the statement of Oskar Helmer (Austrian minister of the interior, 1945–59) on the issue of restitution and the return of Jewish émigrés to Austria: "Ich bin dafür, die Sache in die Länge zu ziehen" (I am for dragging the matter out).[23] For this reason, it is imperative, West argues, to counter forgetting of the Holocaust by speaking about it, and thereby to work against the silence and repression that constituted much of postwar Austrian discourse on the recent past, and was certainly predominant in the early 1980s when the film was made. In a 2007 interview conducted on the occasion of the reissuing of the film as part of a boxed set of Beckermann's documentaries, Beckermann contrasted West's articulacy throughout the course of *Wien retour* with the speechlessness of Austria at the time: "In diesem damals doch sehr sprachlosen Österreich, auch in der Kultur ziemlich sprachlosen

Österreich, in dem eher derb und herb artikuliert wurde, wollte ich gerade jemanden zeigen, der auf dieser Art und Weise reden kann" (In that very speechless Austria, also speechless in terms of its cultural life, where things were being articulated in a rather rough and coarse manner, I wanted to show someone who could speak in the way that he does).[24]

West's words, spoken at a time when the far right was once again gaining in popularity in Austria, point to the unresolved issues of Austria's National Socialist past, which would come spectacularly out into the open in the late 1980s. In the year that *Wien retour* was made, the *Sozialistische Partei Österreichs* (Socialist Party of Austria) lost its absolute majority in the general election of April 1983, and entered into a coalition with the right-wing *Freiheitliche Partei Österreichs* (Freedom Party of Austria). Subsequently, the Waldheim affair of 1986–88 would see the Austrian presidential candidate assert that he had "only done his duty" when accused of war crimes during his time as a Wehrmacht officer in Greece and the Balkans. Beckermann herself, meanwhile, has cited her motivation for making the film as twofold: "Jemandem das Wort zu geben, der in der heutigen gesellschaftlichen Situation in Österreich nur ungern gehört wird ... Und den Zusammenhang herzustellen zwischen der Zerschlagung der Arbeiterbewegung und dem Schicksal der Juden, die Verknüpfung von Minderheiten mit den fortschrittlichen Bewegungen zu zeigen" (to give a voice to someone who in today's society in Austria is only heard reluctantly ... and to make the connection between the destruction of the workers' movement and the fate of the Jews, to show the conjunction of minorities and progressive movements).[25]

Beckermann thereby connects the experience of marginalization to progressive political movements, and serves to counter the marginalization that West has experienced throughout his life, by making him the center of her film. This is something that has resonated in the film's reception, with Peter Turrini writing in *profil*: "Ein Mensch wie Franz West hat in Österreich wenig Öffentlichkeit" (A person like Franz West is given little publicity in Austria).[26] Christina Guenther has asserted that, in her films, Beckermann has been engaged in "working against invisibility" of the Jewish experience in postwar Austria.[27] This focus on marginalized groups has permeated Beckermann's works throughout her career, whether these are African Americans in *American Passages* (2011), women in *Ein flüchtiger Zug nach dem Orient* (A Fleeting Train to the Orient; in English as *A Fleeting Passage to the Orient*, 1999), or asylum seekers in *Those Who Go Those Who Stay* (2013). Meanwhile, Beckermann's earliest films, *Arena besetzt* (Occupied Arena; in English as *Arena Squatted*, 1977), *Auf amol a Streik* (Suddenly, a Strike, 1978), and *Der Hammer steht auf der Wies'n da draussen* (The Hammer is Out There on the Meadows; in English as *The Steel Hammer Out There on the Grass*, 1981), are all concerned with the labor movement and industrial relations in Austria, making the choice to focus on an individual who was strongly involved in the Austrian labor movement in *Wien retour* a logical progression for Beckermann. What was new for Beckermann's filmmaking at this stage, however, was the explicit concern with the protagonist's Jewish identity in addition to his socialist background. The film may therefore be viewed as a turning point in Beckermann's filmmaking; her work over the following two decades would place Jewish protagonists and questions of Jewish identity at the forefront of her films. *Wien retour*, in its melancholic journey to the past, in its privileging both of West's story and that of interwar Red Vienna, constitutes a reflective, critical nostalgia for "the past as it could have been," in Boym's terms, thereby prompting the viewer to reflect on the lessons that may be drawn from West's story for the future.[28]

Die papierene Brücke

In the second film of her trilogy on Jewish identity, *Die papierene Brücke*, Beckermann undertakes a journey from her native Vienna to her father's former home in the historical region of Bukovina, a personal journey that simultaneously traces the once vibrant Jewish communities of central Europe. She visits the Jewish community in Rădăuți (in German as Radautz), northern Romania, and travels to Osijek in Yugoslavia (now Croatia) where an American film company has reconstructed the concentration camp of Theresienstadt for the filming of Herman Wouk's *War and Remembrance* (1988–89). Here Beckermann interviews Jewish Austrians, who have come to act as extras in the film. We also see interviews with Beckermann's mother and father, as well as a sequence showing Beckermann's father participating in a protest in central Vienna, against the election of Kurt Waldheim as president of Austria in 1986. *Die papierene Brücke* is an autobiographical documentary, with Beckermann, in contrast to the use of an impartial narrator in *Wien retour*, narrating her thoughts in voice-over throughout. The film essay begins with a camera pan of Beckermann's attic; then there is a cut to a shot of two men, with their backs to the camera, driving a horse-cart in a misty landscape. As the camera follows the horse-cart, before stopping and letting the cart disappear into the mist, we hear Beckermann relating the parable of Hagazussa (a ghostly figure and storyteller), a story adapted from the recollections of Manès Sperber,[29] which gives the film its title:

> Es ist die Geschichte der Juden im Stedtl, die stolz auf ihre eiserne Brücke sind, doch nach der Ankunft des Messias ohne Zögern die neue Brücke aus Zigarettenpapier wählen, um singend ins ewige Leben zu ziehen, während die Zweifler und die Spötter mit der eisernen Brücke ins Wasser stürzen.[30]

[It is the story of the Jews in the shtetl, who are very proud of their iron bridge, but who upon the arrival of the Messiah choose the new bridge from cigarette paper without hesitation, and cross the bridge, singing, into eternal life, while the doubters and mockers fall with the iron bridge into the water.]

In a similar vein, Beckermann crosses a paper bridge in her film essay, attempting to salvage the fragile memories of her family's past prior to the Holocaust, and to visit the places that her ancestors originated from in a search for a viable identity as an Austrian Jewish woman in contemporary Austria.

Following this sequence, we are again returned to Beckermann's apartment and the view of the Marc-Aurel Strasse in central Vienna from the curtain-covered attic window. As Christina Guenther has highlighted, windows feature prominently in *Die papierene Brücke* and suggest, as in *Wien retour*, "a sense of extraterritoriality" and "separation."[31] A pan of the attic in Beckermann's house, which is clearly undergoing renovation, again shows a number of empty window frames and thereby serves to reinforce the theme of "separation." The feeling of being an outsider in her own city, as a Jewish woman growing up in postwar Vienna, is something that Beckermann has written about in her essay *Unzugehörig*, published just two years after the release of *Die papierene Brücke*. A further sense of disconnection and estrangement is evoked by a camera pan of Vienna's splendid Ringstrasse, shot from the window of a tram, while Beckermann narrates the story of her grandmother Rosa, who, as a Jewish woman, survived the war in hiding. Both the shots of the Marc-Aurel Strasse through the attic window and of Vienna's Ringstrasse from the window of the tram, evoke the image of the outsider looking in. In voice-over, Beckermann describes her growing interest in her family history, which manifested itself in drawing the routes of her family's migrations, interviewing family members, and looking at family photographs. In her study *Family Frames*, Marianne Hirsch posits the photograph as having a unique relationship to postmemory, as the subject, by looking at family photographs, hopes to "find some truth about the past . . . however mediated."[32] This exploration of family history prompts Beckermann to leave Vienna for northern Romania, where her father lived before the war, explaining: "Aber manchmal ist nur die Himmelsrichtung klar, in die man fahren will, oder der Klang einer Sprache, der einen anzieht. Oft sind es Namen, Ortsnamen, die man auf der Landkarte nie gesucht hat." (*PB*; Sometimes one only knows the direction one wants to travel in, or it is the sound of a language that attracts one. Often it is names, place-names that one has never looked for on a map.) These words are spoken immediately following a medium shot of a roadblock in the same misty conditions in which we previously saw the receding horse-cart, to the accompaniment of Romanian voices on a crackly radio, signaling that Beckermann has arrived in Romania. The roadblock in a misty landscape, together with the indistinct voices, evokes an image of an elusive and difficult-to-reach destination. The radio voices give way to the sound of sawing, before we see a medium shot of a tree being felled by workmen along a suburban road.

The place-names that Beckermann is so attached to, allegorically, point to another time, persisting as traces of a submerged topography, that of the Austro-Hungarian Empire from which Beckermann's ancestors originated. The place-names thereby become deeply auratic. Beckermann's privileging of place-names in the quotation above is strongly reminiscent of Ingeborg Bachmann's exploration of the aura of place-names and their status as topographical markers in her fourth Frankfurt Lecture on Poetics, "Der Umgang mit Namen" (The Treatment of Names, 1960). For Bachmann, place-names have an aura that points to a submerged history or imaginary topography that could be revived through literature, forming part of an "Atlas, den nur die Literatur sichtbar macht" (an atlas that only literature makes visible).[33] Beckermann's project, albeit in the genre of the documentary film rather than fiction, is to make the places behind the auratic names visible. In Walter Benjamin's definition, an object's aura is created by an object finding itself in a unique and unrepeatable moment in place and time, and being characterized by a unique appearance of distance.[34] Names such as Bukovina and Czernowitz thereby become particularly auratic, as the historical contingencies that gave rise to their names are now irrevocably superseded. The names become objects of melancholic cathexis, as together with the architecture of the period, they are, in many cases, all that is left of the Habsburg era that Beckermann's father remembers. For Beckermann herself, Czernowitz and the Bukovina constitute a "postmemory," in Marianne Hirsch's terms, a memory that the subject never experienced, that is "indirect" and "belated," but that is vivid enough so that the subject feels he or she really remembers it.[35] Czernowitz, in particular, can be said to function as a model case for postmemory, as Marianne Hirsch and Leo Spitzer illustrate in their 2010 book *Ghosts of Home: The Afterlife of Czernowitz in Jewish Memory*. As Hirsch and Spitzer trace, throughout the twentieth century, the city has been variously named Cernăuți (as part of Romania, 1918–45), Chernovtsy (as part of the USSR, 1945–89), and Chernivtsi (as part of Ukraine, since 1989).[36] Nevertheless, long after the city was no longer part of the Austro-Hungarian Empire, it has been perpetuated as "Czernowitz" in cultural memory (the name it held between 1774 and 1918), and with it "an *idea* of a pre–First World War multicultural and multilingual tolerant city."[37] Beckermann sets off on her personal journey through northern Romania partly in order to ascertain whether these cultural myths correspond with reality.

In Radautz, northern Romania, Beckermann meets the aging Jewish community where a congregation of ten elderly men meet every day in a synagogue built in honor of the Austro-Hungarian Emperor Franz Joseph I. Pensioner Herbert Gropper shows Beckermann the cemetery, a deeply melancholic landscape. At first we see a long shot of Gropper walking among the slanted and weather-beaten gravestones, with the lone human figure among symbols of death and mortality creating a desolate image. Following this we see a medium shot of Gropper explaining the significance of a gravestone that incorporates a statue of a severed tree. The gravestone is that of a man who took his own life, a sin according to both Jewish and Christian teaching, as Gropper explains. As Andrea Reiter has also observed, the severed tree resonates with that of the image of the tree being felled in the opening sequence in Romania.[38] Allegorically, if we take trees to represent life paths, the recurrence of severed trees in the course of fifteen minutes of screen time can be read as an allusion to the lives of Beckermann's relatives who perished in the Holocaust, and to the severing of a central European Jewish tradition, making Beckermann's search for roots all the more problematic. Further, the stony and the wintry landscape of the graveyard evokes traditional associations of melancholy with the earth and the seasons of autumn and winter in medieval humoral cosmology, a conception of melancholy for which Albrecht Dürer's engraving *Melencolia I* (1514) is emblematic.[39] The weather-beaten and age-worn gravestones, some half-submerged into the earth, their inscriptions worn away, also resonate with Walter Benjamin's conception of the ruin as an allegorical symbol of transience and of a submerged history, here that of pre-Holocaust central European Jewish culture.[40] Members of the local community tell Beckermann that the younger generation of Romanian Jews are emigrating, to Israel or the United States. These scenes, filmed in a town that has certainly seen better days, contrast greatly with the stories of a vibrant Jewish community that existed in the Bukovina before the war that we see Beckermann's father relating later on in the film.

In voice-over, Beckermann justifies her desire to travel to northern Romania with the following statement: "Ich glaube, dass ich einfach neugierig war, ob es dort noch Bilder zu den Geschichten gibt, mit denen ich aufgewachsen bin" (*PB*; I think I was just curious to see whether there were still images to the stories I had grown up with). Beckermann finds that there are not, and when she does find images that correspond to the stories she was told, she feels strangely divorced from them: "Wie Fotos, so kamen sie mir vor. Die letzten Juden von Radautz, ganz hoch oben im Norden Rumäniens." (*PB*; Like photos, that is how they seemed to me. The last Jews of Radautz, right up in northern Romania.) These words are spoken during two medium shots showing elderly men sitting in a room in the synagogue built at the time of Emperor Franz Joseph

I. Photographs showing, in Barthes's view, the moment of transformation of subject to object, and the "micro-version of death" that this signifies,[41] are here symptomatic of the moribundity of the community. Beckermann's viewing of the Jewish community of Radautz "like photos" also suggests that these images correspond to the ones that she has previously seen in family albums or books, yet this is not necessarily the right kind of recognition. The fact that individuals resemble people in photographs taken years ago is not symptomatic of a thriving, dynamic community. The journey to northern Romania thereby proves a deeply uncanny experience, in Freudian terms, both homely and, as the frightening defamiliarized manifestation of something that used to be homely, distinctly unhomely.[42] The places she visits and the images she sees in Radautz are unable to make good the loss of members of her family, the loss of home, and the loss of a sense of belonging. As Reiter puts it: "Beckermann can neither find the world that matches the nostalgic memories of their former residents nor can she connect to the world she herself encounters on her journey to Eastern Europe."[43] Reiter reads Beckermann's sense of estrangement from the world of her ancestors as symptomatic for "post-memory" in Hirsch's terms.[44] The projected return to origins that Beckermann had envisaged for her journey turns to disappointment.

The much-vaunted golden age of the multicultural Habsburg Empire cannot be returned to in any concrete sense, and this is made all the more pertinent by the contrast between these stories of the past and the realities of the present. For this reason Beckermann even voices relief when she is unable to film in Czernowitz where her father came from. During a short preliminary visit to Chernovtsy, at that time part of the USSR, Beckermann realized that filming there would be very difficult. As she relates in a conversation, conducted in 1987, with the writer Elfriede Jelinek: "Von der österreichichen und jüdischen Geschichte der Stadt wollte man nichts wissen" (People did not want to know anything about the Austrian and Jewish history of this city).[45] In *Die papierene Brücke*, Beckermann relates: "Es ist gut, von manchen Orten keine Bilder zu haben, so bleiben sie Erinnerung" (*PB*; It is good to have no images of certain places, so that the memories remain). In an article written for the Austrian weekly *profil* in 1985, Beckermann describes her short sojourn in Czernowitz, and relates how her film material was confiscated by the authorities.[46] At the same time, Beckermann's inability to include Czernowitz in her film ensures that the aura of the place is preserved, facilitating the maintenance of what Benjamin termed the "einmalige Erscheinung einer Ferne, so nah sie sein mag" (unique appearance of distance, however close it may be).[47]

Instead we witness an instance of family myth creation as the film narrative of Beckermann's travels is intercut with an interview with her father, Salo Beckermann, born in 1911,[48] conducted in the textile shop that he owns in Vienna. A series of close-up shots show Salo Beckermann arranging stock in his office, before a medium close-up shot focuses in on him as he nostalgically remembers Czernowitz, asserting that it has remained his spiritual home despite decades of living in Vienna, and praising it as a model multicultural site, both during the Habsburg Empire and after 1918, where, prior to the advent of Hitler, "es fast kein Antisemitismus gegeben [hat]" (*PB*; there was hardly any anti-Semitism). He displays a high level of Habsburg nostalgia, remembering how his own father fought in the Austrian Army and was an Austro-Hungarian patriot, just as Beckermann himself was brought up to be. To illustrate this point, Salo Beckermann points out that he has a portrait of Emperor Franz Joseph I hanging on the wall of his office (although we are not shown this), a melancholic reminder of a vanished era that he is unable to relinquish an attachment to. Wilfried Geldner, in his review of *Die papierene Brücke* for the *Süddeutsche Zeitung*, described Salo Beckermann as resembling "ein Held von Joseph Roth, einer der den Kaiser und das Land geliebt hat" (a hero from a Joseph Roth novel, who loved the Kaiser and the country).[49] Having fought in the Red Army during the war, Salo Beckermann ended up in Vienna, which, even after the war, had lost none of its aura for *Altösterreicher* (Old Austrians), those irrevocably attached to the Habsburg Empire. Here he met Beckermann's mother, originally from Vienna, who, together with her mother and sister, had fled to Palestine following the Anschluss, and who was in Vienna for a holiday. Following their marriage, the Beckermanns, largely at the wish of Salo Beckermann, chose to settle in Vienna. As a Jew originating from eastern Europe, Beckermann's father is what the filmmaker has described as typical of the postwar Jewish community in Vienna,[50] the majority of which was made up of those who had migrated to Vienna after the war, and for whom the city was still the iconic imperial capital, untainted with associations of anti-Semitism and the Holocaust:

> Die osteuropäischen Juden, die nach 1945 die Mehrheit der Wiener Gemeinde bildeten, hatten ihre traumatischen Erfahrungen nicht hier vor Ort gemacht, sondern mit ukrainischen und rumänischen Faschisten, ungarischen Pfeilkreuzlern und deutschsprechenden Nazis. Sie hatten keine Vorkriegserfahrungen mit dem österreichischen Antisemitismus und dem Verhalten der Bevölkerung nach dem Anschluß. Sie brachten im Gegenteil ein romantisch verklärtes Bild von der Kaiserstadt mit, die für sie auch nach dem Zerfall der Monarchie Anziehungspunkt geblieben war. Deutsche Sprache und Kultur hatte für die Juden Galiziens und der Bukowina schon vor der nazistischen Machtergreifung eine besondere Bedeutung.[51]

> [The Eastern European Jews, which made up the majority of the Viennese Jewish community after 1945, did not experience trauma

in Vienna itself, but rather with Ukrainian and Romanian fascists, members of the Hungarian Arrow Cross, and German-speaking Nazis. They had no experience of Austrian anti-Semitism before the war and the behavior of the population following the Anschluss. On the contrary, they brought with them a romantic, glorified image of the imperial city, which remained a center of attraction even after the collapse of the monarchy. For the Jews of Galicia and the Bukovina, German language and culture had a particular significance even before the Nazi takeover.]

Elsewhere in *Unzugehörig*, Beckermann has written about the vicissitudes of this elevation of the hallowed past of the Habsburg Empire by Austrian Jews, at the expense of the darker sides of emancipation and assimilation: "Sie phantasieren sich zurück in das geschönte Vorgestern, ohne sich klarzumachen, daß es das Vorgestern war, das zum Gestern der nationalsozialistischen Verfolgung führte" (They fantasize themselves back into an airbrushed ancient past, without realizing that this was an ancient past that led to the past of National Socialist persecution).[52] Yet it is not only the perceived advantages of the past that prompt this idealization, but also the insufficiencies of the present. As emerges in the interviews with Beckermann's parents in *Die papierene Brücke*, both Bety and Salo Beckermann do not feel entirely at home in Vienna. Beckermann's mother, for whom her eleven-year-long emigration, between 1938 and 1949, in Palestine (later Israel), was highly formative, asserts that, despite decades of living in Vienna, Israel has remained her home. Bety Beckermann speaks of her guilt with regard to raising her children in Austria, with its recurrent problems of anti-Semitism, but asserts that she could not persuade Beckermann's father to move to Israel. For her Austria was, and will always remain, the country "wo man mich und meine Familie hinausgeschmissen hat" (*PB*; where my family and I were thrown out). Beckermann's father also feels that his spiritual home is elsewhere: "Ich bin noch immer in Czernowitz" (*PB*; I am still in Czernowitz). It is unsurprising, in this context, that Beckermann herself has described her experience of growing up in Vienna as "exterritorial" (exterritorial).[53]

Yet while Salo Beckermann certainly appears to espouse an uncritical nostalgia with relation to Czernowitz, it is clear that this rose-tinting of and flight into the past allows him to cope with an unsatisfactory present. This is reinforced in *Die papierene Brücke*, upon Beckermann's return from her travels in Romania and Croatia, by black-and-white documentary footage of the protests on Vienna's central square, the Stephansplatz, for and against Dr. Kurt Waldheim as president, in the summer of 1986. This sequence, filmed by Beckermann using a handheld camera largely in one long take (we see the camera swerve jerkily and hands placed over the lens to prevent Beckermann filming), sees Beckermann's father become the target of anti-Semitic abuse. He is called a "Judenbub" (*PB*; Jew boy) by a Waldheim supporter who, prior to addressing him, expounds his views with regard to a worldwide Jewish conspiracy. The fact that the viewer sees anti-Semitism openly expressed in Vienna's central square, with its symbolic function for Viennese and Austrian identity, is testament to the impunity with which individuals felt able to openly express their anti-Semitism at the height of the Waldheim affair, and to the resurfacing of a traumatic and unconfronted historical legacy of the Holocaust in Austria. As Beckermann herself comments in the voice-over: "In diesem Sommer ist es endlich offensichtlich geworden" (*PB*; This summer it finally became obvious).

Beckermann's return to Vienna, following her journey in Eastern Europe, is signaled by a shot of the interior of what Beckermann tells us is her favorite coffeehouse in Vienna, the Café Prückel, which faces out onto a statue of the infamous Viennese city mayor and anti-Semite Dr. Karl Lueger on the eponymous square. Once again, we are shown the statue from an interior window, suggesting a precarious homeliness within the café. This resonates with Hillary Hope Herzog's description of the relationship of Beckermann and that of many other Austrian Jewish writers to their native city as being "simultaneously at home and unhomed in Vienna," allowing them the critical distance to comment upon the cultural environment in which they live.[54] The threatening statue is safely outside the café's walls, but is symptomatic of the filmmaker-narrator's unease within Vienna. In an interview conducted ahead of the release of *Die papierene Brücke*, Beckermann revealed that the film was initially planned as "ein Abschied" (a farewell) to Vienna.[55] Beckermann claims in voice-over that she is no longer disturbed by the statue of the "Patron des Wiener Antisemitismus" (*PB*; patron of Viennese anti-Semites); on the contrary, "man weiß woran man ist" (*PB*; one knows where one stands). However, this sentiment reveals a strong sense of unhomeliness, which is further reinforced by the aforementioned contemporary documentary footage of the protests for and against Waldheim. In *Die papierene Brücke*, Beckermann abandons the conventional documentary genre in favor of the genre of autobiographical documentary, dispensing with an objective narrator and instead narrating her own thoughts in voice-over throughout. The film marks a shift in Beckermann's work toward a much more subjective and autobiographical form of filmmaking. This is a reflection of the political climate of the late 1980s, when the anti-Semitism sparked by the Waldheim affair prompted Austrian Jews like Beckermann to assert and articulate their own Jewish identity much more than they had in the past. In this sense, as Dagmar Lorenz has asserted, the late 1980s marked a coming-of-age for many Austrian Jewish writers and filmmakers of Beckermann's generation.[56]

The sequence immediately following the Waldheim protest shows visitors at the 1985 *Jugendstil* exhibition "Dream and Reality" (Traum und Wirklichkeit) held at the Vienna *Künstlerhaus*, a museum that in 1939 hosted the notorious "Decadent Art" exhibition. This is commented on with dry irony by Beckermann: "Freud, Schnitzler, Schönberg. Das Wien der Jahrhundertwende ist modern. ... Seit der Ausstellung über 'entartete Kunst' wurden hier nicht mehr so viele Juden gezeigt. Jetzt, auf einmal, gehören sie dazu." (*PB*; Freud, Schnitzler, Schoenberg. Fin de siècle Vienna is "in." ... They haven't shown so many Jews here since the "Decadent Art" exhibition. Now, suddenly, they belong.) Viennese Jewish modernism may have been coopted by official Austrian culture as a tourist brand, but Beckermann suggests that there is still some way to go before she and other Austrian Jews can feel that they truly belong in modern-day Austria, as the previous sequence, shot on Austria's most prominent public square, demonstrated. As Beckermann asserted in *Unzugehörig* regarding her status as a member of the second generation in Austria: "Unsere Gefühle und Gedanken, unsere Identität als Kinder der Überlebenden, werden in diesem Land ignoriert und beleidigt" (Our feelings and thoughts, our identity as children of the survivors, are ignored and denigrated in this country).[57] The exhibition is shown via a long shot of an arched marble doorway leading to the rooms where the exhibits are displayed. As we see visitors disappear into the room behind the doorway, we hear *Arvo Pärt's Tabula Rasa*, creating an eerie and melancholic effect, and serving as a reminder that the artists whose works are being exhibited are now dead, and with them the Viennese modernist culture that they instigated. While their legacy is melancholically preserved in exhibitions and museums, the connection to this culture was irrevocably severed during the Holocaust and cannot be returned to.

Die papierene Brücke ends where it began, in the attic of Beckermann's flat, located in the former Jewish textile quarter. As in northern Romania, here too, Beckermann tells us, old traditions are dying out. Most of the textile shops are closing as the proprietors' children choose to attend university or emigrate rather than continue the family business. As if to emphasize her point, there is a medium long shot of one of the elderly proprietors (Adolf Doft, who reappears in *Homemad(e)*) pulling down the blind on his shop front. At the end of her film essay Beckermann is equivocal. The journey has come full circle without having provided the answers she was searching for. Instead, Beckermann's film constitutes an attempt simply to preserve the memories of her family history, to visit the communities and places that her father told her about before there is no one left to corroborate these memories. The end sequence of the film, where we see the camera slowly pan across a series of Beckermann's family photographs laid out on a tablecloth, suggests that the melancholy journey that Beckermann has embarked on to uncover her family history is far from over, with the photographs acting as an imperative to continue her engagement with her personal and collective history.

Homemad(e)

Homemad(e) thematically adjoins *Die papierene Brücke* by returning to the same street from which Beckermann set off and returned from her journey in *Die papierene Brücke*, and by exploring the fate of a textile quarter, which in *Die papierene Brücke* was described as "dying out."[58] In *Homemad(e)*, a further "Vienna film,"[59] made more than a decade after *Die papierene Brücke* and nearly two decades after *Wien retour*, Beckermann ventures no farther than her own street in Vienna, the Marc-Aurel Strasse, a street already introduced in *Die papierene Brücke* as the historical center for the city's Jewish textile merchants. The thematic continuity between *Die papierene Brücke* and *Homemad(e)* is further emphasized, in that the textile shop proprietor Adolf Doft, introduced briefly at the end of *Die papierene Brücke*, reappears to take on a central role in *Homemad(e)*. In voice-over, Beckermann locates the street in the topography of the city with reference to landmarks that serve as inescapable reminders of the city's history, with the only remaining synagogue and the Gestapo Headquarters' memorial located within meters of the street. Yet Beckermann asserts that she is not interested in the street's location within the historical cityscape of Vienna, directing her attention, instead, to the residents of the street: "Was mich interessiert sind die Menschen, die diskutieren und gestikulieren, und intrigieren, und studieren, oder einfach nur vorbeispazieren" (*H*; What interests me are the people debating, gesticulating, plotting, studying or simply walking by). In the course of the film, Beckermann interviews a total of eighteen individuals, among them shop owners, pensioners, writers (Elfriede Gerstl and Franz Schuh), a filmmaker, a photographer, a restaurant owner, a waiter, and a nightclub doorman. Beckermann's conversations with the street's inhabitants, several of them Holocaust survivors, reveal their painful memories of the past beneath the veneer of normality. As Doron Rabinovici, in his review of *Homemad(e)*, comments: "unter der Gegenwart scheint durch, was hier einst geschah" (beneath the present, what once happened here shows through).[60]

Some individuals, such as Adolf Doft, reappear more than once in various settings (the café, the interior and exterior of his shop, the street); others only appear once. For the most part, the film alternates between scenes shot inside or outside the Café Salzgries (taking up a total of forty-nine minutes of screen time in the eighty-four-minute film) or Doft's shop (taking up twenty minutes of screen time altogether), the two other locations being a Persian restaurant and the outside of a bar. At first, it seems as if the film may be a "day-in-the-life" of the Marc-Aurel Strasse, as it opens with Doft and other shop owners conversing outside his shop in the summer morning sunshine, before the action proceeds to the Café Salzgries opposite, where regulars take their morning coffee. However, two-thirds of the way into the film, a shot of snow being cleared in the Marc-Aurel Strasse, and passersby dressed in winter clothing, introduces a twenty-minute sequence dealing with the 1999 general election. The end sequence of the film (where we see restaurant-goers sitting outside in light, summer clothes), adjoins the summertime opening, thereby lending the film, and the street scenes it depicts, an aspect of circularity.

The action remains in the microcosm of this city street throughout the film. The rest of the city figures only as far as it falls within the frame. Occasionally, we can see the Danube canal and the pier in the distance. It is only during these rare moments that the city village is situated within the context of the rest of Vienna. As Hillary Hope Herzog has noted, the title of the film refers both to the film's "homemade quality" (Beckermann makes frequent use of a handheld camera in this film), and its thematic preoccupations.[61] What emerges is a cozy and intimate atmosphere in which the viewer is also invited to share. We hear Beckermann asking her interviewees questions or appearing in the frame herself. Yet beneath the easygoing camaraderie, an underlying sadness and melancholy pervade the street, the epicenter of which is the Café Salzgries, where the regulars are still mourning the passing of the late proprietor, Ernst Göschl. A sequence showing regulars reminiscing about Göschl, who played the function of bringing people together in this Viennese coffeehouse, is introduced through a shot of his portrait on the wall of the café, which serves as a melancholic reminder of his passing. The sense of melancholy is also heightened by the fact that the majority of people Beckermann interviews are elderly, and so their conversations with Beckermann take on the character of life reflections.

Beckermann's microjourney around her own street allows her to show a community in flux, poised between the street's traditional image as a bustling Jewish textile quarter and being part of a twenty-first-century leisure economy. However, in contrast to the previous two films discussed in this chapter, *Homemad(e)* is less melancholic in tone, largely because Beckermann does not make use of nondiegetic music in this film (in contrast to the use of Arvo Pärt's music in *Die papierene Brücke* and, for example, the music of Pierre-Max Dubois in *Wien retour*), but also because Beckermann does not invest her journey around her own street with the same weight of expectation with which the journeys to the Vienna of yesteryear and the journey to northern Romania, in *Wien retour* and *Die papierene Brücke*, respectively, were undoubtedly inflected.

However, the editorial choices in the film mean that the darker sides of some of the inhabitants' experiences are never far away. We see

Adolf Doft in the very first and very last shot of the film. He is the figure who takes up the most screen time, appearing a total of ten times throughout and serving as a unifying figure in the film. In one sequence with Doft, "the last surviving Jewish textile merchant"[62] in the street, it emerges that he spent four-and-a-half years in Auschwitz, Flossenbürg, and Buchenwald. A medium close-up shot shows Doft against a background of shelves containing packaged clothes in his shop, while he relates how his parents and three siblings did not survive the Holocaust, and how he suffers from survivor's guilt, claiming to have lived in vain since 1941 when the rest of his family was murdered. Doft's wife, meanwhile, relates how their children have emigrated from Austria. The trope (already introduced in *Die papierene Brücke*) of the younger generation of Austrian Jews leaving Austria, particularly in this traditional textile-making area, constitutes a deeply melancholic reflection on the fate of the Austrian Jewish community following the Holocaust. The elderly Dofts and Beckermann's parents, featured in *Die papierene Brücke*, know that the businesses they have worked so hard to build up will die with them, and so will the traditional Jewish textile quarter that they represent.

A long sequence shot in the Café Salzgries (taking up seven minutes of screen time, it is by far the longest interview in the eighty-four-minute film), focuses on the pensioner and Holocaust survivor Senta Segall, another inhabitant of the street. Segall describes how she and her neighbors, many of them Jewish, never spoke to each other about what they had gone through, even though they were aware of which concentration camps their neighbors had been in. She relates how what we frequently term repression in the psychoanalytic sense was the norm, necessary even, in the postwar years, when all were primarily concerned with rebuilding their lives. Segall's attempt at confronting her experience through writing failed. Having begun writing her life story, she relished writing about her childhood, yet when the narrative reached the point of her arrival at the concentration camp she could not continue. The trauma of the Holocaust cannot be surmounted; it runs as an undercurrent beneath the veneer of normality of everyday life in the street. By giving a voice to Holocaust survivors like Adolf Doft and Senta Segall, Beckermann, both here and in *Wien retour* and *Die papierene Brücke*, privileges a form of *Eingedenken*, insightful remembrance. *Eingedenken*, conceived by Walter Benjamin in his theses "On the Concept of History" as the opposite of monumental history, in its privileging of individual, subjective memory, is a form of remembering that abolishes clear distinctions between the past and the present, seeking to reactivate the voices of the past in the present.[63] By showing the past to be omnipresent for the victims of the Holocaust, Beckermann's films serve to counteract a historicization of the Holocaust, what Doron Rabinovici has termed "das Vergehen der Vergangenheit" (the passing of the past).[64]

The interview with Senta Segall is followed by a sequence focusing on the impact of the election of the Freiheitliche Partei Österreichs (Freedom Party of Austria), headed by Jörg Haider, into the Austrian coalition government in February 2000. Beckermann takes the pulse among the inhabitants of the Marc-Aurel Strasse, starting with the Café Salzgries, which throughout the film is presented as an exemplary site for civic life. Following an introduction in which Beckermann explains in voice-over that "jeder vierter Wiener hat Herrn Haider gewählt" (*H*; every fourth Viennese voted for Mr. Haider), and during which four individuals at the café come into the frame, she presents a range of responses to the political shift in the country, ranging from resignation and disregard for politics, to active engagement in the protest culture that sprung up in opposition to the FPÖ-ÖVP coalition. Beckermann interviews photographers and filmmakers (notably Franz Novotny and Lisl Ponger) involved in protests and political broadcasts. Whereas an oppositional public sphere was tentatively emerging in 1986, in the wake of Waldheim's presidential candidacy and election, by the 1999 elections an oppositional culture had taken hold to counter what Beckermann herself has termed "Austronazismus."[65]

As Dagmar Lorenz has described, the many Austrian Jews involved in oppositional activities were instrumental in facilitating the establishment of an Austrian civil society.[66] This marked a shift from the parents' generation, which "contemplated how to coexist with and eventually be accepted by the Catholic majority in an increasingly anti-Semitic climate."[67] To some extent, as Beckermann relates in *Unzugehörig*, this sentiment also held true for the "illusions" of Austrian Jews of her generation, who became involved in the left-wing movement around 1968, where individual identity was to be sublimated toward achieving socialist goals.[68] As Beckermann writes: "Wir verschwiegen nicht, daß wir Juden sind, wir sprachen nur nie davon." (We did not hide the fact that we are Jews, we just never spoke about it.)[69] This strategy became unraveled at the time of the Waldheim affair. The demise of Marxist ideology in the late 1980s and early 1990s also prompted Austrian Jewish intellectuals to, as Lorenz notes, "redefine[d] themselves through their Jewish ancestry."[70] The journalists and filmmakers involved in oppositional activities to the Haider government that Beckermann interviews, in their emphatic willingness to thematize the National Socialist past, contrast starkly with the attitude of the parents' generation, represented by Senta Segall. For Beckermann, the long silence on the National Socialist past in Austria was a fusion of victims being *unable* and perpetrators being *unwilling* to talk about the past, coalescing into a coexistence where, as Beckermann describes, the specificity of Jewish suffering during the Second World War was erased.[71]

In Beckermann's film essay on her home street, the Marc-Aurel Strasse stands allegorically for her Austrian homeland. It is at once homely (homemade), yet the persistent lack of a climate in which Austria's past is spoken about openly, and the concurrent ascent of radical right-wing politics, is enough, Beckermann suggests, to drive anyone to distraction, to render the home distinctly unhomely, or to make one "homemad." As Hillary Hope Herzog has written, "the unsteady adjective 'home-mad,' suggests that there is no simple answer" to the question of whether Beckermann and the Austrian Jewish community are really at home in Vienna.[72] While the Marc-Aurel Strasse certainly constitutes a home, it is a highly precarious one. In *Homemad(e)* the writer Franz Schuh describes the Marc-Aurel Strasse as a village in the city, yet, as Herzog has rightly asserted "the Marc-Aurel Strasse does not shield its inhabitants from a confrontation with the nation of which they are a part."[73] More contentious public spaces, such as the Dr.-Karl-Lueger-Platz with its statue of the anti-Semitic mayor, or the Stephansplatz, where Beckermann's father becomes the subject of anti-Semitic ranting in *Die papierene Brücke*, are only meters away from the Marc-Aurel Strasse. While the urban village of the Marc-Aurel Strasse certainly makes the vagaries of Austrian politics easier to bear, it does not preclude a collision with them.

Yet *Homemad(e)* is also the most optimistic of the three films discussed here. The new generation, exemplified by figures such as the filmmaker Franz Novotny and the photographer and filmmaker Lisl Ponger in the film, shows how the civic life existing in the delimited space of the Marc-Aurel Strasse may be transported outward into the rest of the city. While returning the Marc-Aurel Strasse to the vibrant textile quarter of old would neither be possible nor desirable in the context of a globalized economy, the street is shown to be lively and vital, with new restaurants nestling around the remaining textile shop. The film closes with the Jewish Doft conversing with his neighbor, Iranian-born hotelier Djavad Alam. A medium close-up shows the figures talking against a background of tables outside Alam's busy restaurant, with the film offering an alternative model for communal city living to that propagated by Austrian radical right-wing politics.

In *Wien retour*, *Die papierene Brücke*, and *Homemad(e)* the melancholic journeys that Beckermann undertakes function as a search for roots and personal identity in the wake of the destruction wrought by the Holocaust. From the interview with Franz West in *Wien retour* and Beckermann's visit to the Jewish community in northern Romania in *Die papierene Brücke*, to her interviews with the inhabitants of the Marc-Aurel Strasse, all of Beckermann's journeys (whether these are literal or, in the case of Franz West in *Wien retour*, metaphorical) seek to forge a connection to a pre-1938 Austrian and central European Jewish culture. All three films are concerned with returns to origins of various kinds, to places that have a great significance for the filmmaker, whether these are sites invested with the legacy of central European Jewish culture (Romania in

Die papierene Brücke, Vienna's second district in *Wien retour*, Vienna's traditional textile quarter in *Homemad(e)*), or sites connected to Beckermann's familial and personal history [Romania and Vienna in *Die papierene Brücke* and her own street in *Homemad(e)*]). All three films discussed here continually oscillate between the present and the past. They are attentive to a place's particular topographic legacy, yet Austria's present is not neglected, with Franz West's call to remember the Holocaust in *Wien retour* at a time when the Right was gaining ascendancy in Austria, the topical footage of the Waldheim demonstrations in *Die papierene Brücke*, and reflections upon the 1999 elections in *Homemad(e)*.

In reactivating the voices of the past in the present, these early films by Ruth Beckermann constitute an act of insightful remembrance for the victims of the Holocaust. They are suffused with a reflective nostalgia for the missed opportunities of the past, while highlighting the impossibility of returning to or recuperating the past in any way. However, through melancholically preserving the memories of the past, through the places that Beckermann chooses to focus on and the people she gives voice to, her documentaries serve to reintegrate the Austrian Jewish experience into the dominant narrative of Austrian history, and foreground the enduring trauma of the Holocaust. By creating a space in which the victims of Austrian Nazism can tell their stories, Beckermann's films serve to counteract Austria's long silence about its Nazi past.

2: Reconstructing a Home: Nostalgia in Anna Mitgutsch's *Haus der Kindheit*

> *One is always at home in one's past.*
> —Vladimir Nabokov, *Speak Memory*

HAUS DER KINDHEIT WAS THE SIXTH NOVEL published by the Austrian writer Anna Mitgutsch.[1] Mitgutsch who was born in 1948 in the Austrian city of Linz, is an academic and writer who divides her time between Linz and Boston in the United States. Her novels are largely concerned with issues of memory, identity, belonging, and Austria's Nazi past. Her work from the early 1990s onward is frequently concerned with journeys in search of roots, whether these are from the New World to Old Europe, or from Europe to the Middle East. The return to origins, which the protagonists anticipate in Mitgutsch's novels, are inevitably thwarted. In the novel *Abschied von Jerusalem* (Farewell to Jerusalem, 1995), the protagonist's search for roots in Jerusalem ends in tragedy, while in the novel *In fremden Städten* (In Foreign Cities, 1992), Mitgutsch presents the American-born Lillian leaving her Austrian family for the East Coast, yet failing to achieve the homecoming she anticipated.

Mitgutsch's novel *Haus der Kindheit* is no different in this respect. The first of Mitgutsch's novels to center on a male protagonist, *Haus der Kindheit* offers a powerful exploration of place, home, and belonging through the protagonist's quest to regain the house in the Austrian town of H. that his Jewish family left in 1928 when they moved to the United States, when Max was aged five. Max's aunt, uncle, and grandfather remained in the house, but the house was subsequently expropriated by the Nazis, and all three family members perished in the Holocaust. Despite growing up in New York, Max Berman is infected with his mother's melancholy for the Old World and for the home they left behind, and following her death, sets about reclaiming the "Haus seiner Kindheit" (*HdK*, 227; house of his childhood, *HoC*, 209). By the time that Max is ultimately successful in his quest he is nearly seventy, yet the projected return to origins rapidly turns to disillusionment through his experience of contemporary Austria.

The novel was well received upon its publication, with Karl-Markus Gauss asserting in the *Neue Zürcher Zeitung* that the novel "ist einer der wichtigsten Romane der neueren österreichischen Literatur" (is one of the most important novels of modern Austrian literature).[2] Gauss characterizes the novel both as a "Gesellschaftsroman" (social novel) and as a "politischer Roman" (political novel) that renders visible "die österreichische Misere" (the Austrian plight).[3] In addition to these categorizations, Anthony Bushell has also ascribed *Haus der Kindheit* to the tradition of the *anti-Heimat* (anti-patriotic) novel in German-language culture, a genre that serves to unmask any idyllic views of the rural landscape and lifestyle, and where instead "provincial Austria is revealed mercilessly as a place of bigotry and unexamined guilt."[4] Several critics, including Bruno Lässer, praised the novel's thematization of an issue that became very topical in Austria at the beginning of the twenty-first century, namely the restitution of property looted during the Nazi era.[5] As noted by Kristin Teuchtmann in her review of the novel,[6] the painting on the cover of the first edition of the novel was Egon Schiele's *Tote Stadt* (Dead City, 1912), which as Mitgutsch herself confirmed at a reading given at the University of Minnesota, also alluded to contemporary high-profile restitution cases involving Schiele's works.[7] The novel was also published at the time when, as Katherine Elizabeth Evans has highlighted, Jörg Haider's radical right-wing Austrian Freedom Party entered the Austrian coalition government in 2000, and the provenance of Haider's family wealth was subject to public scrutiny in Austria.[8]

Several critics also praised the mature and "unemotional" style[9] with which the novel critiques Austria's treatment of the past: "auf unpathetische, aber gerade deshalb umso überzeugendere Weise zeigt Anna Mitgutsch die verheerenden Folgen der hierzulande so gern praktizierten schlampigen Verhältnisse bei der Aufarbeitung der Nazizeit." (in an unemotional but all the more convincing manner Anna Mitgutsch shows the devastating consequences of the slipshod circumstances, so favored in this country, surrounding the working through of the Nazi past.)[10] Another reviewer similarly highlights the novel's treatment of the "Erinnerungs(un)kultur der österreichischen Nachkriegsjahrzehnte" (the lack of a memory culture in postwar Austria).[11] By contrast, Kirstin Breitenfellner contended that *Haus der Kindheit* lacked the drive of Mitgutsch's previous novels, and that the novel did not have anything to add to the well-trodden topic of exile and memory, calling it an "Exilroman remixed" (exile novel remixed).[12] However, negative reviews of the novel were few and far between. Katherine Evans asserts that with *Haus der Kindheit* Mitgutsch was able to free herself from "the categorization of a writer of *Frauenliteratur* (women's literature) or autobiography" and to "finally establish herself as a writer of serious political fiction."[13]

There have been a number of studies examining Mitgutsch's novel in the context of history, memory and remembrance,[14] photography,[15] postmemory,[16] topography,[17] and Austria's past and contemporary Austrian politics.[18] As highlighted by the critics cited above, issues of memory, identity, and belonging are of key concern to Mitgutsch, and these issues are foregrounded through her treatment of space and place. Topography and personal identity are inseparably linked, as has frequently been elaborated.[19] Often, the search for a stable identity is accompanied by a search for a point of origin that the subject construes as guarantor of this identity. As I have argued elsewhere, the attempt to return to this construed topographical point of origin opens up a fraught topographic experience, complicated by melancholy and nostalgia.[20] In his seminal study of the Baroque mourning play in *Ursprung des deutschen Trauerspiels* (The Origin of German Tragic Drama, 1928), the philosopher Walter Benjamin conceived origin as a dynamic, spatio-temporal process, rather than a finite point of origination or stasis.[21] The search for origin, however, unleashes the dynamic of trying to uncover the original within the complex process of origination, something that, as Benjamin shows, can never be achieved, but can only lead to processes of restoration and reestablishment that will forever remain incomplete. It is, however, precisely this search for a point of origin, which aims for a restoration or reestablishment of roots, which is so prevalent throughout Anna Mitgutsch's work, and in *Haus der Kindheit* especially.

The attempts at reestablishment and restoration, springing from a nostalgia for an imagined past, which we find in Mitgutsch's novel, lend themselves to an exploration of *Haus der Kindheit* in conjunction with Svetlana Boym's theories of nostalgia. While, as described above, a number of critics have sought to situate Mitgutsch's novel in the context of discourses on memory and postmemory, there have been no studies, to my knowledge, of the function of restorative and reflective nostalgia in *Haus der Kindheit*. As outlined in the introduction to this study, in her seminal 2001 work *The Future of Nostalgia* Svetlana Boym coined the terms "restorative" and "reflective" nostalgia to distinguish between two distinct types of nostalgia. Boym characterizes restorative nostalgia as primarily concerned with restoration and a return to origins, which "proposes to rebuild the lost home and patch up the memory gaps."[22] Reflective nostalgia, meanwhile, respects that the past cannot be returned to, while still maintaining a melancholy attachment to and a wish to preserve "shattered fragments of memory."[23] We can observe both types of nostalgia in Mitgutsch's novel, as the central protagonist tries to achieve a very concrete restoration of his childhood home, before realizing the futility of such an endeavor and moving toward a much more reflective engagement with his personal and collective history. The following discussion will examine how restorative and reflective nostalgia function in *Haus der Kindheit*, and what these reveal about the search for home and belonging in the novel.

The first half of *Haus der Kindheit* is concerned with the anticipation of Max Berman's planned reclamation of the expropriated family home in Upper Austria. The novel opens with a description of a photograph of the house that would invariably be put up in every apartment in New York that Max and his mother and brothers would move into, thereby making every new home into "einem weiteren Ort des Exils" (*HdK*, 7; one more place of exile, *HoC*, 3). The ever-present photograph is symptomatic of how the house in Austria becomes subject to processes of idealization throughout Max's childhood. Much has been written about the specific role of photography in the novel, particularly with relation to Marianne Hirsch's concept of postmemory, developed in her 1997 book *Family Frames*.[24] For Monika Shafi, drawing on Susan Sontag's 1973 elaboration of photographs as "das nostalgische Erinnerungsmedium *par excellence*" (the nostalgic medium of memory *par excellence*),[25] the photograph of the lost house represents "die verlorene Heimat Österreich" (the lost home of Austria).[26] Maria Regina Kecht meanwhile likens the use of photographs in *Haus der Kindheit* to the use of photographs in *jiskor bicher* (memorial books written by Shoah survivors about their destroyed communities), combining personal and collective memory, evoking "die vergangene und vernichtete Welt" (the vanished and destroyed world) and constituting a *memento mori*.[27] In addition to the auratic photograph of the house in H., the narrator describes another way in which "postmemories" of the house and of Europe were inscribed in Max's consciousness; his mother would take him to the beach near New York and point to the horizon where Europe and the home they had left behind lay (*HdK*, 7; *HoC*, 3–4). Boym, in *The Future of Nostalgia*, describes the past for the "restorative nostalgic," the nostalgic seeking to return to an enigmatic point of origin, as being "not a duration but a perfect snapshot."[28] For Max and his mother, the photograph of the house in H., mounted in ever-changing New York apartments, indeed becomes this "perfect snapshot" of an ideal past, frozen in time. The house, both for Max's mother and for Max himself, comes to stand for a feeling of homeliness, security, and belonging, everything that their life in the United States lacks:

> Das Haus, in dem er irgendwann in der Zukunft wohnen wollte, war nicht jenes heruntergekommene Gebäude aus den zwanziger Jahren, als dessen Besitzer er sich fühlte, sondern ein Kindheitstraum, gespeist aus der lebenslangen Sehnsucht seiner Mutter nach einem endgültigen Nachhausekommen. (*HdK*, 8)

> [The house he wanted to inhabit at some future date wasn't the dilapidated building from the twenties whose owner he now considered himself to be. It was rather a childhood dream nourished by his mother's lifelong yearning to someday finally go home again. (*HoC*, 4)]

Max's childhood vision of the house is one that seemingly erases the passage of time, the "dilapidation" that the concrete building has been subject to, in favor of a timeless and immutable vision of home, nourished of dreams. This is symptomatic of restorative nostalgia, as described by Boym, whereby "the past is not supposed to reveal any signs of decay; it has to be freshly painted in its 'original image' and remain eternally young."[29] Max's childhood dream of the house in H. becomes, as in the case of his mother, a lifelong yearning, one that is sometimes stronger, and sometimes weaker, but that is a constant in his life nonetheless.

Having first seen the house in Austria again as a twenty-two-year-old when fighting in the US army in 1945, where a woman now residing in the house slams the door on him, Max decides to talk to his mother on his return to the United States with regard to reclaiming the house. However, he finds that his mother has little interest in pursuing a restitution claim. For her, the town of H. becomes synonymous with the murder of her Jewish family: her sister (to whom she had sent affidavits, which her sister did not heed), her brother-in-law, and her father (*HdK*, 36; *HoC*, 28–29). Max devotes his youth to his career as a successful interior designer and to the pursuit of various love affairs, and imagines that his mother's yearning for the house in Austria has subsided, since she no longer mentions it. However, in her final years his mother begins talking about the house again, and Max realizes that she never really forgot it. Following his mother's death Max, now aged fifty-one, returns to the town of H. in Austria with the intention of regaining the house. He is warned by Arthur Spitzer, the secretary of the local Jewish community, that he will face difficulties in reclaiming the house, and, indeed, Max encounters various officials hell-bent on making Max's pursuit of his case as difficult as possible. One bureaucrat explains to him (in the 1970s) that the house was expropriated legally because of tax fraud (the pretext under which thousands of properties belonging to Jews were expropriated under the Nazis). The house then passed into the ownership of a *Gauhauptmann*, before passing to another Nazi Party member, whose descendants Max finds still living in the house. In the town itself, meanwhile, Max is confronted with a wall of silence and embarrassment from the local population:

> Wie soll ich mir das erklären, fragte er Spitzer. Einerseits wissen sie von nichts, andererseits behandeln sie einen mit dieser Mischung aus Unterwürfigkeit und Überheblichkeit. Und wenn man sie anspricht, schauen sie beleidigt weg. (*HdK*, 78)

> ["How do you explain it?" he asked Spitzer. "On the one hand they claim to know nothing, on the other they treat you with this mixture of subservience and arrogance. And when you talk to them, they act insulted and look away." (*HoC*, 67)]

The year of Max's first extended visit to the town is given as 1974 (*HdK*, 59; *HoC*, 49), and Mitgutsch's novel captures the prevailing climate in postwar Austria when Austria's involvement in the Holocaust, in which 65,000 Austrian Jews were murdered, was largely not spoken about. At this time, the "first victim" thesis, the idea that Austria had been "the first free country to fall a victim to Hitlerite aggression," as stated in the 1943 Moscow Declaration,[30] was predominant in Austrian culture. The characterization of postwar Austria as a "Schweigensreich" (realm of silence) by Mitgutsch's contemporary, the Austrian writer Gerhard Roth, is echoed very strongly in *Haus der Kindheit*.[31] The changing climate in the early 1990s, following the Waldheim affair in Austria of the 1980s, where the revelations that the Austrian presidential candidate had lied about his Nazi past sparked a belated confrontation with the country's wartime history, are also reflected in Mitgutsch's novel. At this point in time the local population in H. is presented as taking more of an interest in the past (particularly the younger generation, which is represented by the historian Thomas in the novel), but many of these attempts to engage with the history of the Holocaust and with Jews living in Austria today are shown to be deeply problematic. After Max has succeeded in regaining the house in H. and is fulfilling his wish of spending at least a year there, he is invited to a panel discussion on "Judentum heute" (*HdK*, 233; Judaism today, *HoC*, 214), where Max is asked how he as a Jew would like to be treated, and where one of his Austrian Jewish co-panelists is asked whether he considers himself to be Austrian (*HdK*, 247–49; *HoC*, 227–28). Further, Max's seventieth birthday is marked in the town by the mayor placing a ribbon with a large cross (a Christian symbol) around his neck (*HdK*, 238–39; *HoC*, 219–20). Max is feted as a prodigal son of the town, both at the civic ceremony (*HdK*, 239; *HoC*, 219) and in an article that Thomas writes about him for the local newspaper entitled "Zum siebzigsten Geburtstag eines verlorenen Sohnes unserer Stadt" (*HdK*, 234; A Lost Son of Our Town Turns Seventy, *HoC*, 214). Max is somewhat perturbed by the "liebevolle[r] Sentimentalität" (loving sentimentality) with which he is depicted, but decides not to confront the historian about the "gut gemeint" (meant well) article (*HdK*, 234; *HoC*, 214–15). While it is made clear that the local population's actions stem from ignorance rather than malice—"Man kenne so wenig Juden" (*HdK*, 248; one knew so few Jews, *HoC*, 228)—relationships between Jews and non-Jews, apart from those immediately associated with the Jewish community in H., are presented as deeply uneasy throughout the novel.

Despite the various bureaucratic hurdles put in front of him in 1970s Austria, Max persists in his efforts to regain the house, safe in the certainty that the last remaining inhabitants will die sooner or later, and the house will then belong to him:

Bald würde er das Haus besitzen, nach dem sich Mira ihr ganzes Leben lang gesehnt hatte. Dennoch, es war ein fremdes Haus in einer fremden Stadt, die ihm wie ein Lebewesen vorkam, das sich stur fortpflanzte und die Vergangenheit überwucherte, ein dumpfes, manchmal bösartiges, manchmal geschundenes Geschöpf mit einer unverwechselbaren Ausdünstung, für die er allmählich eine Witterung bekommen hatte. (*HdK*, 105–6)

[Soon the house that Mira had spent her whole life yearning after would belong to him. But it was a foreign house in a foreign city, a city that seemed to him like a living being, overgrowing the past in stubborn proliferation, a dull, sometimes malicious, sometimes abused creature with an unmistakable scent he had learned to recognize. (*HoC*, 93)]

The quotation above displays how the house is anthropomorphized, taking on a life of its own for the protagonist. The house becomes an obsession, an idée fixe that he is unable to free himself from, and a way for him to take vengeance upon the expropriation of the family home in Austria, the subsequent murder of his relatives who did not leave Austria in time to escape the Holocaust, and the loneliness and estrangement of exile that his mother in particular found so difficult to bear. In *The Future of Nostalgia*, Boym describes how the word "restoration" is derived from *restaure* (reestablishment), signifying "a return to the original stasis, to the prelapsarian moment."[32] The first half of Mitgutsch's *Haus der Kindheit*, focalized primarily through the perspective of Max, is certainly permeated with a sense that if only the house in H. could be repossessed and restored, then the past, returned to the static frame of the photograph that graced Mira's and Max's desolate New York apartments, could also be restored.

Max returns to New York from his first extended visit to H., safe in the knowledge that each day is bringing him closer to the day that he will live in the house in Austria. Finally, aged sixty-nine and having just recovered from a heart attack, Max receives a letter informing him that the last inhabitant has moved out of the house. The interior designer intends to experience every season at least once in the Austrian town, making the renovation of the house into his life's work:

Das Haus stand leer. Es gehörte ihm, er würde noch heute einziehen. Er hatte Spitzer gebeten, es provisorisch mit dem Nötigsten auszustatten. Die Renovierung sollte die Krönung seines Berufslebens werden, er brachte fertig gezeichnete Pläne mit, und unentwegt hatte er Ideen. Es würde seine letzte Arbeit sein, und er würde zusehen, wie sie sich entfaltete, ihn wie ein ganz und gar auf seine fernen Erinnerungen abgestimmtes Gehäuse umschloß und

den Zauber seiner Kindheit wiederbelebte, heitere Gegenwart, die
keine Zeiteinteilung kannte. Er war überzeugt, er kehre an den Ort
zurück, an dem er sterben werde. (*HdK*, 167)

[The house stood empty. It belonged to him. He would move in
today. He'd asked Spitzer to furnish it provisionally with the bare
minimum. Its renovation would be his crowning achievement. Max
brought plans that he'd already drawn up in New York and he was
still brimming with ideas. It would be his final project, which he
would watch as it grew and began to enclose him like a shell, completely attuned to his distant memories. The house would restore
the magic of his childhood, recreate a serene present ignorant of the
passage of time. He was convinced that he was returning to the place
where he would die. (*HoC*, 150)]

The quotation above reveals yet again how the protagonist's nostalgia is
strongly restorative at this point of the narrative. The renovation of the
house aims to "restore the magic of his childhood, recreate a serene present ignorant of the passage of time" (*HoC*, 150). These lines are strongly
symptomatic of the nature of restorative nostalgia, as defined by Boym,
whereby the past for the restorative nostalgic becomes "a value for the
present," with the passage of time ignored entirely, and the aim of supplanting the present for the past.[33] However, when Max enters the house
for the first time the expected feelings of homecoming are absent, he
is left cold by kitchen objects that must still have belonged to his aunt
Sophie, and he perceives the house as decidedly unhomely:

Max ging durch die Zimmer. Keines entsprach den Vorstellungen,
die er sich all die Jahre gemacht hatte. . . . Das Haus war fremd und
abweisend, es enttäuschte ihn. (HdK, 170)

[Max walked through the rooms. None of them corresponded
to what he had imagined all these years. . . . The house was alien,
inhospitable. He was disappointed. (*HoC*, 153–54)]

The experience of the house is uncanny, in Freudian terms, distinctly
unhomely precisely because the house was previously regarded as a
home.[34] As Monika Shafi writes, for Max the house becomes symptomatic of both the "glückliche[n] und friedliche[n] Zeiten von einst" (the
erstwhile happy and peaceful times) and of the destruction of this era.[35]
"Heimat und Ausgrenzung" (home and exclusion) overlap, thereby making the house into a place where "sowohl Heim(at)liches wie das ihm eng
verwandte Unheim(at)liche aufeinander [treffen]" (both the homely/
canny and the closely related unhomely/uncanny meet).[36] Simply regaining the physical entity of the house his family had to abandon, he is unable

to make good the loss of members of his family, and the loss of home. The projected return to origins that Max had envisaged turns to disappointment. His childhood cannot be returned to in any concrete sense, and this is made all the more pertinent by the contrast between the hallowed past and the realities of the present. Max's restoration project does little to assuage the unhomeliness he experiences with regard to the house. Despite beginning to feel comfortable in certain rooms of the house such as the veranda, the bathroom, and the kitchen (*HdK*, 185; *HoC*, 168), Max perceives the house as "ein ausgebeulter, vererbter Anzug [an ihm], sperrig und muffig" (*HdK*, 185; still hanging on him like a baggy hand-me-down suit, musty and cumbersome, *HoC*, 168). The whole house, and by extension "dieses ganze Land" (the whole country), remain for Max "sehr fremd und unbegreiflich" (*HdK*, 200; foreign and incomprehensible, *HoC*, 182).

As signaled by the quotation above, it is not merely the hard-won house in H. that proves distinctly unhomely for Max. The librarian and historian, Thomas, shows Max the city's most beautiful parks, courtyards, and façades. However, unlike Thomas, who has an unbroken family line, stretching back centuries, connecting him to the city, Max lacks a personal connection to the city, and is only able to experience it in a secondhand way, through the memories of his mother, declaring to Thomas that his mother loved the town very much (*HdK*, 184; *HoC*, 166). In contrast to Thomas, Max's own family connection to the town of H. was severed by the Holocaust. In a similar manner, he listens attentively to Spitzer's reminiscences of the town, surmising that these must be very similar to those of his mother. Max reflects that the more life years, experience, and memories that bind an individual to a city, the more this creates within the individual "jene starke Zugehörigkeit . . . die sich auf keinen anderen Ort übertragen ließ" (*HdK*, 179; that powerful sense of belonging that couldn't be transferred to any other place, *HoC*, 162). While this sense of belonging to a place is something that Max attributes to his mother and to Spitzer, it is something that Max himself lacks. This highlights the futility of his restoration project of the house in H., as restoring the house cannot give him the feeling of belonging to his native town that he may have had if his extended family had not been deported from their home and from the town. Max's own connection to the city can only ever be fragmented and broken, and for this reason he is drawn to people who have a similarly broken and fragmented relationship to the city, and to buildings and objects that serve as fragments of history. On his first visit to H. in 1974 he begins a relationship with Nadja, who feels out of place in H. and who had turned up at the Jewish community in H. as a teenager asserting that her mother's ancestors were Jewish. Nadja's lifelong search for identity and belonging mirrors that of his own. She follows him to the United States, and later dies in a mysterious car accident during a trip to Eastern Europe, where she photographs the places from which Max's family originated. On his second extended visit to H. in the 1990s, Max develops a friendship with Diana, a woman whose late Jewish father causes her to seek out the Jewish community in H., but to feel equally unaccepted by both the Jewish community and her husband's Catholic family. These women, in their conflicted and uneasy relationship to the town of H., reflect Max's own sense of unhomeliness in the town.

In the same manner that Max seeks out individuals whose own fragmentary relationship to the town of H. corresponds to that of his own, on his daily walks through the city, his attention is not directed to the beautiful surface of the city, its splendid façades and courtyards, but rather to buildings that sit uneasily in and disturb the townscape. On one of his walks, Max discovers a crumbling row of houses and a former Jewish prayer house on the edge of the town. The row of houses forms a contrast to the restored castle, which it backs onto, and is described as being "so dörflich und abgelegen, als wolle sie sich geduckt davonschleichen in eine ferne Zeit" (*HdK*, 180; as rural and isolated as if they wanted to creep cowering back into a distant time, *HoC*, 163). In contrast to the restoration of the castle, which erases the passage of time for this historic building, the houses and prayer house are irrevocably marked by the passage of time, which cannot be erased. While "ihre romantische Verwahrlosung" (*HdK*, 180; their romantic dilapidation, *HoC*, 163) appeals to the restoration architect in Max, he suspects that the houses will soon be renovated by the town authorities, effacing the particular aura of the buildings that Max so cherishes. The fact that Max favors these buildings, which serve as remnants of the town's submerged Jewish past, is symptomatic of reflective nostalgia, which in contrast to restorative nostalgia, is not concerned with return or restoration of a "prelapsarian moment"[37] (in the way that Max attempts to restore his childhood home, or in the way the town's castle has been restored, oblivious to the passage of time), but rather with a meditation on the passage of time and what might have been. As Boym describes in *The Future of Nostalgia*, the reflective nostalgic is not "nostalgic for the past the way it was, but for the past the way it could have been."[38] Certainly, the submerged buildings that Max sees are testament to a more vibrant Jewish culture than that of present-day H., but that is one side of the coin. The unvoiced assumption is that these buildings located on the edge of the town were part of the former Jewish ghetto, symptomatic of the marginalization of Jewish culture both in the past and in the present, as the buildings lie neglected and uncared for.

In the same manner that Max feels compelled to return to the prayer house with its yellow walls and Moorish windows on his daily walks through H. (*HdK*, 180–81; *HoC*, 165–66), he is drawn to objects at flea markets whose value is overlooked by others, such as the kiddush cups that Max spots in a market stall, whose Hebrew inscriptions are dismissed as squiggles by the seller (*HdK*, 184–85; *HoC*, 167). Similarly he is able to spot the inscription on a Jewish gravestone, which has been used as the cornerstone for a building (*HdK*, 186–87; *HoC*, 169). This hidden and neglected Jewish history is one that Spitzer, the secretary of the Jewish community in H., is also sensitive to, as he feels that the history of the Jews in H. may be best studied in the cemetery, where graves are inscribed with "geschichtsträchtige Daten" (*HdK*, 244; dates... pregnant with history, *HoC*, 224), such as March or November 1938, or where gravestones only bear the place names of concentration and death camps, such as Theresienstadt and Treblinka. The work of Max as amateur historian closely follows Walter Benjamin's historical materialist model of brushing history against the grain, and of privileging an attention to seemingly trivial objects that point toward a hidden or neglected history, the objects and traces of the past that society threatens to destroy.[39] This Benjaminian historical model is closely aligned to reflective nostalgia as defined by Boym, where the reflective nostalgic turns his or her attention to "ruins, the patina of time and history," to "the dreams of another place and another time."[40]

The discovery of the hidden street in H. (*HdK*, 180; *HoC*, 163) marks a pivotal point in the novel, signaling Max's move from restorative to reflective nostalgia. He becomes less concerned with the restoration of his house in H. and instead turns his attention to writing a chronicle about the history of Jews in the town, a history that he discovers is one of "Siebenhundert Jahre Mord und Vertreibung in seiner Stadt, in regelmäßiger Wiederholung" (*HdK*, 187; seven hundred years of regularly recurring murder and expulsion in his city, *HoC*, 170). As Katrien Vloeberghs has pointed out: "Das Aufgeben der Illusion, das Haus seiner Kindheit durch Renovierungsarbeiten zurückgewinnen zu können, führt zu seiner Entscheidung, die Chronik der verschwiegenen jüdischen Geschichte von H. zu schreiben." (Giving up the illusion of regaining the house of his childhood through renovation work, leads to the decision to write the silenced Jewish history of H.)[41] Here again, as in the case of Max's growing collection of Jewish ritual objects, rescued from the town's flea markets, his concern is for the neglected and ignored aspects of history: "die ausgeblendete Geschichte von H. . . . über die die überlieferte Geschichte hinweggeht, so daß ihr Fehlen nicht einmal bemerkt wird" (*HdK*, 259; the supressed history of H. . . . the things that traditional history has ignored so thoroughly that their absence is not even noticed, *HoC*, 238–39). His attention is given over to the marginal, to the fragments of history, to "einzelne[n] knappe[n] Randbemerkungen in den Annalen" (*HdK*, 186; some terse marginal note in the annals, *HoC*, 168), and to "Einzelschicksale, die nur für Augenblicke, in historischer Zeit gemessen, ans Licht getreten sind, manchmal nur im Augenblick ihres Todes" (*HdK*, 259; the fates of individuals that are illuminated for a mere moment when measured in historical time, sometimes only at the moment of their death, *HoC*, 238).

Writing the chronicle is symptomatic for Max's move from restorative to reflective nostalgia, as not only does it allow him to focus on the past as past, rather than on an attempted restoration of the past in the present (that the regaining and restoration of the house in H. constitutes), but it also allows him to see that there is no golden age, point of origin or "prelapsarian moment," in Boym's formulation,[42] to return to, "daß die Geschichte seiner Generation sich schon seit siebenhundert Jahren wiederholte" (*HdK*, 238; that the history of his generation had been repeating itself for seven hundred years, *HoC*, 218) and that his chronicle constitutes "die Geschichte einer durch die Jahrhunderte nachgetragenen, unerwiderten Liebe der Juden zu diesem unwürdigen Ort, dem keine andere Erwiderung einfiel als Raub, Plünderung und Mord" (*HdK*, 219; the story of the Jews' love for this unworthy town, a love they had borne through the centuries, unrequited, a love the town could only think to requite with rape, plunder, and murder, *HoC*, 200). This acceptance that there is no hallowed point of origin to return to, and an attention to countless missed opportunities of the past, in this instance, the failure of the town of H. to treat its Jews as equal citizens, makes Max's chronicle a reflective nostalgic account of what might have been. It may seem paradoxical to describe Max's chronicle as in any way a nostalgic project, but this would be a misinterpretation of what nostalgia is. As Boym highlights, while restorative nostalgia puts its emphasis on the *nostos* (which means "return home"), reflective nostalgia resides in *algia* (a painful feeling), "in longing and loss, the imperfect process of remembrance."[43] It is precisely this pain that is bound up with the native home and a sense of irredeemable loss, when confronted with the history of the town's Jewry, which makes Max's project of writing the chronicle one of reflective nostalgia. As the narrator describes, the history of the Jews in H. is the only history that connects Max to H. (*HdK*, 216; *HoC*, 197), the history that fashions a home out of the foreign Upper Austrian town, albeit one that seems to negate the very idea of the home as being homely. This connection to his native town, this "return home," is a painful homecoming, reaffirming the literal meaning of nostalgia (*nostos*, "return home"; and *algia*, "pain").

While Max continues to work on the chronicle and to forge friendships with the inhabitants of the town, the restoration of the house becomes ever more of a disappointment:

> Hatte er nicht das Haus restaurieren wollen, um in die Vergangenheit zurückzukehren, die Träume seiner Mutter zu beleben? Aber das Haus seiner Kindheit ließ sich nicht zurückgewinnen. Je weiter die Restaurierungsarbeiten voranschritten, desto mehr verblaßten die

alten Bilder. . . . Die Zeit hatte sich verlangsamt, ganz so, wie er es sich in früheren Jahren gewünscht hatte, aber der Stillstand war wie eine Lähmung. (*HdK*, 227–28)

[Hadn't he wanted to restore the house in order to return to the past, to revive his mother's dreams? But the house of his childhood was not retrievable. The further his renovations progressed, the more the old images faded. . . . Time was slowing down, just as he had once wished it would, but its stagnation was like a paralysis. (*HoC*, 209)]

Moreover, the deaths first of Spitzer, the secretary of the Jewish community, and later Nadja, Max's former lover, finally prompt him to leave Austria. He is terrified by the thought of dying and being buried in the town (*HdK*, 265; *HoC*, 243), and now perceives the house that he had fought so hard to regain as being "so fern und fremd . . . als habe es nichts mit ihm zu tun" (*HdK*, 312; remote and foreign . . . as if it had nothing to do with him, *HoC*, 290). On the day of Nadja's funeral, he decides to leave the town and the house of his childhood before it is too late:

An diesem Nachmittag beschloß Max, nach New Zork zurückzukehren, solange er die Kraft besaß, sich gegen die Lähmung und den Schmerz der Verluste zur Wehr zu setzen. . . . Er mußte sich vor dieser Stadt und diesem Haus retten, wenn er leben wollte. (*HdK*, 314)

[It was on this afternoon that Max decided to return to New York while he still had the strength to resist the paralysis and pain of his losses. . . . He had to escape this town and this house if he was to survive. (*HoC*, 292)]

The return to New York is framed as an escape and a rescue (*HdK*, 314; *HoC*, 292), with the town of H. and the house framed as endangering his sense of self, which he needs to abandon if he is to survive. The house of childhood is thereby presented to be pathologizing, giving rise to paralysis and an overwhelming "Schmerz der Verluste" (*HdK*, 314; pain of losses, *HoC*, 292) The past cannot be made good or returned to, as Max discovers, and his search for origins through his project of restoring the house of childhood fails because there is no point of origin to return to. As Max is told by Thomas, the young historian: "Wir suchen Verlorenes immer am falschen Ort" (*HdK*, 316; We always look for what we've lost in the wrong place, *HoC*, 294). Although the architectural entity remains, the house of childhood cannot be returned to in any physical sense. The novel ends with Max sitting in an airplane bound for New York, anticipating his return to his home of choice, where he plans to finish his chronicle of H.'s Jewish history. Having fulfilled his promise of experiencing all the seasons of the year in the house, he is content to return to New York, where he would look out from Coney Island Beach, and know that his house was waiting for him across the ocean should he wish to visit it again. While Mitgutsch's *Haus der Kindheit* shows us that knowledge of one's roots is vitally important, a geographical point of origin is ultimately not presented as constituting a home.

3: Silencing the Past: Margarete Heinrich's and Eduard Erne's *Totschweigen* and Elfriede Jelinek's *Rechnitz (Der Würgeengel)*

> *Es ist mir und wahrscheinlich auch Ihnen oft durch den Kopf gegangen, wohin der Virus Verbrechen gegangen ist.*
>
> [The thought has often crossed my mind, and doubtless yours as well, where the virus of atrocity has got to.]
>
> —Ingeborg Bachmann, Preamble to *Das Buch Franza*

Toward the end of the Second World War, on the night of March 24–25, 1945, days before the arrival of the Red Army, approximately two hundred Jewish slave-laborers were murdered in a small Austrian village on the Hungarian border, purportedly in the context of a party hosted by Countess Margit Batthyány at Rechnitz Castle. The exact events of that night remain shrouded in mystery, the perpetrators have not been brought to justice, and the mass grave has not been found to this day. Instead a wall of silence has descended on the village regarding the events of that time, with Rechnitz serving as a model case for the repression and silencing surrounding the Nazi past in postwar Austria.

As Walter Manoschek has pointed out, the Rechnitz massacre was by no means a unique case in Austria in the final stages of the Second World War.[1] It was one of a series of what Christiaan Rüter has termed "Endphasenverbrechen" (end-phase crimes) that took place in Austria in the spring of 1945.[2] In contrast to the concentration camps largely situated in Eastern Europe (with notable exceptions, such as Mauthausen-Gusen and Ebensee in Austria), far away from the eyes of the Austrian and German civilian population, thereby creating a "räumliche, soziale und emotionale Distanz" (spatial, social, and emotional distance) from the events, the camp evacuations and death marches of tens of thousands of Hungarian Jews to Eastern Austria, which began in the summer of 1944, meant that the last phase of the Holocaust "spielte sich . . . vor der Haustüre ab" (played out . . . in front of the house door).[3] The two hundred victims of the Rechnitz massacre were engaged in building the so-called Southeast Wall fortifications, designed to stop the Soviet advance. As Teresa Kovacs describes in a chronology of the events, on March 24,

1945, one thousand Hungarian Jewish slave-laborers were transported from Köszeg in Hungary to Rechnitz in order to work on the wall section there, of which 180 were determined as no longer fit for work and murdered on the night of March 24–25 by fourteen or fifteen guests (led by local Gestapo chief Franz Podezin) attending a party hosted by the Batthyány family for local Nazis and Hitler Youth at Rechnitz Castle.[4] A further eighteen, who had to bury those killed the previous night, were murdered on the following day (March 25, 1945).[5]

As Manoschek describes, the Rechnitz massacre was just one of a number of atrocities against Jews that took place in Deutsch Schützen, Engerau, Hofamt Priel, and dozens of other places in Austria in the spring of 1945, constituting the largest number of killings on Austrian territory carried out during the Holocaust, a fact often neglected by historical discourse.[6] Due to a number of factors, the Rechnitz massacre has, however, received the most media attention. One reason for this, as Manoschek highlights, has been the repeated search for the mass grave where the victims were buried,[7] with the first search, as Kovacs notes, beginning in 1969.[8] Related to this has been the lack of information about the possible location of the gravesite from the local population, which has made Rechnitz into a "pars pro toto für den Umgang Österreichs mit dem Nationalsozialismus: Schweigen und Verdrängen" (*pars pro toto* for Austria's approach to National Socialism: silence and repression).[9] The massacre also attracted renewed international attention in 2007 through the publication of a book examining the Thyssen dynasty (from which Rechnitz's Countess Margit Batthyány was descended) by British journalist David Litchfield, in which he asserted that the countess personally took part in the massacre, leading to a surge of media interest in the figure of Margit Batthyány.[10] In the media representation of Litchfield's book, Batthyány has been labeled "the killer countess,"[11] "Gastgeberin der Hölle" (hostess from hell),[12] and a "Monster" (monster) in an account by her nephew Sacha Batthyany.[13] As Manoschek has asserted, the danger of this stylization of the massacre into a "sadistische Sex & Crime-Geschichte" (sadistic sex-and-crime story) risks a historical decontextualization and its designation as a "bizarre[r] Ausnahmefall" (bizarre, exceptional case).[14] Yet it is not least the medial presence of the Rechnitz massacre that has led to a number of artistic treatments of the events of March 24–25, treatments that have, in all cases, gone beyond journalistic cliché to explore the extremity of the massacre as well as its legacy in the postwar era.

This chapter will examine perhaps the two most important artworks, of diverse genres, that have thematized the Rechnitz massacre: Margareta Heinrich's and Eduard Erne's documentary film *Totschweigen*, and a play by the Nobel laureate Elfriede Jelinek, *Rechnitz (Der Würgeengel)*. Both works highlight the difficulty of uncovering the truth about the past through unreliable witnesses, and the culture of what has been termed "geschwätziges Verschweigen" (garrulous silencing).[15] Yet, through their diverse genres, the two works are able to offer distinctive perspectives on the massacre. While Heinrich's and Erne's sensitive documentary depicts the fraught endeavor of unearthing the past in Rechnitz, with poignant images of an excavator fruitlessly digging up earth on purported sites of the mass grave, Jelinek is able to use the poetic license offered by fiction to provide a radical treatment of the Rechnitz massacre in her postdramatic play, illuminating the self-exculpatory strategies of the perpetrators and their successors, who continue to obfuscate and cover up the past. My chapter will explore the intersections and diverse possibilities of the filmic and theatrical texts for confronting the past and representing the continuing repercussions of the past in the present.

Totschweigen

Totschweigen, a film made by the Austrian documentary filmmakers Margareta Heinrich and Eduard Erne, arose out of the directors accompanying the search for a mass grave (initiated by Holocaust survivor Isidor Sandorffy and continued, following Sandorffy's death in 1993, by Rabbi Simon Anshin), containing the bodies of the victims of the Rechnitz massacre, over the course of three years, from November 1990 through to the summer of 1993. The documentary was well received in Austria, with reviewers praising its treatment of an issue that may be regarded as symptomatic for Austrian history,[16] its poetic language,[17] and its profound engagement with its subject matter.[18] As Michael Omasta comments in his review, the film does not only show "die bloße Oberfläche von Ereignissen" (the mere surface of events); instead it becomes an "Ereignis" (event) itself by taking part in the search for a mass grave.[19] The directors' own participation in the search for the mass grave certainly stretches the limits of the documentary film genre as we commonly understand it, which we associate with documenting events rather than actively participating in them. Erne has asserted that, initially, the directors had hoped that their film would document the successful excavation of the bodies and the local population's reactions to this event.[20] When it became clear that this was not going to be possible, the directors proceeded to interview the local population with regard to the events of the night of March 24–25, 1945, and to document Isidor Sandorffy's continued efforts to find the mass grave.

Exactly what constitutes a documentary film has been a perennial source of debate, with Bill Nichols asserting that "documentary is what we might call a 'fuzzy concept,'" whose definition has changed over time.[21] Patricia Aufderheide similarly underlines the fluidity of the concept of the documentary film genre, providing only a very broad definition for a documentary as a film that "tells a story about real life, with claims to truthfulness."[22] Some of the formal elements that we typically associate with the documentary film include "voice-of-God" narration, an analytical argument, interviews with experts (talking heads), stock images, and serious classical music.[23] However, as Aufderheide describes, many of the best documentary films (Aufderheide mentions Luis Buñuel's *Land without Bread* [1932], the BBC's *The Spaghetti Story* [1957], and Scott Barrie's *In Search of the Edge* [1990]) have self-consciously parodied these conventions.[24]

Totschweigen does make use of a number of classic documentary film conventions. These include partial voice-over by Erne. However, for the most part, the film dispenses with an omniscient narrator and allows the interviews with the Rechnitz population to speak for themselves. An analytical argument is, in any case, not presented. Viewers are thereby invited to draw their own conclusions from the words of the interviewees and the images presented on screen. As Jiranek and Scheucher describe, in this manner, *Totschweigen* avoids "d[ie] Gefahr jedes Dokumentarfilms, mit der Moralkeule die Zuseher und Zuseherinnen zu bevormunden" (the danger of every documentary film of patronizing its viewers with a moral club).[25] Apart from interviews with victims' relatives and the initiators of the search for the mass grave, the interviews are not with individuals who can be described as experts, but rather with local Rechnitz residents who, instead of shedding light upon the events of the night of March 24–25, 1945, serve to obfuscate the past by talking around the issue and effectively communicating very little. Stock archive photographs of the death marches in Burgenland are used to punctuate the recollections of victims' relatives, and photographs of Franz Podezin are used in a sequence in which the filmmakers travel to the former Gestapo chief's new home in South Africa. Similarly, the melancholy and haunting main title theme music, composed by Peter Ponger, punctuates the fruitless search for a mass grave depicted in the film throughout, underlining the lack of progress and closure with regard to finding the burial site of the two hundred slave-laborers.

Yet while the film makes use of certain documentary conventions, it dispenses with others. This is most evident in the interviews with the Rechnitz residents, who are not introduced either by means of voice-over narration or by captions. They are not differentiated in this manner, underlining the fact that what they say and communicate differs very little from the statements of their neighbors. Instead, the Rechnitz population is shown to espouse essentially very similar views with regard to the massacre. These may be summed up as follows: a denial of personal culpability ("Ich weiß nichts" [*T*; I don't know anything] and "Des hab' ich nicht gesehen" [*T*; I didn't see that] are recurring phrases), a manner of talking about the past that fails to register the extremity of what happened ("Die waren sehr arm" [*T*; They [the victims] were very unfortunate]),[26] and a desire to lay the unpalatable past to rest. The latter sentiment is best exemplified by the words of one local man: "Aber das eine Glück hat Gott dem Menschen gegeben, dass er das verdrängen kann. Man kann das verdrängen im Bewußtsein." (*T*; However, God has given man one blessing, that one can repress it. One can repress it in one's consciousness.) This standpoint is underscored time and again in the film, with a shop owner telling the filmmakers to "get lost," and asking why the past should be "stirred up" again, a sentiment echoed by a coworker in the store: "Es soll Ruhe geben, genau" (*T*; They should let it rest, exactly). Disapproval toward the grave search is voiced repeatedly by several residents: "Es wirbt mehr Staub auf und macht mehr Negatives wach, als was Positives zum Durchbruch käme" (*T*; It blows up more dust and rouses too many negative things than anything positive that could break through).

The metaphor of uncovering a troubling past, buried in Rechnitz ground, is used consciously throughout the film. The image of an excavator fruitlessly digging up earth is one that recurs time and again, illustrating the repeated excavation and search attempts that Erne and Heinrich witnessed in the course of making *Totschweigen*. The remains of the murdered slave-laborers, which Isidor Sandorffy and his colleagues look for, constitute the past that some of the Rechnitz residents, interviewed by Erne and Heinrich, would prefer to keep repressed and hidden. While the search for the mass grave for the purpose of exhuming the bodies and giving them a dignified burial in accordance with Jewish burial rites is unsuccessful, the mere "Aufrühren" (*T*; stirring up) of the ground (as one interviewee puts it), where the truth regarding Austrian complicity in the crimes of the Holocaust lies, ensures that, even if the full truth about the past cannot be brought to the surface, the presence of the excavators and the disturbance that they instigate serves to ensure that the past is not laid to rest (as, again, some of Erne and Heinrich's interview partners would wish it to be), but rather that the "open wound" of the Austrian National Socialist past remains open.[27] As Erne has asserted: "Es ist auch fast wie eine Metapher für den gesamtösterreichischen Umgang mit der Vergangenheit. Die Vergangenheit wird mit diesem Massengrab konkret ans Tageslicht geholt, und das wird abgewehrt. Die Toten kehren zurück, und man kann das alles nicht mehr so leicht abtun." (It [the search for the mass grave] is also almost like a metaphor for the way the whole of Austria deals with the past. The past will be brought to light in a concrete way with this mass grave, and that is fended off. The dead return, and all of this can no longer be dismissed so easily.)[28] The sheer number of times that we see sequences featuring the excavation of Rechnitz ground, panoramic shots of the field and the Kreuzstadl homestead, near which the massacre took place and where the bodies are thought to be buried, emphasizes the presence of the past in its purported absence. As such, the film finds powerful visual images for the ongoing and complex process of coming to terms with the past in Austria, and is testament to the capacity of the documentary film genre not only to depict, but also to illuminate, aspects of reality.

The film opens with a close-up of a cross in a cemetery where a Catholic burial is taking place. We see a grave digger digging up the earth in preparation for a burial, something that is emphatically denied the two hundred victims of the Rechnitz massacre. As the grave digger digs up the earth, he uncovers the bones of those who have previously been interred in the ground and comments that they will have to be put back as, once they have been blessed, they cannot simply be thrown somewhere else. His words anticipate the statements of Rabbi Simon Anshin at the close of the documentary, who explains how he considers it his duty to search for and uncover the places where people were killed because they were Jews, and to give them a proper burial. Following this opening there is a sequence evidently shot from the window of a car, where we see a snowy road illuminated by the headlights. As the car makes its journey toward Rechnitz, we hear the disembodied fragments from the interviews with local residents, which will later feature in the film. These narrative fragments, together with the partially illuminated landscape, suggest that those looking for the mass grave have to piece fragments and clues together in a similar manner. This sequence precedes the title frame, which merely shows an aerial shot of the Kreuzstadl homestead in a snowy, inhospitable landscape, while the wind can be heard moaning around it. The motif of a snow-covered landscape concealing a dark past is a recurring one in postwar Austrian literature. A notable example can be found in Thomas Bernhard's debut novel *Frost* (1963), where snow serves as a master trope for repression, covering over all evidence of a mysterious cattle rustling incident, as well as all traces of the central protagonist, Strauch, who goes missing in driving snow.[29] As such, the opening of *Totschweigen* establishes the central thematic concerns of the film: the issue of a proper burial, the search for the mass grave, and the inhospitable landscape that covers rather than yields the secrets buried within it, in a similar manner to the open hostility and obfuscation of the past practiced by some of the local population. It is this eerie atmosphere of the documentary that has led some critics to label the film an unintentional "historische[r] Thriller" (historical thriller),[30] and a "Krimi[s], in dem sehr wenig entdeckt . . . wird" (a crime story, where very little is detected).[31] However, while the piecing together of information to arrive at definitive knowledge regarding a crime, as depicted in the documentary, shares similarities with a detective story, the Rechnitz massacre, which occurred in the context of the industrialized mass murder of the Holocaust, precludes *Totschweigen* being read as a "crime thriller."

Through its visual imagery the film attests to the loss caused by the Holocaust in Rechnitz, which, as Neumüller describes, had a sizable Jewish community until 1938.[32] The only testament to this today is the dilapidated Jewish cemetery, which is shown twice in the film. The first instance occurs near the beginning of the documentary, as the fate of Rechnitz's Jews, who were deported from the village in 1938 to a "Niemandsland an der jugoslawischen Grenze" (*T*; no-man's-land on the Yugoslavian border), is narrated in voice-over. The second time is in the middle of the film, following a sequence shot near Podezin's villa in South Africa, where the reasons given by a district attorney in Kiel for not mounting a case against the former Gestapo chief are narrated in voice-over: that it is better not to risk an acquittal in "der jetzigen politischen Situation" (*T*; the current political situation). The precise nature of the political situation is shown in the following shot: we see desecrated gravestones in the Jewish cemetery in Rechnitz, covered in graffiti reading "Sieg Haider" (*T*; Victory to Haider), "Juden raus" (*T*; Jews out), and "Gas" (*T*; gas). *Totschweigen* was filmed in the early 1990s, a period that saw the rise of the populist Austrian Freedom Party led by Jörg Haider, which culminated in the entry of his party into the Austrian coalition government following the 1999 general elections. In another sequence we see a florist ambiguously referring to a new generation of Haider supporters. These sequences shot in Rechnitz attest to the legacy of a past which, because never properly confronted, resurfaces in grotesque forms.

Throughout *Totschweigen*, the portrayal of Rechnitz is distinctly antiidyllic. Immediately following the title sequence, we see a panoramic aerial shot of the village come into view, with the church spire rising into the sky. Rechnitz appears as an unassuming, pretty village in a beautiful, rural part of the country, a place that we would certainly not associate with mass murder, although historical facts prove otherwise. This fallacy of viewing the Austrian rural landscape as allegedly untainted by the Second World War is one that was successfully exploited in postwar Austria with the aim of furthering mass tourism. The beauty of Rechnitz in contrast to the brutality of the massacre that occurred there is underlined by the words of the Hungarian relatives of two victims of the massacre (who refuse to have their faces shown on camera, at the time of the making of *Totschweigen* in the early 1990s, due to the renascent anti-Semitism in Hungary and Europe) who carried out their own searches for the mass grave after the war: "Upon our arrival we were surprised at how beautiful this little village looked, well-to-do, attractive, clean. It was hard to imagine, how, in the town square, where there was a beautiful church, people could be battered and beaten to death."[33] As the sequence in the living room of the Hungarian couple is followed by scenes of nighttime Rechnitz, the vision of the village that is now presented is one that is dark, inhospitable, and sheltering a dark secret. As this sequence of shots finishes back in the living room of the Hungarian couple, this montage of images, a favored technique of documentary filmmakers, further underscores the contrast between the surface image of Rechnitz and its legacy of brutality and violence, which continues to impact the lives of those far removed from the village.

The village on the Austro-Hungarian border is presented as an inhospitable and heavily guarded territory, with the barbed wire of the Cold War era mutating into the border posts of the Austrian army on the lookout for illegal immigrants. Further images underline this anti-idyllic presentation of Rechnitz, for which the recurring aerial shot of the Kreuzstadl homestead (also used in the title frame), cutting a bleak, austere figure in the snow-covered landscape, is emblematic. Rather than focusing on the buildings and architecture, the filmmakers repeatedly choose to direct their attention to the field where the Kreuzstadl is located, emphasizing that the village's real essence is to be found in its ground rather than in the façades of its buildings and architecture. Repeated pans and aerial shots of the sweeping landscape emphasize the enormity of the task faced by Isidor Sandorffy and his team, as do recurring medium shots of the ploughed fields surrounding the Kreuzstadl. As Heinrich and Erne document the search attempts over several years, shots of the snow-covered field alternate with the scorched earth of summer, thereby accentuating the changing of the seasons and the passing of time as Elke Schüttelkopf highlights.[34] All the while, the grave site remains undiscovered.

As we have seen, *Totschweigen* adheres to some genre conventions of the documentary film (through its use of music, stock images and, to some extent, voice-over), but it dispenses with others, such as presenting an analytical argument. It depicts an attempt to confront the past that remains frustratingly incomplete and unresolved, and that precludes any "voice-of-God" commentary. Instead, Erne and Heinrich are able to find a powerful visual language for the repression of memory in Rechnitz, the impenetrability of the landscape and its people, and the dark secret that lies at the heart of the village. The film's narrative is circular, with the closing shot showing Rabbi Anshin walking along the field near the Kreuzstadl, having vowed to continue the search for the mass grave. Together with the interviews, which serve as oral testimonies of "geschwätziges Verschweigen" (garrulous silencing),[35] the documentary succeeds in finding images for the ongoing confrontation (or lack of it) with a deeply fraught historical legacy.

Rechnitz (Der Würgeengel)

Rechnitz (Der Würgeengel) is a play by the Austrian Nobel Prize for Literature laureate Elfriede Jelinek, which premiered at the Munich Kammerspiele on November 28, 2008, under the direction of Jossi

Wieler. Jelinek was awarded the coveted Mühlheimer Dramatikerpreis (Mülheim Dramatist Prize) for the play in 2009, and Wieler was awarded the Nestroy Theater Prize for his production. Jelinek, who has had a fraught relationship with the Austrian state and its media throughout her literary career, decided not to stage the work in Austria, where she expected a negative media reaction to it.[36] *Rechnitz* was, however, very well received in Vienna during a guest performance by the Munich Kammerspiele in May 2010, and the first Austrian production of the play premiered in Graz in March 2012. There have also been notable productions in Düsseldorf and Chemnitz in Germany. Extracts from the play have also been performed by the British theater company *aya* at the Austrian Cultural Forum London in 2014.[37]

The first and longest section of the play is set in a castle in Austria, filled with an unspecified number of messengers. As Jelinek has elucidated in an interview, it was theater director Jossi Wieler's idea to pick up on Luis Buñuel's film *El ángel exterminador* (The Exterminating Angel, 1962) for the 2008–9 season at the Munich Kammerspiele,[38] and, as such, the subtitle to Jelinek's play alludes to Buñuel's 1962 film, where, during a dinner party at the home of Señor Edmundo Nobile, the servants inexplicably disappear, leaving the dinner party guests and their hosts trapped in the house. In Jelinek's play, however, it is the messengers (who, among the multiple identities that they take on in the play, also identify themselves as the absent masters' servants) who are left behind to communicate their knowledge of the events of the night of March 24–25, 1945, to the audience. The masters of the castle have fled, and the castle set on fire prior to the arrival of "die Russen" (the Russians).[39] This echoes the historical narrative of the Rechnitz massacre and its aftermath, as Countess Margit Batthyány left Rechnitz Castle together with her husband on March 25, 1945, eventually settling in Switzerland, while the castle itself was set on fire by the German anti-aircraft defense on March 31, 1945, in the course of fighting with the Red Army.[40]

However, as Pia Janke has asserted, *Rechnitz* should not be understood as a work trying to reconstruct historical events; rather, it asks questions about how knowledge about historical events is communicated.[41] As Gerhard Scheit has argued, this occurs specifically through the *Botenberichte* (messenger reports), which allow for the integration of witness statements, memories, stories, historical analyses, media debates, and television reports.[42] Like many of Jelinek's previous works, *Rechnitz* is a play that is insistently preoccupied with the discourse that is constructed about the past and transmitted by the media. This is signaled, in *Rechnitz*, in a "Danksagungen" (R, 205; acknowledgments) section at the end of the published play, in which Jelinek makes reference to a newspaper interview with German philosopher Hans Magnus Enzensberger, which is reproduced almost verbatim in the words of the "Ausnahmebote" (R,

78; exceptional messenger) in *Rechnitz*. This is just one of a number of intertextual references, to works belonging to diverse genres, in *Rechnitz*, which are explicitly acknowledged by Jelinek. These include Litchfield's biography of the Thyssen dynasty, Friedrich Nietzsche's philosophical text *Thus Spake Zarathustra*, the ancient Greek drama *The Bacchae* by Euripides, T. S. Eliot's poem "The Hollow Men," Friedrich Kind's libretto for Carl Maria von Weber's opera *Der Freischütz* (The Marksman), and a book entitled *Interview mit einem Kannibalen* (Interview with a Cannibal) by the Austrian filmmaker and author Günter Stampf in which he interviews the infamous "Rothenburg Cannibal" Armin Meiwes. In addition to this, Jelinek has also highlighted the profound influence of Erne's and Heinrich's *Totschweigen*, from which she first learned about the Rechnitz massacre.[43]

The range of intertexts in *Rechnitz* is generically diverse, and the play itself similarly resists straightforward genre delimitation. It lacks any of the features that we would typically associate with a play, such as clearly defined *dramatis personae* (the "Ausnahmebote" [exceptional messenger] is the only named messenger in the play) or dialogue. Instead, for the majority of the play, the audience is confronted with long, unbroken passages of text (forty-seven in total), which collectively have been described as "ein einziger langer Sprachstrom, ohne Figurenzuschreibungen, ohne Bildvorgaben, ohne Handlung im klassischen Sinne." (one long current of language, without the attribution of roles, without scene specifications, without action in a classic sense.)[44] It is for this reason that Jossi Wieler and his team of actors at the Munich Kammerspiele had to spend a significant amount of time working with Jelinek's text, breaking it up, determining which actor could speak which section, and transforming it into a performance text.[45] Making her director into a "Co-Autor" (co-author) of her play in this manner is something that Jelinek views as very important.[46] All of these formal features of *Rechnitz*, from its necessity for director's theater to the lack of action or clearly defined roles, would place it within the category of postdramatic theater as defined by Hans-Thies Lehmann in his 1999 study.[47] However, in contrast with a central aspect of postdramatic theater, as defined by Lehmann, whereby the text itself is deemed no longer primary, in Jelinek's *Rechnitz*, as in all her plays, the dramatic text itself is of crucial importance, with her dissecting language being the main vehicle for her social and cultural critique. From her earliest plays in the 1970s, Jelinek has never favored nuanced characterization, instead making her characters into "Sprachflächen" (linguistic surfaces) where what is said is not associated with an individual, but rather where characters are the sum of existing social and media discourses.[48] For Jelinek, such a mode constitutes the only fitting way to write about the Holocaust: "Die massenhafte Tötung von Menschen hat, für mich jedenfalls, das Ich ausradiert, und sie hat das individuelle Sprechen des

Schauspielers, der Schauspielerin auf der Bühne zerstört" (The mass murder of people has, for me at least, erased the I, and destroyed the individual speech of the actor or actress on the stage).[49]

Nowhere is this more evident than in *Rechnitz*, whose primary concern is how knowledge about the Second World War and the Holocaust is transmitted to the "Nachgeborenen" (those born after) as we approach an age in which, as Jelinek describes in an interview, "Botenberichte" (messenger reports) will replace eyewitnesses.[50] Through the multitude of voices contained in the messengers' words, Jelinek is able to portray strategies of repression and denial of the past, negation of guilt or personal culpability. Eschewing any psychological depth, in her play she indeed uses her messengers as "linguistic surfaces," in Julianne Vogel's terms,[51] to reflect how the Rechnitz massacre and the Holocaust more broadly are remembered today. Through the staged performance the audience is confronted with discourses that it will instantly recognize from the media and elsewhere which, through Jelinek's virtuoso play with language, are regurgitated and exposed for what they really are. With no dramatic action or character development to "distract" the audience, it is forced to focus entirely on what the messengers communicate. The messengers address the audience or speak in a collective "we" form. In Jossi Wieler's 2008 Munich production, they wave and smile to the audience, speaking in a light-hearted tone and eating throughout, all the while talking about the Rechnitz massacre. Indeed, Norbert Mayer (2012), reviewing the 2012 Graz production of *Rechnitz*, has asserted that the audience members are made into "Komplizen" (partners in crime), provoking shame and recognition of the "Ungeheure, an dem Österreich noch immer würgt" (the monstrosity on which Austria continues to choke).[52] The audience finds itself in the uncomfortable position of being invited to sympathize with the messengers, played by popular actors, while identification is precluded by the nature of what the messengers say. Jelinek utilizes the genre of the theater play to full effect by addressing her Austrian and German audience in this way, forcing her viewers to confront the obfuscation, repression, and falsity that, in her view, characterize contemporary discourse about the Nazi past. In this manner she follows in the footsteps of the late Austrian author and dramatist Thomas Bernhard (1931–89), who in his last play, *Heldenplatz* (1988), which provoked the biggest scandal of his career, confronted his audience with the long shadow of Austrian history by thematizing the continuing and inescapable effects of the Holocaust on an Austrian Jewish family.

The messengers in *Rechnitz*, who may be described as perpetrators or bystanders, emphatically deny any suggestion of personal culpability, with one messenger insisting that she or he "sowas auch nur mit angesehen hätte, wobei die Betonung auf mit liegt, denn es waren auch andre da" (*R*, 185; only saw something like that *as well*, whereby the emphasis is on the *as well*, since others were there too). They engage in a relativizing of history, which functions as a strategy of repression and denial of the past: "Es ist egal, es ist heute egal, das weiß man ja, wer Henker und wer Opfer war. . . . Denn Wahr und Falsch gibt es auch nicht mehr, es gibt auch hier nur noch ein Dazwischen." (*R*, 85; It's all the same, it's all the same nowadays, as we all know, who was the hangman and who the victim. . . . Since there is no longer right and wrong, there is only an in-between here.) As Allyson Fiddler has pointed out, Jelinek is "writing hard against the relativizing of values" in her play.[53] Moreover, the messengers assert that they will contradict one another, that some will not say anything, "doch ohne uns wüßten Sie überhaupt nichts" (*R*, 143; but without us you would know nothing at all). As such, Jelinek highlights the difficulty of the endeavor of trying to find out historical facts about the Rechnitz massacre, specifically the location of the mass grave, when clues have to be pieced together from the words of the perpetrators and their descendants. The victims are dead and, as such, emphatically absent from her play: their story is told from the perpetrators' perspective.

Through replicating "die Sprache der Täter" (the language of the perpetrators),[54] who deny the victims' their humanity and dignity, Jelinek illustrates how the victims are murdered a second time. The messengers employ the Nazi discourse of "Vernichtung durch Arbeit" (destruction through work), and the Nazi ideology of racial superiority to justify the massacre: "Zur Arbeit waren diese Hohlen, die ich dort gesehen habe, ohnedies nicht mehr, nicht mehr zu gebrauchen" (*R*, 167–68; Those hollow ones, that I saw there, could, in any case, no longer be used for work). For the messengers-as-perpetrators, the Rechnitz victims are alternately T. S. Eliot's "hollow men" (*R*, 131), "schäumenden Narre[n], die sich ihre Abstammung nicht besser ausgesucht haben" (*R*, 130; frothing idiots, who could not choose their ancestry better), "Nullen" (*R*, 129; zeros), "200 Stück" (*R*, 141; 200 pieces), and "Wild" (*R*, 94; wild game), In *Rechnitz*, Jelinek replicates the dehumanization to which Holocaust victims were subjected on a linguistic level: "Menschen sind das keine mehr. Menschen sind sie nicht mehr. Menschen werden sie nicht mehr." (*R*, 141; These are not people any more. They are no longer people. They will not be people any more.) The use of anaphora functions as a means of performing social and cultural critique by emptying out language to reveal the real issues at stake, or engaging in a play with words as, for example, with the term "schwindeln" (which means both "to feel dizzy" and "to tell fibs" in German),[55] as one of the messengers reports rising to "Schwindelhöh" (dizzying heights) to watch the mass grave being dug, but asserting "ich werde immer schwindeln, wenn ich später davon rede" (*R*, 124–25; I will always tell fibs when I talk about it later on). In this manner, Jelinek shows how "garrulous silencing" about the past, which is documented in *Totschweigen*, may become a virtuosic performance masking terrible atrocities.

Another characteristic that the play shares with the documentary *Totschweigen* is its focus on the mass grave, with Jelinek's use of language emphasizing the covering up of the past that the grave symbolizes. The messengers, whose narrative switches between past, present, and future throughout the play, predict that the mass grave will prove difficult to find: "Wir graben ein Grab, das keiner findet, das alle übersehen" (*R*, 124; We are digging a grave that no one will find, that everyone will overlook). The attitudes of some sections of the Rechnitz population are parodied through the messengers' concerns: "Daß die bloß nichts ausgraben, wenn sie schon so lang graben! Aber solang sie an der falschen Stelle graben, ist es mir im Prinzip wurscht." (*R*, 132; That they don't manage to unearth something, when they've already been digging for such a long time! But as long as they're digging in the wrong place, I basically couldn't care less.) These statements echo the words of a farmer interviewed in *Totschweigen*, who summarizes the views of some of the local Rechnitz population regarding the search for the mass grave as follows: "Lass sie graben bis sie deppert werden, na, die hören von alleine auf, dann ist die Sache erledigt für uns." (Let them dig until they lose their minds, they'll stop of their own accord, then the whole matter will be settled for us.) Similarly, the messengers' words in *Rechnitz* are hauntingly prophetic: "Dieses Grab will nicht gefunden werden und wird auch nicht gefunden" (*R*, 133; This grave does not want to be found and will not be found).

By making language, rather than characterization or action, the real "protagonist" of her drama, an aspect noted by André Jung, one of the actors in the Munich Kammerspiele production of *Rechnitz*,[56] Jelinek offers a critique of contemporary discourse in Austria and Germany about the Nazi past. Jelinek has repeatedly voiced the view that despite concerted efforts to confront the past in Germany and Austria, this process has become ritualized and devoid of meaning:

Indem man diese Sünden der Väter und Großväter gebetsmühlenhaft immer wieder hervorholt, ohne ihnen wirklich analytisch auf den Grund gehen zu wollen oder ihr Fortwirken in der Gegenwart zu untersuchen, deckt man Geschichte zu, statt ihr die Kleider vom Leib zu reißen.[57]

[By rolling out these sins of the fathers and grandfathers again and again, like a mantra, without really wishing to probe these analytically or investigate their continuities in the present, one covers over history, instead of laying it bare.]

Jelinek borrows a term from German philosopher Hermann Lübbe, who used the concept of "Sündenstolz" (literally: "pride in one's sins";

metaphorically: "pride in rituals of remembrance") to refer to Germany's remembrance culture, and reaffirms its literal meaning, as the messengers voice their pride in committing atrocities during the Third Reich: "und doch sind wir stolz auf unsere Sünden und reden darüber, denn welchen Sinn hätte es zu sündigen, wenn man danach nicht darüber reden dürfte" (*R*, 131; and yet we are proud of our sins and talk about them, since what would the point of transgressing be, if one couldn't talk about it afterward). In her analysis of the play, Allyson Fiddler describes how *Rechnitz* constitutes a "critique of what might be summed up as mere lip-service to the project of atonement or of 'mastering'/overcoming the past."[58]

In *Rechnitz*, Jelinek strives to work against the rationalization that she sees as now dominating the discourse on the Holocaust, for which Hannah Arendt's concept of "the banality of evil" has become emblematic.[59] There is an explicit allusion to Arendt in *Rechnitz* through Jelinek's reference to "unsere tägliche Sendung von der Banalität des Bösen" (*R*, 99; our daily program about the banality of evil), as Fiddler has also observed.[60] As Hermann Schmidt-Rahmer, the director of the 2010 Düsseldorf production of *Rechnitz*, describes,

> Es ist commonsense geworden, den Holocaust als einen gut geschmierten, deutsch-perfekt organisierten Verwaltungsakt zu beschreiben, der relativ emotionslos ist und einem delirierendem Pragmatismus folgt. Das ist im Grunde der Blick der Historiker. . . . Das heißt aber, wenn Jelinek die Verbindung zieht zwischen dem Kannibalen von Rotenburg und der Gräfin Batthyány und einem Fest, bei dem Menschen getötet wurden, evoziert sie automatisch—natürlich auch durch die Einführung des Euripides-Textes über die Bakchen—den Gedanken, die Judenvernichtung im Nationalsozialismus sei ein dionysischer, lustvoller, orgiastischer Vorgang gewesen, der metaphorisch in ihrem Text—nein, ganz konkret in ihrem Text—kulminiert im Kannibalismus. . . . Sie stellt also diese polemische Behauptung auf als Gegensatz zum Holocaust als Verwaltungsakt. Sie sagt nicht, die Täter waren nüchtern, sondern sie waren lustbesessen, dionysisch und haben lustvoll gefressen. Es ist eine absolut polemische, politisch inkorrekte Meinung, mit der sie meinen Aufschrei provozieren möchte.[61]
>
> [It has become common practice to describe the Holocaust as a perfectly organized Germanic administrative machine, running like clockwork, which is relatively emotionless and follows a delirious pragmatism. That is essentially the view of the historians. . . . This means, however, that when Jelinek draws the connection between the cannibal of Rotenburg, and the Countess Batthyány, and a party during which people were murdered, she automatically evokes—also through the introduction of Euripides's Bacchae text—the thought

that the Holocaust under National Socialism was a Dionysian, sensual, orgiastic process, which culminates metaphorically in her text—no, actually in a very concrete way in her text—in cannibalism. ... She therefore sets up this polemical assertion in contrast to the Holocaust as an administrative process. She does not say, the perpetrators were levelheaded, rather that they were lustful, Dionysian, and that they sensuously gorged themselves. It is an absolutely polemical, politically incorrect view, with which she wants to provoke my outrage.]

Through her radical depiction of the Rechnitz massacre as an orgiastic killing, Jelinek presents a challenge to an established understanding, notably developed by historian Raul Hilberg, of the Holocaust as an "administrative process,"[62] yet her treatment of the massacre is not sensationalist in the manner of Litchfield. Instead her play reaffirms the Rechnitz massacre as something that, as Jelinek herself has asserted, exceeds human comprehension,[63] and that therefore radically destabilizes the ritualized and sanitized forms of remembrance that she criticizes. At the close of the play the messengers depart, following in the footsteps of the Countess Batthyány, Podezin, and Oldenburg (manager of the Rechnitz estate), who, as the messengers relate, are happy and unrepentant of their actions. The audience, meanwhile, leaving the theater, gains an appreciation of the ways that the past may be consciously obfuscated, distorted, repressed, and relativized.

This chapter has examined how both Heinrich and Erne's film and Jelinek's play have sought to utilize the possibilities of their respective genres in order to thematize the Rechnitz massacre, and explore its repercussions and legacy in the present day. As we have seen, *Totschweigen* is able to find a powerful visual language for the repression and denial of the past, as well as for the difficult endeavor of searching for the mass grave. Through its oral testimonies from local eyewitnesses as well as from relatives of the victims of the Rechnitz massacre, the film documents strategies of repression, and offers a sensitive treatment of the pressing need to uncover the past. *Rechnitz*, meanwhile, is a work of fiction—with no compulsion to document reality, as is the case with *Totschweigen*. Jelinek presents her audience with a radical treatment of the Rechnitz massacre, with messengers using the language of the perpetrators to recount an orgiastic killing, for which they show no remorse. Almost fifteen years after *Totschweigen* was made, Jelinek utilizes the unique power of theater as a public forum in order to confront her audience with ongoing strategies of self-exculpation, denial, and relativizing of the past. For this purpose she stretches the genre of the theater play to its limits, making language itself rather than action the main focus. *Totschweigen* also does not adhere to all the genre conventions of the documentary film, dispensing, for example, with an authoritative commentary. In both cases, the subject matter exceeds the formal conventions of the particular genre. At the same time, both works fully utilize the potential of their respective genres. While *Totschweigen* harnesses film's unique ability to document reality in order to provide a moving portrayal of the confrontation with the past in one Austrian village, *Rechnitz* utilizes the power of performance to reveal hidden truths about our existence; in this case, the empty rhetoric and rituals of talking about the past, which mask the true horror of historical events.

4: Historicizing the Waldheim Affair: Robert Schindel's *Der Kalte*

Vielleicht wird es sieben Generationen brauchen, um das wirklich aufzuarbeiten; wie es in der Bibel steht, bis ins siebente Glied hinein.

[Perhaps it will take seven generations, in order to really work through this; as it says in the Bible, unto the seventh generation.]
—Robert Schindel (1944–)

As ELABORATED IN THE INTRODUCTION to this study, the Waldheim affair of 1986–88 was a turning point in Austrian society, sparking the beginning of a belated process of coming to terms with the country's National Socialist past. The debates that the exposure of the presidential candidate Dr. Kurt Waldheim's Nazi past provoked, signaled the end of the postwar era in Austria and led to "eine massive Umwertung zentraler Werte" (a wide-ranging reassessment of central values), as Robert Schindel has asserted in an interview.[1] Robert Schindel's *Der Kalte* offers a literary treatment of the Waldheim affair, which, nearly three decades on, has become historical.[2] While it is certainly not the first literary treatment of the Waldheim affair, as some critics have asserted,[3] it is the first novel to offer such a sustained literary exploration of the political scandal. However, as this chapter will demonstrate, by drawing attention to the events of the late 1980s in Austria and the disturbance of the past that they provoked, Schindel's fictional narrative in turn disturbs and challenges our interpretation of this period in Austrian history, refusing to lay the ghosts awakened during that time to rest. Ultimately, Schindel's performative interventions, reinscribing aspects of the Waldheim affair, serve to draw attention to the work that remains to be done in order for Austria to fully confront its past.

Der Kalte is Robert Schindel's second novel in his planned trilogy focusing on the legacy of the Second World War and the Holocaust in Austria, entitled *Die Vorläufigen* (The Provisional Ones), reflecting the provisory, transitional nature of societal models in the twentieth century, and also the characters' ultimate mortality.[4] The first part of the trilogy, *Gebürtig* (Native, 1992; in English as *Born-Where*, 1995), appeared in 1992, and was made into a highly successful film by Schindel and the director Lukas Stepanik, released in 2002.[5] *Der Kalte*, published in

February 2013, had a long gestation period, as can be gleaned from a 1998 publication of the opening pages of the novel in a literary journal.[6] It is unclear when the third volume, given the provisional title *Genia und die lichte Zukunft* (Genia and the Bright Future), will appear.[7] Schindel was born in April 1944 in Bad Hall, Austria, to Austrian Jewish communists active in the resistance.[8] He was able to escape the Holocaust, following his parents' arrest near Linz and subsequent deportation to Auschwitz, thanks to the efforts of Franzi Löw, who worked for the Jewish Community in Vienna, and brought him to an "Aufbewahrungsort für jüdische Säuglinge ohne Eltern" (holding place for Jewish infants without parents) from where he and the other children held there were meant to be deported to Theresienstadt concentration camp.[9] However, if a child was sick, deportation was delayed until the child recuperated, and Franzi Löw sought to report Schindel and the other children sick before every deportation.[10] As Schindel described in an interview: "Und ich habe eine Krankheit nach der anderen gehabt. Und habe durch wirkliche Krankheit, fälschliches Kranksein oder auch beides überlebt." (And I had one illness after another. And whether through real illness or false illness, or both, I survived.)[11] Schindel spent the first year of his life in this *Aufbewahrungsort* (holding place) and with a foster family, before his mother (who survived Auschwitz and Ravensbrück) was able to return to Vienna and find her son in August 1945.[12] Schindel's father was murdered at Dachau in March 1945.[13] Schindel has described himself as irrevocably "geprägt von der NS-Zeit" (marked by the Nazi era), having lost "einen Großteil der eigenen Familie im Holocaust" (the majority of my own family in the Holocaust), and it is for this reason that his fiction is preoccupied with the question of "wie die Überlebenden, Nachkommen miteinander umgehen" (how the survivors, the descendants, interact with each other).[14]

Schindel began his literary career writing poetry, but it was the publication of his second novel, *Gebürtig*, that led to his literary breakthrough, a novel that has subsequently been hailed by Matti Bunzl as "the most critically and commercially successful product of the Jewish literary renaissance [in Austria] and arguably its definitive text."[15] In *Gebürtig* Schindel explored the problematic relationships between Jews and non-Jews of the second generation in postwar Austria, and the lack of a proper confrontation with the National Socialist past in the country, symbolized through the novel-within-a-novel that sees exiled composer Hermann Gebirtig make a painful return to Vienna to testify against notorious *Oberscharführer* (senior squad leader) Anton Egger, only for the *Schädelknacker* (skull-cracker) to be acquitted. While the narrative time of the novel, set in the early 1980s, does not extend to the Waldheim affair proper,[16] the film adaptation, produced nearly a decade later, makes a number of subtle references to the political scandal, in the wake of which *Gebürtig* was undoubtedly written, through the film's dialogue and mise-en-scène.[17]

The Waldheim affair was, in many ways, a coming of age for artists and intellectuals of the second postwar generation. Confronted with the open anti-Semitism that the Waldheim affair brought to the surface, many Austrian Jewish writers and intellectuals, such as Doron Rabinovici and Robert Menasse, became heavily involved in the protest movement against Waldheim. Austrian Jews of the second generation were no longer prepared, as Andrea Reiter describes, to "keep a low profile."[18] Instead, as Dagmar Lorenz has traced, "a highly visible, discursive Jewish culture" emerged in opposition to Waldheim's candidacy and presidency.[19] Schindel himself has asserted that he only played a marginal role in the *Republikanischer Club–Neues Österreich*, the leading opposition movement to Waldheim, founded in 1986.[20] However, the writer has emphasized time and again the significance of the Waldheim affair and the protest movement it sparked for Austria's historical development, asserting that Austria would not be what it is today without the debates that took place around the "Gedächtniskünstler" (memory artist) Kurt Waldheim.[21] It is this fascination with both the figure of Waldheim and the processes his candidacy unleashed in Austria that is the subject of Schindel's *Der Kalte*.

Initially an uncontroversial presidential candidate for the *Österreichische Volkspartei* (Austrian People's Party), Dr. Kurt Waldheim appeared to be, as Beller has traced, "someone who would make an ideal Austrian president" because of his previous credentials, having served as Austrian foreign minister in the Austrian People's Party between 1968 and 1970 and two terms as UN secretary general between 1972 and 1981.[22] Waldheim went into the presidential election as "the clear favorite,"[23] campaigning under the slogan "ein Österreicher, dem die Welt vertraut" (an Austrian whom the world trusts),[24] a motto that was to come spectacularly undone when Waldheim's past was uncovered. In his autobiography *Im Glaspalast der Weltpolitik* (In the Glass Palace of World Politics, 1985; in English as *In the Eye of the Storm*, 1985), he glossed over his period in the Wehrmacht, claiming to have been injured on the Russian front and returned to Vienna in 1941, where after his recovery in 1942 he remained until the end of the war to complete his doctorate in law.[25] However, in March 1986, Hubertus Czernin, investigative journalist for the *profil* news weekly, who had found Waldheim's *Wehrstammkarte* (military record card), published a major exposé of Waldheim's wartime record, which showed his membership in Nazi organizations, namely the *SA Reitersturm* (SA riding unit) and the *Nationalsozialistischer Deutscher Studentenbund* (National Socialist German Students' League) from 1938 to 1945.[26] In an article published in the *New York Times* on March 4, 1986, it emerged that Waldheim had served on the staff of General Alexander Löhr (a convicted war criminal who was executed in 1947) between 1942 and 1944, when brutal atrocities against Yugoslav partisans and deportations of Greek Jews were taking place.[27] Waldheim had omitted more than two years of his life from his autobiography.

Following these revelations, some Western media and the World Jewish Congress claimed that Waldheim was a war criminal.[28] Waldheim defended himself throughout by maintaining that he had only done what his fellow countrymen at the time had done, his "duty."[29] Waldheim's team also resorted to anti-Semitism to fend off attacks, focusing their efforts above all on the World Jewish Congress, and dismissing American media criticism as coming from the "Ostküste" (East Coast), which, as Beller describes, played on historic prejudice against "Ostjuden" (Eastern European Jews).[30] Waldheim's campaign posters asserted "Wir Österreicher wählen, wen wir wollen!" (We Austrians vote for whom we choose!) and "Jetzt erst recht!" (Now more than ever!).[31] The Waldheim affair polarized Austrian society, prompting a belated and grotesque confrontation with Austria's Nazi past directly proportional to its repression since the Second World War. On June 8, 1986, Waldheim was elected president. The Waldheim affair did not go away at this point, however. An "informal ban" was instituted by Western governments on meetings with Waldheim, and the Vatican, several Arab countries, and Cyprus were the only countries he visited during his six-year presidential term.[32] Waldheim was similarly put on the US Watch List as a suspected war criminal, and therefore not permitted to enter the United States.[33] In February 1988 an international historians' commission, which had been called to examine Waldheim's war service, stopped short of identifying Waldheim as a war criminal, but concluded that he must have been very well informed about Nazi atrocities committed in the Balkans and deportations of Jews from Thessaloniki.[34] In the course of the historians' commission's investigations, Michael Graff, then general secretary of the Austrian People's Party, expressed the view, in an interview conducted in November 1987, that "Solange nicht bewiesen ist, daß er eigenhändig sechs Juden erwürgt hat, gibt es kein Problem." (As long as it is not proved that he [Waldheim] strangled six Jews with his own bare hands, there's no problem.)[35] Graff was subsequently made to resign from his post. As outlined in the introduction to this study, Waldheim's initial covering up of his Nazi past, followed by denial of any wrongdoing, may be seen as symptomatic of a country that founded its postwar identity on the *Lebenslüge* (life-sustaining lie) of being "the first free country to fall a victim to Hitlerite aggression,"[36] despite all the evidence to the contrary. Austrian participation in all echelons of the Nazi war machine and in the Holocaust is widely documented, and the historian Tony Judt has asserted that half of all concentration camp guards were Austrians, despite Austria having just one-tenth of Germany's pre-war population.[37]

The Waldheim scandal, dominating Austria's political stage in the late 1980s, also reverberated in the cultural arena. Schindel identifies three *Kulturkämpfe* (cultural battles) in total, which dominated that period: the Waldheim affair itself; the premiere of Thomas Bernhard's play *Heldenplatz*, which addressed Austria's unconfronted National Socialist past and provoked a scandal at its premiere at Vienna's *Burgtheater* on November 4, 1988; and, in the same month, the unveiling of Alfred Hrdlicka's controversial *Mahnmal gegen Krieg und Faschismus* (Monument against War and Fascism).[38] In *Der Kalte*, Schindel presents the different spheres of Austrian politics, journalism, and culture nestling side by side, particularly through their topographic proximity in a capital city whose main political and cultural institutions may be located within a one-mile radius. The various tribulations of the Burgtheater, Vienna's national stage, are given as much weight as the scandal surrounding the figure of Johann Wais, the Austrian presidential candidate. This is symptomatic of a nation in which, as Stefan Zweig described in *Die Welt von Gestern* (The World of Yesterday, 1942), the theater has had as much, if not more, importance than the country's political institutions.[39] Robert Schindel's *Der Kalte* effortlessly spans the political and cultural arenas in Vienna in which the Waldheim affair played out, including the chancellery, the headquarters of various political parties, the Burgtheater, the *Musikverein*, numerous cafés and bars, and the private apartments of the protagonists. Yet Schindel's novel is not only focused on Austria's capital, but takes in the Austrian countryside, as well as Israel and New York, in order to trace the reverberations of the Waldheim affair upon the Austrian nation and Austria's image across the world. The places and localities in Schindel's novel are rendered in great detail, which has provoked criticism in one review of the novel.[40] This exact rendering of locality, place, and milieu (to the extent that the novel, published by the German publishing house Suhrkamp, has a sixteen-page glossary aimed specifically at the non-Austrian reader), means that *Der Kalte* may be ascribed to the genre of the Viennese city novel, and indeed the novel in its detailed representation of Vienna's topography has drawn comparisons with the work of Heimito von Doderer.[41] The novel has also been widely read as a *Schlüsselroman* (roman à clef),[42] although Schindel himself has rejected this label.[43] However, in common with the genre of the roman à clef, *Der Kalte*'s success as a novel undoubtedly rests on the reader's identification of the fictionalized and very thinly veiled characters and events, such as, for example, the figure of Johann Wais, who is unmistakably modeled on Waldheim.

The characters who populate *Der Kalte* are drawn from three generations: the generation that experienced the Second World War and the Holocaust firsthand; its sons and daughters (the second postwar generation); and in the case of high-school students Stefan Keyntz and Dolly

Segal, the third postwar generation. Through these diverse constellations Schindel is able to show the effect of the Waldheim affair at every level of Austrian society. The narrative of *Der Kalte* coalesces around the story of Edmund Fraul, a (fictional) former Communist and concentration camp survivor, who was *Lagerschreiber* (camp writer) for the *SS-Standortarzt* (SS doctor) Eduard Wirth in Auschwitz. Fraul, loosely modeled on the Austrian resistance fighter Hermann Langbein,[44] is married to Rosa, "eine unpolitische Jüdin" (*DK*, 64; an unpolitical Jewess), who also survived Auschwitz. Despite never having seen each other in Auschwitz the couple were drawn together by their shared past. Edmund Fraul is, due to the nature of his past experiences, emotionally cold and distant, giving the novel its title, and is unable to forge a bond with his son Karl, an actor, who regards him as self-righteous and an "antifaschistische[s] Heldenarschloch" (*DK*, 540; antifascist hero-arsehole). In the course of the novel, however, Fraul becomes less emotionally distant through his acquaintance, termed by Robert Schindel a "Schicksalsgemeinschaft" (companionship of fate),[45] with Wilhelm Rosinger, who was formerly an SS-officer at Auschwitz. Having been detected by Fraul and the "Nazijäger" (*DK*, 54; Nazi-hunter) David Lebensart (clearly modeled on Simon Wiesenthal), arrested in 1960, and tried in the Auschwitz trials, Rosinger was sentenced only to three-and-a-half years' imprisonment—despite his personal involvement in crimes such as the murder of children through phenol injections—which he had already served by the time of the trial verdict. In Rosinger's self-perception he belongs to the "Wichten, nach denen sich nach fünfundvierzig keiner umgeschaut hat" (*DK*, 55; the little wretches that no one looked for after 1945), while former concentration camp inmates had described him "als Menschen in SS-Uniform" (*DK*, 55; a human being in an SS uniform) at Rosinger's trial. Fraul's conversations with Rosinger about Auschwitz function as a talking cure, allowing Fraul, in particular, to free himself from his nightmares of the past. Throughout the novel, the past is presented as being omnipresent for Fraul and his wife, Rosa:

> Der Novemberregen fiel auf die ganze Wienerstadt . . . und der November von Auschwitz-Birkenau mit seinem stürzenden Himmel. . . . Wenn der Himmel in Wien im November sich öffnete, dann prasselte all das Vergangene herunter wie zu anderen Zeiten auch. (*DK*, 32–33)
>
> [The November rain fell on the whole city of Vienna . . . and the November of Auschwitz-Birkenau with its pouring sky. . . . When the heavens opened in Vienna in November, then all the bygone times pattered down, as at other times as well.]

The past imposes itself on the Frauls with a cyclical regularity, with the climatological invariability of November rain reminding Edmund Fraul of autumn in Auschwitz. Similarly, Fraul habitually sees former friends and adversaries from his time in the concentration camp among Vienna's pedestrians. The former SS doctor Wilhelm Rosinger is also haunted by the past. His dreams are plagued by the voices of the children he murdered in Auschwitz (*DK*, 55).

The furor surrounding the presidential candidacy of Johann Wais does not provoke a strong reaction from Fraul and Rosinger. They are too preoccupied with working through their own past from that time to be overly concerned with that of Wais. Fraul is not surprised by the scandal since, as he describes to journalist Roman Apolloner, he views his own generation as irrevocably blighted by the National Socialist era:

> der Nationalsozialismus hat meine ganze Generation verdorben, ihr gesamtes Denken und Handeln ist mit Wegschieben, Verdrängen und Lügen beschäftigt. . . . Meine Generation ist verloren. Wir müssen ihr Abtreten abwarten und höchstens darum kämpfen, dass sie nicht den Träumen ihrer Jugend treu bleibt und die früheren Zustände wiederherzustellen versucht. (*DK*, 250–51)

> [National Socialism ruined my whole generation, its entire thought patterns and actions are geared toward pushing aside, repression, and lying. . . . My generation is lost. We have to wait for them to make their exit and, at the very most, see to it that they don't remain true to the dreams of their youth and try to turn the clock back.]

Fraul is not surprised by Wais's lying, which he sees as symptomatic of that of many of his generation, describing Wais as "ein normaler Österreicher" (*DK*, 250; an ordinary Austrian) among his own kind. Fraul pursues his efforts to find and bring old Nazi criminals to justice through his work in Vienna's historical archives, and has little time for what he sees as the self-righteous anger of the younger generation, advising the journalist Apolloner to join with others to oppose Wais (*DK*, 252), rather than merely lamenting the state of Austrian politics. He himself is absolutely convinced of his own moral rectitude in his actions as a resistance fighter during the Second World War, and advocates that Apolloner's generation should fight resurgent Nazism with the same level of commitment (*DK*, 393).

Other figures belonging to Fraul's generation include his wife Rosa, the sole person to survive the Holocaust in her family, who tries to avoid being overwhelmed by painful memories of the past through her devotion to her son and through losing herself in her work, cataloging books in the backroom of a bookshop. For Rosa, unlike her husband, the past is not something she can draw anything positive from; rather, it is something that she tries her utmost to suppress. However, even she cannot escape the precarious political climate in the country, and is confronted with the anti-Semitism unleashed by the Waldheim affair while running an errand. When passing the Stephansplatz, Vienna's central square, in order to pick up a book from a nearby distribution center, she finds herself in the middle of a demonstration for and against Waldheim, of the kind filmed by Ruth Beckermann in *Die papierene Brücke*, discussed in chapter 1 of this study. Here Rosa overhears an elderly Austrian, wearing a traditional Styrian hat, advise a young man, who is handing out leaflets against Wais (Waldheim), that he should not be helping "die Juden" (the Jews) since "die haben doch eh alle auf ihrer Seite" (*DK*, 368; they have everyone on their side anyway). She intercedes, telling the man to be quiet, at which point she is subjected to anti-Semitic abuse on the basis of her appearance, with the elderly man echoing the racial stereotyping propagated during the Nazi era: "Da ist ja eine. Dieses Gesicht. Das sieht man sofort. Merkst du das, Burscherl?" (*DK*, 369; There's one. That face. One sees it straightaway. Do you notice it, lad?) In this manner, Schindel draws attention to the experience of many Jews living in Austria in the late 1980s, who had to face increased anti-Semitism in the wake of the Waldheim affair.

Rosinger, the repentant ex-SS officer, is another representative of the war generation, who tries to provide Fraul with details of surviving Nazis. Through his Nazi-sympathizing sister he is connected to the dark underworld of unapologetic Nazis who meet annually at Carinthia's Ulrichsberg, and who are given new hope by the ascent of Jupp Toplitzer (clearly modeled on Jörg Haider), new leader of the Austrian Freedom Party. Mountains and the Alpine landscape, with their perennial association with Austrian identity and the Alpine Republic, take on a central function in *Der Kalte*, as was the case in Schindel's earlier novel *Gebürtig* (1992). In *Gebürtig* the notorious Ebensee *Schädelknacker* (skull-cracker) Anton Egger was discovered by the former resistance fighter Karl Ressel and his daughter Susanne during a walk on the Rax mountain range. In *Der Kalte* we see Egger meet his end on the Rax, when he decides to flee to Argentina due to the resumed efforts of Nazi hunters during the Waldheim affair to track down Nazi criminals. Deciding to walk through the mountains on foot before traveling to the airport, from which he would travel to Bariloche with his wife, the former skull-cracker slips and falls on a rock, fracturing his skull in the process. In this instance at least, Fraul's thesis about the need to wait for perpetrators of his generation to meet their end, is proven correct.

Other members of the generation that experienced the Second World War directly include the sculptor of the *Denkmal gegen Krieg und Faschismus* (Memorial against War and Fascism) Herbert Krieglach, whose father was arrested for socialist activities in 1938 and sent to the Dachau concentration camp for two months (*DK*, 201); the Czernowitz-born architect Ernst Segal, the only one in his family to survive the Holocaust, who decides to take his family away to Israel immediately upon Wais's election; and the star columnist of the populist right-wing newspaper *Die Stunde*, Martin Moldaschl, who launches an anti-Semitic campaign against Wais's detractors, and frequently dreams about his experiences of fighting in Hitler's army on the Eastern front (*DK*, 408). The latter character is evidently modeled on then-editor of the populist *Kronen Zeitung*, Hans Dichand, a figure, who, as Walter Manoschek has described, defended *das Wehrmachtskollektiv* (the Wehrmacht collective), having himself been in the *Kriegsmarine* (Nazi German navy) and, as editor of Austria's largest-circulation newspaper, had considerable media power with which to do so.[46] In this manner, Schindel shows the responses of the war generation to the Waldheim affair to be irrevocably shaped by its experiences in the Second World War and, most importantly, by its attitude to these at the time. For this generation in *Der Kalte* the Waldheim affair constitutes a continuation of the unconfronted legacy of the Second World War and the Holocaust in displaced form. Displacement, which Freud saw as symptomatic of a repressed trauma,[47] is exemplified in *Der Kalte* through the finding of Johann Wais's *Wehrstammkarte* (military record card), with the intrepid journalist Apolloner rightly assuming "dass die Karte nicht verschwunden, sondern woanders verborgen war" (*DK*, 212; that the card had not disappeared, but was hidden somewhere else). These words closely echo Freud's ideas about the psycho-logic of trauma, whereby the repressed traumatic symptom must eventually manifest itself, albeit in another time and place, "an eine andere Stelle" (at another point), "anderswohin" (somewhere else).[48] It is this belated manifestation of a trauma, repressed by the war generation, that *Der Kalte* is concerned with.

The second postwar generation in *Der Kalte* is shown to be deeply critical of Wais's (Waldheim's) candidacy and presidency, whether this is expressed in political action or merely in private circles of friends and acquaintances. These include Roman Apolloner (recognizably modeled on *profil* journalist Hubertus Czernin), who publishes an exposé of Wais's wartime record in the (fictional) Austrian weekly *Signal* (clearly modeled on the Austrian news weekly *profil*); the doctor and political activist Boaz Samueli, and cultural journalist Judith Zischka, who found an opposition movement to Wais, under the name of *Club Diderot: das andere Österreich* (Club Diderot: the other Austria); and Johannes Tschonkovits, secretary of the (socialist) Austrian chancellor, who has an ideological interest in defaming the presidential candidate of the opposition party. The banker-cum-writer Emanuel Katz and poet Paul Hirschfeld (figures who also feature in *Gebürtig*, the first volume in Schindel's novel trilogy) are similarly exercised about Wais in private conversations in Vienna's fashionable bars, but while Hirschfeld decides to join the *Club Diderot* in combating Wais, Katz merely takes refuge in humor and irony. Meanwhile the ensemble of actors on Vienna's foremost stage, the Burgtheater, led by director Dietger Schönn, act in a number of plays selected to draw the audience's attention to the country's political situation. The opposition to Waldheim is presented in *Der Kalte* largely as a generational conflict between the war generation and its descendants, as the following monologue by Apolloner illustrates:

> Da wachsen wir auf im Nachkrieg unter den Blicken einer zugleich stummen und verlogenen Generation. Wie die sich herausputzten, nachdem sie erst dem Führer zugelaufen waren, auf sein Geheiß sowohl die Andersdenkenden denunziert, die Juden verjagt und umgebracht hatten oder es billigend in Kauf genommen hatten, bis Stalingrad gelatscht waren oder in den Bombennächten mit vollgeschissener Wäsche in den Kellern gesessen sind, die Gräuel gesehen, mitgemacht, erlitten hatten, und als der Krieg zu Ende war, sich eben herausputzten und schwigen. Sie schwigen uns alle frech ins Gesicht, diese verbrochene und zerbrochene Generation. Im Züge dieses Herausgeputzes schau dir doch die Politiker an. Das Gelüge, die Machtspiele, das hohle Reden, diese Grundfeigheit, alles eine Folge der österreichischen Staatslüge, damit die sich alle herausputzen: Wir Österreicher, das erste Opfer Hitlers, wir Österreicher, die im Herzen immer Österreicher waren, zwar Heil Hitler gerufen, aber O du mein Österreich gedacht haben. (*DK*, 100)

> [We grew up in the postwar era under the eyes of a simultaneously mute and mendacious generation. How they all scrubbed themselves up, after they first ran after the Führer, denounced the dissidents at his bidding and expelled and murdered the Jews, or gave it all their seal of approval, traipsed to Stalingrad or sat in the cellars in their dirty underwear through the nights of bombing, they saw the atrocities, joined in, endured, and then when the war ended, they just scrubbed themselves up and kept quiet. They all insolently kept silent right in front of our faces, this criminal and broken generation. And in the wake of this scrubbing up, take a look at the politicians. The lying, the power games, their empty words, this fundamental cowardice, all of this is a consequence of the Austrian state lie, so that they could all scrub themselves up: We Austrians, Hitler's first victim, we Austrians, who were always Austrians in our hearts, who admittedly had shouted "Heil Hitler," but were really thinking "O thou, my Austria."]

For the second generation in *Der Kalte*, which did not experience the Second World War directly, but had to grow up with its consequences, including emotionally distant parents, the Waldheim phenomenon constitutes the bursting of the surface of the "first victim" myth to uncover the latent violence and repression beneath.

Despite the novel's focus on the interdependency and interconnectedness of Viennese politics, media, and cultural life, the narrative does not remain centered on these spheres. Instead, through the weave of the characters' personal relationships, the narrative extends to the lives of those far removed from the epicenters of power. This is particularly evident through the representatives of the third generation in *Der Kalte*, in the shape of adolescent Stefan Keyntz and his girlfriend Dolores (Dolly) Segal, whose love story is told via means of Keyntz's diary entries. The non-Jewish Keyntz begins a relationship with Dolly Segal whose Jewish family immigrates to Israel following the election of Kurt Waldheim, leaving the young Keynz heartbroken. Keynz and Segal are the only representatives of the third postwar generation in the novel, yet the effect that Waldheim has upon their relationship is symptomatic of the inescapable impact of the Waldheim affair upon every generation living in Austria at the time.

Schindel's novel is strongly satirical in its treatment of the Austrian cultural and political establishment, and the tragicomic is his preferred mode for dealing with the insufficiencies of Austria's confrontation with its historical legacy. Nowhere more is this the case than in Schindel's depiction of Johann Wais (Kurt Waldheim), with his surname, Wais (homophonic to the word *weiß*, meaning the color white), ironically evoking associations with moral purity and a whiter-than-white image. The collective whitewashing of the past that Waldheim symbolizes, meanwhile, is underlined in *Der Kalte* through reference to Wais's supporters as "die Waiswäscher" (*DK*, 340; the whitewashers). Johannes Tschonkovits, secretary of the Austrian chancellor Theodor Marits (Fred Sinowatz), initially laments that nothing can be done to destroy Wais's whiter-than-white image, but he is unable to abandon his "Idée fixe, vom Bedrecken des Doktor Johann Wais" (*DK*, 210; his idée fixe of dirtying Doctor Johann Wais). Both Tschonkovitz and the intrepid journalist Roman Apolloner are delighted when it emerges that Wais was a member of the SA. From there the depictions of Wais become ever more grotesque as Waldheim's historical press statements are given almost verbatim in *Der Kalte* in assertions such as that his initial experiences in the SA extended to "nichts anderes ... als an Sportveranstaltungen, also Reitveranstaltungen teilzunehmen" (*DK*, 285; nothing more ... than taking part in sports events, that is, in equestrian events). When Wais's advisors show him a map in order to demonstrate the proximity of his wartime villa in Thessaloniki to the train station from which the area's Jewish population was deported to Auschwitz, Wais can only plead the excuse of having been too preoccupied with his doctoral thesis and his burgeoning relationship with his future wife: "'Ich habe es nicht bemerkt,' sagte Wais. 'Was soll ich denn tun? Ich weiß auch nicht, wieso mir das nicht aufgefallen ist. Ich kann es mir lediglich mit meiner Dissertation erklären, mit Aglaja.'" (*DK*, 449; "I didn't notice it," said Wais. "What am I to do? I don't know why it didn't strike me either. I can only explain it with my dissertation, with Aglaja.")

The constant assertions by Wais about his inability to remember or to have witnessed any of the atrocities going on around him are parodied by the organization *der Club Diderot* (which closely resembles the *Republikanischer Club–Neues Österreich*, the opposition movement that emerged at the time of Waldheim's candidacy and presidency). Similar to their real-life counterparts, who introduced a performative, humorous aspect into their protests by adopting a wooden horse, a symbol for Waldheim's "equestrian" participation in the SA, designed by Alfred Hrdlicka, as their mascot (an aspect of the club's activities that also finds its way into *Der Kalte*, with the mascot designed by the architect Herbert Krieglach), *der Club Diderot* devises a series of initiatives in order to improve Wais's memory. These include encouraging all schoolteachers to hang portraits of the new president upside down in Austria's classrooms: "Bekanntlich hebt eine rasche Blutzufuhr zum Kopf das Erinnerungsvermögen" (*DK*, 367; As is well known, a sudden rush of blood to the head improves memory function).

However, Schindel does not portray the Waldheim affair as merely unfolding in public arenas. While the political and cultural intrigues are centered in Vienna's first district, spreading out from the chancellery, parliament, and Burgtheater into the cafés and bars surrounding them, the depiction of private space extends to the residential districts of Vienna, in particular the second, third, and sixth districts. The lunchtime meetings between Rosinger and Fraul, which take place in a little-frequented *Beisl* (pub) near the Danube Canal, which Fraul has to reach using a ferryboat taking him from the second to the third district of Vienna, have the air of transgression about them, not least because of the numerous topographical boundaries that are being crossed (of city districts, of land and water) prior to the meetings. While the Waldheim affair is shown to dominate the country's and the world's media, more subtle confrontations with the nation's collective past in *Der Kalte* take place in private, whether this is in insalubrious pubs where no tourist or fashionable bohemian would venture, or the living room of the Segal family where Dolly's boyfriend Stefan watches the election results coverage with the Austrian Jewish family, which leaves them in a state of shock: "Die Mutter hat zu weinen angefangen und ist verschwunden, der Vater hockte stumm da mit einem Gesicht, als wäre der Hitler soeben an die Macht gekommen" (*DK*, 329; The mother started crying and disappeared, while the father sat there in silence with an expression on his face as if Hitler had just come to power).

However, Schindel does not only retrace the topography of the Waldheim era in *Der Kalte*, he also reinscribes the Viennese topography through his depiction of the installation of Alfred Hrdlicka's controversial *Mahnmal gegen Krieg und Faschismus* (Monument against War and Fascism, 1988). Planning for "an anti-fascist monument" in the Austrian capital began in 1972,[49] with the monument being formally commissioned by the Vienna City Council on September 30, 1983.[50] Among the many controversies that would plague the monument before and after its execution was the issue of its location. The planned monument would be erected on the Albertinaplatz, behind the Vienna State Opera, a site that, as James E. Young has described, is notable for the multiple "layers of historical memory repressed and buried there."[51] The proposed monument would not only be located on the site of the former Philipphof residential building (which collapsed on the night of March 12, 1945, during an Allied bombing raid, burying alive approximately two hundred Viennese in the bomb shelter below), but also on the site of a pogrom, during which Jews were burned at the stake on the same day (March 12) in 1421.[52] As such the Albertinaplatz is a particularly fraught *lieu de mémoire* or site of memory in Pierre Nora's definition.[53] Following Aleida Assmann, the square may also be understood as a spatial archive, with the space acting as a placeholder for the memories that some would prefer to forget.[54] Both Nora and Assmann construe sites of memory as spaces where different versions of the past may be uncovered and contested. Hrdlicka's decision to erect his monument on this historically laden site, constituted precisely such an uncovering and disturbance of the past since, as Eva Kuttenberg notes, "the history of the Albertinaplatz as an unmarked grave of persecuted Jews in the 1400s and of civilian casualties after an Allied air raid in 1945 only gained prominence in national consciousness through Hrdlicka's monument."[55] The monument, unveiled on November 24, 1988, is a "walk-in-space" consisting of four sculptures,[56] beginning with the *Tor der Gewalt* (Gate of Violence), passing to the *Straßenwaschender Jude* (street-washing Jew), and *Orpheus betritt den Hades* (Orpheus Enters Hades), and ending with the *Stein der Republik* (Stone of the Republic, showing the text of Austria's Declaration of Independence, signed on April 27, 1945). The implied teleology, that the violence of the Second World War and the Holocaust was somehow redeemed by the birth of the Second Republic, has been widely criticized,[57] as has the fact that, as David Art describes, "the monument does not draw any distinctions between the victims of racial persecution, fallen Austrian soldiers, or the victims of Allied bombings."[58]

The monument has also remained highly controversial, not least among Austria's Jewish community, because of its statue of a Jewish man scrubbing the pavement, symbolizing the anti-Semitic violence of the *Anschlusspogrom* following Austria's annexation by Germany. The views of filmmaker Ruth Beckermann, written in her 1989 book *Unzugehörig*, are emblematic of the anger that the monument sparked amongst

Austria's Jewish community: "Was immer dieses Denkmal den Wienern sagen will, mir sagt es: Im Staub seid ihr gelegen. Auf dem Bauch seid ihr gerutscht. Und das ist heute unser Bild von euch. Fünfzig Jahre danach formen wir euch nach diesem Bild." (Whatever this memorial wants to say to the Viennese, to me it says: there you lay in the dust, crawled on your belly. And that is our image of you today. Fifty years on we make you in this image.)[59] As Heidemarie Uhl has traced, the failure of Hrdlicka's monument to adequately commemorate Austrian Holocaust victims ultimately led to the commissioning and unveiling of a Holocaust memorial, designed by Rachel Whiteread, on Vienna's Judenplatz in 2000.[60] In Beckermann's assessment, what is missing from Hrdlicka's monument, which equates all victims of war in an undifferentiated manner, is any depiction of the perpetrators, who have been cut out of the picture:

> Da nahm einer die Photos der knienden Juden, die mit Zahnbürsten zur Belustigung der Wiener die Straßen waschen mußten, zur Hand, in die andere Hand die Schere und schnitt die Grinser, die ganz Unpolitischen in ihrer Alltagskleidung ohne Abzeichen und die in den Kniebundhosen mit den weißen Stutzen, die schnitt er weg. Der ewige Jude wurde zum ewigen Opfer anonymer Gewalt. . . . Wo ist das grinsende Publikum geblieben?[61]

> [One took in one's hand the photo of the kneeling Jews who had to wash the streets with toothbrushes for the entertainment of the Viennese, and took the pair of scissors in the other, cutting out the smirkers, the completely unpolitical in their workaday clothes without insignia and those in their knickerbockers, with their white knee-length socks, he cut them out. Thus the eternal Jew became the eternal victim of anonymous violence. . . . Where has the smirking public got to?]

In Schindel's depiction of the unveiling of Herbert Krieglach's *Denkmal gegen Krieg und Faschismus* (*DK*, 93; Memorial against War and Fascism) in *Der Kalte*, he seems to answer the question posed by his friend Beckermann and, on a fictional level, corrects the failure of Hrdlicka's memorial to represent the perpetrators of what journalist and eyewitness G. E. R. Gedye has described as the "terror unchained" that followed Austria's annexation by Nazi Germany.[62] In *Der Kalte* the statue of the Jewish man scrubbing the pavement is surrounded by three further figures:

> Um den gedemütigten Juden hatte Krieglach drei Wienerleute aufgestellt, zwei Männer und eine Frau. Einer der Männer trug einen Hut mit Gamsfeder, der zweite eine Sportkappe, die Frau hatte aufgesteckte Haare, die am Hinterkopf in einem kropfgroßen

Dutt verknotet waren. Der Wiener mit Hut zeigte auf den Juden und hatte ein höhnisches Lachen im Gesicht. Der Wiener mit der Sportkappe deutete einen Tritt in den Hintern des Knienden an, die Frau hielt die Hände so vor den Körper, als würde sie entweder zu klatschen beginnen oder den Juden packen wollen. (*DK*, 638)

[Krieglach had arranged three Viennese, two men and a woman, around the humiliated Jew. One of the men wore a hat with a chamois feather, the other a sports cap, the woman had her hair pinned up in a goiter-sized bun at the back of her head. The Viennese man with the hat pointed to the Jew and had a mocking laugh on his face. The Viennese man with the sports cap looked as if he was about to kick the kneeling man in the backside, the woman held her hands in front of her body in such a way, as if she was either going to start clapping, or was about to grab the Jew.]

Schindel's fictional memorial thereby reinstates the perpetrators of anti-Semitic acts, which paved the way for the Holocaust, into the picture, rather than making the perpetrators disappear and turning the victims into subjects of "anonymer Gewalt" (anonymous violence) as Hrdlicka's memorial does.[63] To emphasize that this amendment to Hrdlicka's monument constitutes a wish fulfilment, in Schindel's novel the jeering Viennese onlookers are removed four months after the monument's unveiling (having provoked considerable dismay among the country's political establishment), and the statue of the Jewish man is, as was the case with Hrdlicka's monument,[64] covered in barbed wire to prevent tourists from sitting on the statue. Yet in his depiction of this albeit temporary monument to Austrian complicity in the Holocaust, Schindel highlights the unrealized possibilities of remembering and drawing attention to the extent of Austria's participation in the Second World War and in the Shoah. Although the mocking Viennese figures are removed (perhaps in order to uphold the realism principle), through his imaginary installation Schindel underlines the absence of a monument in the Viennese cityscape, or a public discourse more broadly, that would challenge the long-prevalent Austrian self-understanding as first victim of fascism. The presence of the jeering Viennese figures also symbolically counters Waldheim's avowed absence at the scene of the crime during his time in the Wehrmacht. The temporary addition of the sneering onlookers to Hrdlicka's *Mahnmal gegen Krieg und Faschismus* in Schindel's *Der Kalte*, in its transient nature, foregrounds the precise lack of a sustained public discourse in contemporary Austria regarding the country's complicity in Nazi crimes. As we shall see in chapter 5 of this study, a temporary amendment to Hrdlicka's monument, of the kind envisaged by Schindel, was finally realized by Ruth Beckermann in 2015, thereby continuing their dialogue on the inadequacy of the monument, in which both Schindel and Beckermann have engaged in their fiction and nonfiction works respectively.

Schindel's depiction of the *Mahnmal gegen Krieg und Faschismus* is not the only instance of wish fulfilment in the novel. Another notable instance of this in *Der Kalte* is the resignation of Johann Wais on December 23, 1989, thus ending Wais's presidential term two-and-a-half years earlier than that of his real-life counterpart. Similarly, Schindel also has Wais die nearly four years earlier than Waldheim did. Wais dies on March 14, 2003, on the sixty-fifth anniversary of Hitler's arrival in Vienna in March 1938, following Austria's Anschluss with Nazi Germany. The forgetful former president, who persistently denied his involvement in the Nazi war machine, is thereby irrevocably associated with the Nazi regime, even in his hour of death. The epilogue of the novel ends in a conciliatory tone, with Wais, on his deathbed, asking "alle um Verzeihung, die er gekränkt und verletzt hatte" (*DK*, 643; all those for forgiveness, whom he had offended and hurt). This is one of several reconciliations that dominate the closing section of the novel. Prior to this we see Fraul shed tears following the death of Rosinger, who is run over by a car. The unlikely friendship between the erstwhile resistance fighter and the SS officer ultimately enables the former to achieve a sense of closure with regard to his past and to reconnect with his family emotionally. The epilogue concludes with the reported deaths of Edmund Fraul in 2004, and Rosa Fraul in January 2013. The various reconciliations (that of Fraul with his past, that of father and son in the Fraul family, and that of the former president and his countrymen) and the hasty exit of Wais from the Austrian political stage in *Der Kalte* may also be regarded as poetic license and wish fulfilment. In reality, the Waldheim affair created waves in Austrian life that did not subside as easily, with Waldheim paving the way for the rise of right-wing populist Jörg Haider in the following decade,[65] culminating in the entry of his Austrian Freedom Party into the coalition government in 2000. As Dagmar Lorenz has asserted, "Waldheim's self-justification as a Nazi collaborator" allowed Haider to succeed "on a racist populist platform that appealed to xenophobes and revisionists eager to vindicate the Nazi generation and to normalize Austria's history."[66] At the same time, as Lorenz has traced, the oppositional culture that emerged in Austria during the Waldheim affair was instrumental in the formation of a civil society in the country, which would play a crucial role in the movement against Haider more than a decade later.[67] The Waldheim affair arguably drew up the battle lines between liberal progressive forces and right-wing populists in Austria, along which political battles in the country continue to be fought.

Schindel's novel returns to a time in recent Austrian history when Austria's postwar consensus on the National Socialist past was severely disturbed. Through the novel's panoramic focus on several generations and on the places and spaces where the Waldheim affair unfolded, Schindel highlights the extent to which the political scandal came to dominate every sphere of Austria's national life over a period of several years, and which began a long-overdue process of confronting the past in Austria. Schindel's novel draws attention both to recent Austrian history (the Waldheim affair), and to the country's National Socialist past more than seven decades earlier. By fictionalizing Austria's recent past and staging his own interventions in it, specifically through his treatment of Hrdlicka's *Mahnmal gegen Krieg und Faschismus*, Schindel disturbs narratives of Austrian victimhood. By means of his playful reinscription of historical events and personages, Schindel evaluates the Waldheim affair from the perspective of today, seventy-five years on (at the time of the novel's publication in 2013) from Austria's Anschluss with Nazi Germany in 1938, and highlights missed opportunities for reflecting on Austria's National Socialist legacy. As such, Schindel invites his readers to a continual engagement with the past and upon the way that we remember and commemorate it.

5: Missing Images: Memorials and Memorial Projects in Contemporary Vienna

> *Vielleicht ist jedes Gedenken, sind alle Rituale und Mahnmale immer Instrumente des Vergegenwärtigens und des Vergessens zugleich.*
>
> [Perhaps every form of commemoration, all rituals and monuments, are always instruments both of remembering and forgetting at the same time.]
>
> —Doron Rabinovici, *Ohnehin*

As EXPLORED IN THE INTRODUCTION to this study, the decades since the Waldheim Affair of 1986–88 have been marked by a change in attitudes in Austria toward its National Socialist past and its complicity in the Holocaust. This has been reflected not only in the literary and cinematic works explored in the previous chapters of this study, but also in Austria's public spaces, with Austria's increased historical consciousness leading to an increased desire to commemorate victims of National Socialism, and Holocaust victims in particular, in public space. Heidemarie Uhl has termed this "die Wiederentdeckung der Orte" (the rediscovery of place), the refocusing of attention on the concrete places where Nazi persecution occurred.[1] Often springing from grassroots initiatives investigating persecution in concrete places or localities within the cityscape, these memorials draw attention not only to the fact that Holocaust victims lived in streets that one may walk down every day, or indeed live in, but to the "lokale[n] Verstrickung in den Holocaust" (local involvement in the Holocaust),[2] the fact that without the support of ordinary men and women who lived in the selfsame streets and neighborhoods, the Holocaust could not have happened. This, for Uhl, constitutes "die verstörende Dimension der Orte" (the disturbing dimension of places),[3] and accounts for the impact of these local memorial projects.

Public monuments and memorials are symptomatic for how a nation or group of people perceives its past at a given moment in history. As Heidemarie Uhl has traced, developments and conflicts in Austria's attitude vis-à-vis its own history have been reflected in the postwar Austrian memorial landscape.[4] The prevalent memorials in Austria, up until the

1980s, were, as Uhl describes, *Kriegerdenkmäler* (war memorials), which commemorated the war dead of the Second World War as "heroes," who had been doing their duty for their homeland.[5] As Uhl, writing in 1997, notes, "Denkmäler für die Opfer von Widerstand und Verfolgung sind—außerhalb von Wien—wenig präsent" (memorials for the victims of resistance and persecution are—outside of Vienna—few and far between).[6] The first official memorial to commemorate all victims of National Socialism in Austria, the *Mahnmal gegen Krieg und Faschismus* (Monument against War and Fascism) by Alfred Hrdlicka, was unveiled in 1988. The unveiling followed years of disputes between supporters and opponents of the monument,[7] and, as described in the preceding chapter, has remained controversial because of its undifferentiated presentation of victimhood (Wehrmacht soldiers and Jewish victims are symbolically equated in the monument) and lack of adequate commemoration of Holocaust victims. It is this lack of a fitting memorial for Holocaust victims that ultimately led to the erection of Rachel Whiteread's *Mahnmal für die 65.000 ermordeten österreichischen Juden und Jüdinnen der Shoah* (Monument to the 65,000 Austrian Jews Murdered in the Shoah) on Judenplatz in 2000.[8]

Since Heidemarie Uhl wrote her 1997 article on memorials as symbols of the Austrian Second Republic's historical consciousness,[9] memorials for victims of resistance and persecution have proliferated substantially, particularly in Vienna, which will be the focus of this chapter. The past decade has seen a surge in decentralized memorials and memorial projects commemorating Holocaust victims in Austria. An ongoing project (2014–), based at the Institut für Staatswissenschaften (Institute for Political Sciences: in English as Department of Government) at the University of Vienna, aims to investigate and offer a quantitative analysis (as well as offering a qualitative analysis of a small number of selected case studies) of this proliferation of memorials in the Viennese cityscape.[10] In a paper given at the 2015 German Studies Association conference in Washington, DC, historian and political scientist Peter Pirker illustrated the sheer number of monuments that have sprung up in Vienna, in the last ten years in particular, using an interactive, digital map created as part of the project.[11] As mentioned above, many of these memorials have their roots in grassroots initiatives, but institutional support, such as that by the municipal organization *Kunst im öffentlichen Raum Wien* (Art in Public Space Vienna), which was established in 2004, has played a significant role in the support of these projects.

The importance that Vienna's municipal government affords Vienna's memorial culture can be gleaned from a bilingual publication produced by the Vienna City Council in 2014.[12] The brochure details various projects funded by the Vienna City Council, in addition to "zahlreiche Initiativen aus der Zivilgesellschaft" (numerous initiatives from civil society).¹³ These span topics such as "digital remembrance on the Internet,"¹⁴ a section on Jewish Vienna, the renaming of controversial street names, and numerous memorial projects in Vienna's public spaces. The publication is a salient reminder that public memorial projects cannot be regarded in isolation but need to be viewed in the context of Austria's broader remembrance culture. Additionally, *Gedenkjahre* (commemorative years) serve to prompt renewed discussions of and focus on the National Socialist past. The years 1988 (fifty years since the Anschluss), 2005 (sixty years since the end of the Second World War, fifty years of the *Staatsvertrag* [Austrian State Treaty]), 2015 (seventy years since the end of the Second World War, sixty years of the *Staatsvertrag*) have all been notable recent Gedenkjahre. Meanwhile, the institutionalization of Holocaust remembrance, with May 5 (the day of the liberation of the Mauthausen concentration camp in Upper Austria) becoming a day for Holocaust remembrance in Austria since 1997, has served to further integrate remembrance of Austria's complicity in the Holocaust into the Austrian collective consciousness. The official refashioning of May 8 (Victory in Europe Day) into a *Fest der Freude* (Festival of Joy), celebrated on Vienna's Heldenplatz since 2012, is also symptomatic of a change in attitude.¹⁵ The day previously saw violent clashes between right-wing university fraternity groups commemorating the so-called fallen heroes (Wehrmacht soldiers) of the Second World War in the *Weiheraum* (consecration chamber) of the *Äußeres Burgtor* (outer castle door) and anti-fascist groups protesting against this practice. Magnus Koch has described this as a conflict about what May 8 signifies in Austria (a *Tag der Besetzung* [occupation day] or a *Tag der Befreiung* ([liberation day] in the view of the respective groups) played out on the historically freighted Heldenplatz.¹⁶

Investigations into and the consequent renaming of historically freighted street names in Vienna should also be viewed in the context of Austria's evolving memory landscape. Between 2011 and 2013, a commission led by historian Oliver Rathkolb examined Viennese street names named after individuals,¹⁷ focusing particularly on "personalities with historically charged biographies."¹⁸ The commission's findings were published in a guide to controversial Viennese street names in 2014.¹⁹ As a result of the commission's findings, a small number of streets have been renamed in recent years, the most notable being the part of the Ringstrasse on which the University of Vienna is located, which was renamed from *Dr.-Karl-Lueger-Ring* (after the anti-Semitic Viennese mayor) to Universitätsring in July 2012. The former street sign is now part of the permanent exhibition in Vienna's Jewish Museum.²⁰ The fact remains that in other places in the Viennese cityscape we can still find a statue and a square (the *Dr.-Karl-Lueger-Denkmal* on the eponymous Dr.-Karl-Lueger-Platz), named after the infamous anti-Semitic Viennese mayor, Dr. Karl Lueger, as highlighted in Ruth Beckermann's 1987 film *Die papierene Brücke*, discussed in chapter 1 of this study. This is not to mention the *Dr.-Karl-Lueger-Gedächtniskirche* (Dr. Karl Lueger Memorial Church) at the Vienna Central Cemetery.

The renaming of controversial street names and the contextualization of others,[21] should be seen in the context of investigations by notable Austrian institutions, such as the University of Vienna and Vienna's Musikverein, into their own history. A number of research projects have been undertaken at the University of Vienna in recent years, examining the institution during National Socialism, including one resulting in the publication of a memorial book and database of (primarily) Jewish students and faculty who were excluded from the university in 1938.[22] In light of these investigations, a number of memorial projects addressing the University's Nazi past have been undertaken on the university's premises. These include the contextualization of the controversial *Siegfriedkopf* (Siegfried's Head) monument, housed within the *Arkadenhof* (arcade court) of the University of Vienna's main building, and the renovation of a former Jewish prayer house, located on its grounds, into a Holocaust memorial. The latter was opened in 2005 and, since 2009, has housed the above-mentioned "Memorial Book for the Victims of National Socialism at the University of Vienna in 1938."[23] In March 2013, the world-famous Wiener Musikverein published the findings of a historical investigation into its National Socialist past on its website, and a documentary on the same topic was aired by Austrian state broadcaster ORF at the same time.[24] Ongoing discussions in the Austrian media about the planned *Haus der Geschichte* (House of History), which is due to be unveiled in 2019 in the *Neue Burg* (New Castle) section of Vienna's Heldenplatz,[25] can also be viewed as symptomatic of a changed historical consciousness, and the desire to address problematic aspects of the Austrian national past. The debates include how best to incorporate the so-called *Führerbalkon* (Führer balcony, from which Adolf Hitler proclaimed the Anschluss of his native Austria into the Third Reich on March 15, 1938) into the museum.

Scholars have frequently turned their attention to an examination of the monuments and memorials in a given country because these are deeply symptomatic of a country's attitude to its past at a given moment in time. An artist wishing to construct a monument or memorial in public space needs to be given permission by the authorities in order to do so; the artist(s), architects, and their material costs need to be funded (quite often all or at least some of this funding will come from municipal authorities); and if a competition for a memorial design is advertised, the associated administrative costs of advertising and judging the competition need to be factored in. Put simply, the erection of any monument or memorial in public space requires more resources and approval from various bodies than the writing and publishing of a novel, or even the making of a film. For this reason, memorials are frequently the focus of scholarly attention by historians and cultural scholars. James E. Young's influential study *The Texture of Memory* (1993) analyzed Holocaust memorials in Germany (Austria, inexplicably, is subsumed under Germany in his investigation), Poland, Israel, and America, examining how these reflect "not only national and communal remembrance . . . but also the memorial designer's own time and place."[26] With regard to Holocaust memorials in Germany, Young identified a specific kind of monument and memorial that positions itself in opposition to everything that a traditional monument or memorial stands for: the countermonument. These countermonuments seek to avoid "the possibility that memory of events so grave might be reduced to exhibitions of public craftsmanship or cheap pathos,"[27] and seek to counter the tendency to assign "memory work" to a monument or memorial rather than encouraging the viewer to do this him or herself.[28] Young views this passive form of remembrance, which he associates with traditional monuments, as symptomatic for the "impulse to memorialize events like the Holocaust" springing "from an opposite and equal desire to forget them."[29] In opposition to this, the countermonument "flouts any number of cherished memorial conventions: its aim is not to console but to provoke; not to remain fixed but to change; not to be everlasting but to disappear; not to be ignored by passers-by but to demand interaction; not to remain pristine but to invite its own violation and desanctification; not to accept graciously the burden of memory but to throw it back at the town's feet."[30]

This definition of the countermonument, posited by Young in the 1990s, as resisting fixity, disrupting public spaces, and engaging us in "memory work," rather than the monument doing the work for us, can be said to hold true for Holocaust memorial projects more than two decades on. Young's terminology at times conflates the monument and the memorial, with the author explaining that a statue, for example, can take on the function of becoming both "a monument to heroism and a memorial to tragic loss."[31] In the following discussion, I will be referring to the case studies under consideration as memorials and memorial projects, as I do not consider the art projects under consideration to be heroic or monumental in any way. Young does, however, consistently use the term countermonument to refer to artworks that challenge the aesthetic and accompanying memorial practices of the traditional monument or memorial. Occasionally, as noted by Bill Niven, Young has used the term "countermemorial" analogously to the term "countermonument," but there is no discernible distinction between these two terms and, as Niven rightly points out, it is not clear how a countermemorial could be "understood to 'counter' existing memorials to Jewish victims of Nazism."[32] In the following discussion only the term "countermonument" will be used to describe memorial projects that challenge the monumental commemorative practices predating the late twentieth century, practices that would, in any case, be inappropriate when dealing with the Holocaust.

One important matter to bear in mind when examining memorial projects in contemporary Austria is the fact that these are projects carried out by members of the second or third generation and as such they are, as Niven describes, much more concerned with "the problem of memory for those not involved in the Holocaust, either as victim nor perpetrator."[33] Niven even posits that the term "mnemorials" would be more appropriate to describe these memorial projects (rather than "countermonuments" and "countermemorials"): "an amalgam of 'mnemonic' and 'memorial,' encapsulates better their preoccupation with processes of memory and draws attention to their origins in the mid-1980s and early 1990s, when interest in memory, both in the academic and public realms, was on the increase."[34] Niven is writing about Germany, where the discourse surrounding memorialization of the Nazi past was notably ahead of that of Austria in the mid-1980s and 1990s. As will emerge in the following discussion, a number of the artists engaged in memorial practices in Austria today, in the early twenty-first century, view their artworks as anamnestic—they feel it is imperative to draw attention to the lacunae in Austria's collective memory, to bring "missing images" to our attention,[35] or to otherwise "make memory visible."[36] As we shall see, often they incorporate topical events into their memorial artworks to highlight the contemporary relevance of their projects and to draw attention to "the long shadow of the past" in Austrian culture. The multifaceted nature of some contemporary memorials has led Niven to coin a new term for them, the "combimemorial," a type of memorial that incorporates elements of the museum and begins "to dissolve the traditional boundaries between memorials on the one hand, and archives and exhibitions on the other."[37] As we shall see in the following discussion, a number of memorial artists do indeed combine artworks with practices that are more associated with the museum, including educational outreach activities, digital exhibitions, and tours.

In the following discussion, I will focus on a number of memorials and memorial projects that have been undertaken in Vienna in recent years, specifically on Ulrike Lienbacher's *Idylle* (Idyll, 2002), the *Steine der Erinnerung* project (Stones of Remembrance, 2005–), Julia Schulz's *Schlüssel gegen das Vergessen* memorial (Keys against Forgetting, 2008), Maria Theresia Litschauer's *transkription* (Transcription, 2010), Iris Andraschek's and Hubert Lobnig's *Turnertempel Erinnerungsort* (Turner Temple Memorial Site, 2011), Karen Frostig's *The Vienna Project* (2013–14), Ruth Beckermann's *The Missing Image* (2014–15), and Catrin Bolt's *Alltagsskulpturen* (Everyday Sculptures, 2014). Focusing on these case studies, I will examine the specific strategies that the memorials use, whether this is contextualization of existing problematic memorials or another intervention in public space, a drawing attention to the historical legacy of a particular site, or an engaging of the public in a communal process of remembrance through a range of participation initiatives. The aim of this chapter is to evaluate the contributions of the various memorial projects to the Viennese memorial landscape and explore what these reveal about Austria's changing memorial culture.

Contextualizing Nazi Art: Ulrike Lienbacher's *Idylle* (2002) and Maria Theresia Litschauer's *transkription* (2010)

As has already been mentioned in the case of the renaming of Viennese streets, at times, a contextualization of remnants of a problematic history is more appropriate than a renaming. Not removing a street name or a problematic statue means that history is not merely erased, but that it remains an open wound in the cityscape. This section will examine two memorials that draw attention to the former omnipresence of Nazi ideology (which pervaded every sphere of citizens' lives, including their living quarters) in the Viennese cityscape, through their engagement with and commentary on Nazi art. The first example deals with Ulrike Lienbacher's *Idylle* (Idyll, 2002; see fig. 1), which is a contextualization of a Nazi-era wall painting by Rudolf Böttger on the façade of a municipal apartment block in the Brandmayergasse in Vienna's fifth district. Böttger was part of the *Wiener Gaukulturrat* (Vienna Gau Council for Culture) with special responsibility for painting.[38] The painting upon the wall of the apartment block (fig. 2) shows the idyll of family life as propagated by the National Socialist Party. We see a man and a woman surrounded by three children, with the woman also holding a babe in arms. The eldest boy is wearing a *Hitlerjugend* (Hitler Youth) uniform, the younger boy holds a model airplane in his hand, while the girl is holding a doll. The roles that the children are destined to take in life, in the eyes of the Nazi party, are all too clear. The representation of the two adult figures is also highly gendered. The man's well-built, muscular frame embodies the ideal of the Aryan man, while the woman, holding a young baby and surrounded by three other young children, is symptomatic of the Nazi ideal of womanhood as associated with child rearing and domesticity. The tallest of the two young boys is carrying a Nazi Party flag. Today, a hole in the mural marks the place where the swastika used to be. The swastika was removed in 1945, the rest of the mural remained as it is.[39]

Lienbacher's memorial was unveiled on May 8 (Victory in Europe Day) 2002, following a competition for an appropriate artistic intervention in the wall painting, a competition initiated by the apartment block

Fig. 1. Ulrike Lienbacher, *Idylle* (Idyll, 2002).

tenants, district administration authorities, and the Culture Department of the City of Vienna.[40] Lienbacher's intervention in the mural consists of a glass panel placed in front of the painting, which contains the words *Idylle* (idyll) written back-to-front on the glass, so that, as the explanatory plaque describes: "aus der Perspektive der dargestellten Figuren ist an der 'IDYLLE' scheinbar nichts verkehrt" (from the perspective of the represented figures, there is ostensibly nothing amiss in this idyll). Our image of this "idyll" is, however, distorted by the striking through of part of the painting by the letters forming the word *Idylle*. This disturbance of the

Fig. 2. Ulrike Lienbacher, *Idylle* (Idyll, 2002),
on the wall of Brandmayergasse 27, Vienna.

original mural (which, apart from the removal of the swastika, remained unchanged since the time of its erection in 1939) serves to draw attention to the incongruity of the Nazi painting in contemporary Vienna. The glass panel and lettering radically estrange the painting, which may otherwise go unnoticed by residents who have lived in the apartment block or blocks nearby for a considerable length of time, and serve to remind residents and passersby just how pervasive Nazi ideology was in all spheres of public and private life. As well as a contextualization, it is difficult not to view the writing placed over the original painting as at least a partial defacement, as it obscures parts of the painting. It recalls the defacement of so-called degenerate art during the Nazi period, and as such it pronounces judgment on the aesthetic merits of Böttger's wall painting with its presentation of family life under National Socialism.

A memorial from 2010 located in the ninth district of Vienna functions in a very similar fashion to Ulrike Lienbacher's *Idylle*. Maria Theresia Litschauer's *transkription* (Transcription, 2010) consists of a glass panel placed in front of, as well as two large square brackets painted around, a Nazi wall sculpture from 1939 (see figs. 3 and 4). The sculpture, as in the case of Böttger's painting, is located on the wall of an apartment block. The apartment block, named the Thury-Hof, was built in 1925– 26 as part of the municipal housing program instigated by the governing

Social Democrats, which dominated Vienna's City Council in the 1920s and early 1930s. The erection of a National Socialist statue at the Thury-Hof was therefore meant to signal the triumph of National Socialism in this bastion of Red Vienna.[41] As Litschauer asserts, the statue "irritiert als nationalsozialistisches Implantat im Baukörper sozialdemokratischer Identität" (irritates as a National Socialist implant in a building of social democratic identity).[42] The statue by Alfred Crepaz, which, as Litschauer describes, is characterized by a *Blut und Boden* (blood and soil) aesthetic,[43] shows a man-at-arms holding a sword in his hands. The inscription on the plaque beneath his feet is a quotation from Adolf Hitler about steadfastness and duty to National Socialism: "Wir bitten Dich Herrgott, laß uns niemals wankend werden und feige sein, laß uns niemals die Pflicht vergessen die wir übernommen haben." (We ask you Lord God, never let us waver and become fainthearted, never let us forget the duty that we have taken on.) In 1945, the letters bearing Adolf Hitler's name, directly below the quotation, were removed, in a similar vein to the swastika in Rudolf Böttger's wall painting. Prior to Litschauer's intervention, the average passerby would have most likely not been aware of the statue's origins in the Nazi era or come close enough to the statue to read the provenance of the quotation; the missing letters forming Adolf Hitler's name are still visible today, present in their absence.

Litschauer's intervention in this Nazi sculpture consisted of painting two square brackets in bright white paint around the statue, which has the effect of drawing attention to the statue, which may otherwise go unnoticed. Further, Litschauer installed a concrete plank on the ground that leads the visitor from the wall where the statue is mounted to an upright glass plate installed a few yards away. This glass plate contains a text explaining the history and origins of Alfred Crepaz's statue, as well as the fate of the "nicht arische[r] Mieter' (non-Aryan residents) of the council flats during the Nazi era who, in the middle of June 1938, were given notice to vacate their flats by August 1, 1938, as part of the Nazi policy of "Aryanization."[44] The text details the fates of the Thury-Hof's Jewish residents in the 1930s, from those who managed to flee successfully, to those who, like Isidor Nelken, found themselves unable to enter Palestine (due to British government policy at the time) and were sent to an internment camp in Mauritius, where Nelken died. The text further details how another resident was able to survive in Vienna due to his non-Jewish wife, while a mother and daughter took their own lives a week before the deadline for vacating their flat, due to the lack of options that they saw open to them. Litschauer explains that she wanted the text on the glass panel to be read in view of Crepaz's statue (the viewer must stand facing the statue in order to read the text on the panel).[45] In this manner, Litschauer draws a clear connection between the Nazi ideology propagated by Crepaz's statue and the persecution and murder it ultimately led

Fig. 3. Maria Theresia Litschauer, *transkription* (transcription, 2010).

to. The statue can therefore no longer be dismissed as kitsch Nazi art, but instead as the glorification of a violent ideology, the effects of which upon those judged as not belonging to the Aryan race (as espoused by the warrior in the statue) are made all too apparent in Litschauer's *transkription*. The brackets around the statue in bright white paint, and the accompanying text on the glass panel, draw attention to all that has been "bracketed out" in postwar Austria with regard to facing up to the Nazi past. As

Fig. 4. Maria Theresia Litschauer, *transkription* (transcription, 2010), on the wall of the Thury-Hof, Marktgasse 3-7, Vienna.

historian Oliver Rathkolb describes, the erasing of Adolf Hitler's name in the original statue is symptomatic for the *Schlussstrich* (clean break) mentality in postwar Austria, drawing a line under the past or sweeping the past under the carpet.[46] Litschauer's *transkription* does the opposite. The word "transcription" means both to "transfer (information)," and to "rewrite" something "for an instrument or medium other than that originally intended."[47] Just as a transcription of an oral interview often allows more insights than listening alone, so Litschauer's transcription has the effect of estranging the statue and allowing the viewer to reflect on its genesis and meaning in the more reflective medium of the written word.

Litschauer's and Lienbacher's interventions, or "permanent intervention[s]" in Rathkolb's formulation,[48] in Nazi-era artworks serve a number of purposes. They visibly counter the impulses for erasure and obfuscation of the Nazi past by drawing attention to these Nazi artworks (and the pernicious ideology underpinning them) that may otherwise go unnoticed in the cityscape. Their interventions have a distancing and estranging effect, prompting reflection on these reminders of a haunting past in the city, in the precise places where everyday persecution took place, such as in municipal apartment blocks. Like many of the memorial projects that have sprung up in Vienna since 2000, as highlighted by Heidemarie Uhl,[49] Lienbacher's and Litschauer's memorials are located in the concrete everyday spaces where persecution occurred. As such, they can be ascribed a mnemonic function, their purpose being to alert viewers to the traumatic history of a seemingly innocuous everyday place, such as a housing block (particularly in the case of Litschauer's memorial, which makes the connection between the Nazi ideology propagated by the Nazi wall painting and the racial persecution it led to explicit). Litschauer's and Lienbacher's contextualizations of Nazi art serve to draw attention to the persistent remainders (despite the superficial removal of swastikas and Adolf Hitler's name) of a pernicious ideology that once pervaded every sphere of public and domestic life, and the destruction and death that it led to.

Localized Decentralized Memorials: Julia Schulz's *Schlüssel gegen das Vergessen* (2008) and Elisabeth Ben David-Hindler's *Steine der Erinnerung* project (2005–)

Another localized memorial called *Schlüssel gegen das Vergessen* (Keys against Forgetting, 2008) in Vienna's Servitengasse in the ninth district (which, like the second district, had a large Jewish population prior to 1938), designed by Julia Schulz, is constituted of a glass case set into the ground, containing 462 keys, which are attached to name tags bearing the names of those who lived and worked in the street, and who were subsequently driven from their homes. The name of the memorial, *Schlüssel gegen das Vergessen*, implies that the memorial's aim is to counter forgetting of the Holocaust. The memorial grew out of an organization called Servitengasse 1938 in which residents researched the history of their street (similar to the research undertaken for the *Idylle* and *transkription* memorials) and of the Austrian Jews who lived there prior to the Holocaust. Schulz's memorial was constructed following a competition organized by the Servitengasse 1938 association in conjunction with the University for Applied Arts Vienna.[50] The *Schlüssel gegen das Vergessen* memorial, with its anamnestic concerns, may be described as a "mnemorial," to follow Bill Niven.[51] The wordplay on the word "keys" in the memorial's title draws attention to the mnemonic function of objects (in this case facsimile apartment keys) and to the anamnestic intentions of the memorial. The memorial, like that of Litschauer's *transkription* and Lienbacher's *Idylle*, draws attention to the everyday domestic spaces and living quarters where anti-Semitic persecution took place, thereby also highlighting the active or passive complicity of non-Jewish Austrians in the persecution that led to the Holocaust. The sheer number of victims remembered in Schulz's local memorial (462 evicted citizens in a single, rather small street), renders untenable the idea that their non-Jewish neighbors were unaware of the crimes being committed against their fellow citizens, thereby serving to undermine Austria's "first victim" myth. More recently, investigations into the history of the ninth district's Jewish history, through engagement with the history of residential buildings, have expanded with the foundation of a new organization named *Volksopernviertel 1938* (Volksoper Quarter 1938).[52] The project has so far resulted in a *Gedenkstele* (memorial stele[53]) being placed in front of a house in the Fluchtgasse, listing the names of the twenty Jewish residents who lived in the building and were expelled from their apartments following the Anschluss.[54]

The *Steine der Erinnerung* (Stones of Remembrance) project, instigated by Elisabeth Ben David-Hindler in 2005, is another localized Holocaust memorial project, yet it is also a larger-scale and more decentralized project than the memorials discussed hitherto. It takes its inspiration from the German artist Gunter Demnig's *Stolpersteine* (stumbling blocks) project, which has been running since 1994, and which, with over 55,000 stones laid in twenty countries across Europe, constitutes the world's largest decentralized memorial.[55] As part of the *Steine der Erinnerung* project, cobblestone-sized brass stones are placed in the pavement (or, more rarely, on house walls) in front of the former homes of Holocaust victims. Stones are placed in front of houses or buildings following suggestions from members of the public for a stone to be placed there, with the costs for this largely covered by members of the public themselves.[56] Leopoldstadt and Brigittenau, areas of Vienna which, as Sidney Rosenfeld describes, had the largest Jewish population prior to the Holocaust,[57] have their own *Erinnerungswege* (paths of remembrance) where, in addition to the *Steine der Erinnerung*, path markings similarly embedded in the ground serve to commemorate Jewish institutions (temples, theaters, cafés) destroyed in the Holocaust. Other areas of Vienna also have their own *Stationen der Erinnerung* (stations of remembrance).[58] The project is augmented by guided tours, an audio guide to *Steine der Erinnerung* in Vienna's second district, and visits by survivors to schools.[59] The project is a means of commemorating the victims for their children and grandchildren, where no grave is present; often the stones are unveiled in the presence of victims' relatives. Most importantly, the memorial serves to remind passersby coming across the stones that persecution and deportations of Austrian Jews took place under the eyes of the local population, thereby altering our perception of everyday buildings and streets in the city.

These grassroots initiatives, once again focusing on the everyday domestic sphere of housing and living quarters, serve to localize and make tangible the dispossession and persecution that took place in the city of Vienna, in the buildings and areas where today's Viennese continue to live. The processes of "Aryanization" and discrimination, which paved the way for the Holocaust, are made palpable, ensuring that remembrance is not limited to visiting a memorial in the center of the capital, such as Whiteread's Holocaust memorial on Judenplatz, but rather that remembrance remains both habitual (for instance, if a *Stein der Erinnerung* is placed in front of a house where one lives) and disruptive (if a particular *Stein der Erinnerung*, commemorative stele, or other memorial, is "discovered" by a passerby for the first time). Collectively, these localized memorials, which only scratch the surface with regard to marking the addresses of the 65,000 Austrian Jews who perished in the Holocaust and the 130,000 who were able to flee,[60] raise more questions than they answer, prompting passersby to reflect on the history and provenance of their own property, and tourists to wonder about the Jewish history of the street where their hotel may be located. The memorials bring remembrance into our daily lives, ensuring that "memory work" (Young) remains a continual process.

Making Memory Visible: Karen Frostig's *The Vienna Project* (2013–14)

A further decentralized memorial project, which seeks to raise awareness of Nazi-era persecution in the everyday places and spaces of Vienna, is Karen Frostig's *The Vienna Project* (2013–14). The project seeks to make us look anew at the everyday places in the Viennese cityscape that surround us and, in the words of *The Vienna Project*'s initiator, Karen Frostig, "to make memory visible."[61] *The Vienna Project* began when Frostig inherited her father's letters written to him by her grandparents in Austria between 1938 and 1945. Frostig's father, Dr. Benjamin Frostig, was expelled from Austria in June 1938, and ended up in the United States, after being arrested by the Gestapo in 1938 as part of "an early wave of arrests targeting Austria's intelligentsia."[62] Through her father's sixty-nine letters,[63] Frostig was able to find out about a large extended family, all of whom perished in the Holocaust. This prompted a "journey of return to Vienna in 2006," and the reclamation of Austrian citizenship in 2007.[64] This rapprochement between Frostig and the country that her father originated from led to what Frostig describes as a "social-action memorial project developed to mark the seventy-fifth anniversary year of the Anschluss."[65] The multimedia *Vienna Project*, which was conceived in 2009,[66] set out to commemorate seven different victim groups (Jews, Roma and Sinti, Jehovah's Witnesses, the physically or mentally handicapped, homosexuals, persons persecuted on political grounds, and Carinthian Slovenians[67]) and included video projections, performance art, stencil sprays, a series of public engagement events, and a concluding Naming Memorial. This was accompanied by an active Internet and social media presence (in English), which contributed significantly to the project's international reach, particularly in Vienna, which has large numbers of expatriates from around the globe, for whom English is the lingua franca. The project was also partly funded through crowd funding, a practice that is widespread in the Anglophone sphere, but that remains unusual in the Austrian context.[68] The project's orientation toward an international audience (whether these be expatriates or tourists) was underlined through the most visible manifestation of the project in the Viennese cityscape: the thirty-eight stencil sprays at historically significant sites included the project's axiom, "What happens when we forget to remember?" written in twelve languages (fig. 5). These were German, Yiddish, Romani, Slovenian, Polish, Russian, Serbian, Croatian, Bosnian, Turkish, Hebrew, and English. These languages both reflect the ethnic origin of victim groups persecuted under National Socialism and render the memorial accessible to international visitors.

The thirty-eight sites, chosen following research by a team of historians led by Jérôme Segal,[69] are, as Frostig describes, localities "where public instances of exclusion, aggression, humiliation, and theft, as well as instances of rescue and resistance began in 1938, taking place between Austrians subscribing to a Nazi ideology and the targeted victim groups."[70] These sites include train stations in Vienna from which Jews

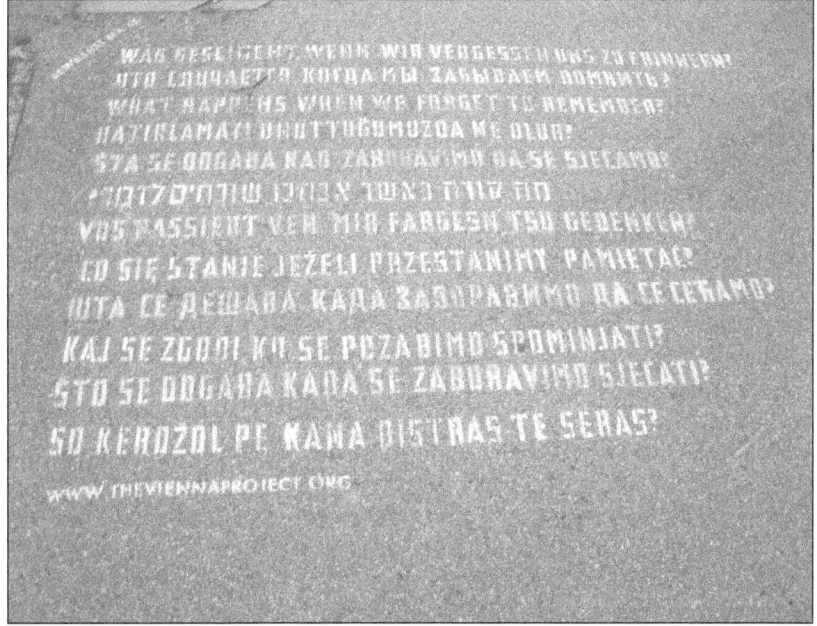

Fig. 5. *The Vienna Project* stencil spray.

were deported to concentration camps, the Central Synagogue, and the former seat of the Gestapo headquarters. Stenciled and sprayed in the pavement in front of these sites is the axiom "What happens when we forget to remember?" *The Vienna Project*'s stencil sprays, like Julia Schulz's memorial, are insistently concerned with remembering, with their aim being to counter forgetting of the Holocaust as it recedes from living memory. Essentially, the question that Frostig's memorial poses is how the Holocaust can be remembered, when it recedes from the collective memory of those who lived through and witnessed it, be it as survivors, perpetrators, or bystanders. The means by which to counter this forgetting, Frostig believes, is to "make memory visible."[71] The need for this making-visible-of-memory stems from Frostig's own experiences of visiting Vienna following the discovery of her grandparents' letters:

> I walked for hours on end, looking for the evidence of memory on the streets of Vienna, looking for some clues about my family's past. What I found was the absence of memory. I saw beautiful street art, Vienna is an incredibly artistically alive city, but I did not see a connection between the street art and my family's story. And it was at that point that I became involved with the ideas of *The Vienna Project*, as a way of using street art to bring memory back to the city of Vienna. Mapping 1938 Vienna is about making memory visible on the streets of Vienna.[72]

In this manner, the most visible aspect of Frostig's project functions as a decentralized "mnemorial" in Niven's terms.[73] The stencil sprays in front of sites of persecution and resistance, with their insistent questioning "What happens when we forget to remember?," serve to alert passersby to the fact that the site that they are standing upon was the historical scene of something that is worth remembering, even if the historical significance of the place is not immediately obvious, if the site, for example, contains an otherwise inconspicuous residential house. The URL of *The Vienna Project*'s website can be found at the bottom of every stencil spray, directing the curious passerby to the source of further information about the memorial project, where one can find out why the stencil spray has been placed in the location one is standing in. On the same website, the visitor is also able to download a smartphone app, which includes an interactive "memory map" detailing the thirty-eight sites on a Google map of Vienna.[74] *The Vienna Project* thereby follows educational practices common to modern museums and other educational institutions. The Jewish Museum Vienna has developed a "Between the Museums" smartphone app, which uses geolocation to offer a guide for visitors to points of interest in Viennese Jewish history, as they make their way between the two sites of the Jewish Museum Vienna.[75] We can see how *The Vienna*

Project incorporates aspects more commonly associated with a museum or educational institution and, out of all the projects described in this chapter, it most closely fits the description of a "combimemorial" proposed by Bill Niven.[76]

Both the designers of the Jewish Museum Vienna smartphone app and the initiator of *The Vienna Project* understand that history can best be reimagined through topographical and architectural traces. The buildings that were the sites of violence and persecution may still exist in their original function, for example, as a center of learning (as in the case of the University of Vienna), a cultural or political institution (as in the case of the Austrian Parliament and the Vienna State Opera), or judicial institution (the Vienna Regional Court, where nearly twelve hundred people were executed in the period 1938–45; see fig. 6). Alternatively, their purpose today may differ radically from their historical function. This is the case, to mention just a few examples, with the former Gestapo headquarters on Morzinplatz (now a *Gedenkstätte für die Opfer der Gestapo Wien* [Memorial Site for the Victims of the Gestapo in Vienna]), the Palais Ephrussi (Ephrussi Palace, which once belonged to the Ephrussi family—as described by descendant Edmund de Waal in his best-selling book *The Hare with Amber Eyes*[77]—and is now owned by Casinos Austria), or Eichmann's "Central Office for Jewish Emigration" located in the "Aryanized" Palais Rothschild (Rothschild Palace) on Prinz-Eugen-Straße (now the seat of the Austrian Chamber of Labor). Some of *The Vienna Project*'s thirty-eight sites, such as representative cultural and political institutions, may be very well known to the native Austrian; others, such as the building that formerly housed the Sanatorium Fürth in the eighth district, whose owners took lethal injections on April 3, 1938, following their forced participation in a so-called *Reibpartie* (scrubbing game; cynical name for the street washing that Jews were subjected to in Vienna following the Anschluss in March 1938), will likely be unknown to those unfamiliar with this district of Vienna. The purpose of the spray stencils in *The Vienna Project* is to alert the viewer to the importance of these locations as sites of memory, and to encourage the visitor to find out why a stencil spray has been placed in front of a building. In this manner, the stencil sprays render these sites visible, alerting the passerby to the fact that there is something worth remembering about the building, and that the building may have had a radically different function in the past than the one it is known for today.

The stencil sprays were applied in a series of so-called *Sprayaktionen* (spray actions),[78] recalling actionist art performances, beginning in October 2013. These spray actions were widely advertised to members of the public, as were a series of performances and installations that later took place at these sites, including silent witness vigils, thematic guided tours, film screenings, and a reading marathon.[79] One such performance, for

Fig. 6. Vienna Regional Court building, where 1,184 people were executed between 1938 and 1945. One of the thirty-eight sites of *The Vienna Project*.

example, was the Israeli artist's Ossi Yalon's "The Well/ Der Brunnen," which took place at the Marpe Lanefesh Memorial (a former Jewish prayer house located on the site of the old General Hospital, now the University of Vienna campus) on August 27, 2014. As part of the performance (which I attended), visitors were encouraged to "leave a memory" by writing it down on a piece of paper attached to a glass crystal and placing it in a bowl in the center of a table, which contained wineglasses and other glass items. A soundtrack of glass smashing was played in the background, clearly meant to evoke associations with the November pogroms, which began across the Third Reich on November 9, 1938, euphemistically referred to as *Kristallnacht* (Crystal Night) by the Nazis. Through incorporating elements of therapeutic art practice, the performance thereby invited visitors to reflect on memory and trauma, and to combine a delving into one's own personal "well of memory" with a consideration of the traumatic events of 1938.

Further initiatives of *The Vienna Project* similarly placed public participation at the heart of their activities. This can, not least, be observed in Nikolaus Gansterer's memory map, a two-by-three-meter construction that features excerpts from archival letters written by Holocaust victims and survivors.[80] The excerpts were scanned and the text was then cut into strips and mapped onto a map of Vienna, thus evoking the memories of those who had to leave the city behind. The majority of the archival letters came from families of Holocaust survivors in the United States.[81] The tangible mapping of archival letters across a map of Vienna, creating a multitude of (silent) voices, underlines the fact that the city is now bereft of these voices that once occupied it, which are now only preserved as letters on a page. At the same time, as Frostig describes, "the letters, reading literally as pathways of remembrance, provide a direct testimony to the past, challenging viewers to imagine the lives of the writers who inhabited this city, abruptly expelled and deported from their homes."[82] The letter fragments serve to activate memory, and remembrance of the victim groups, in the present. Following the conclusion of *The Vienna Project*, the memory map was placed in the Jewish Museum Vienna, as part of its permanent exhibition "Unsere Stadt! Jüdisches Wien bis heute" (Our City! Jewish Vienna up to the Present).[83]

The closing ceremony of the project also made use of personal letters and archival materials, as the names of "91,780 persecuted Austrian victims and dissidents retrieved from five databases . . . murdered between 1938–1945,"[84] were projected onto the façades of the Austrian National Library buildings on Josefsplatz, part of the former imperial *Hofburg* Palace, and meters away from where Hitler proclaimed the Anschluss to an assembled crowd of an estimated 200,000 on March 15, 1938. The choice of site for this Naming Memorial is therefore deeply symbolic. Today, the Hofburg complex also houses the president's and chancellor's offices and, as such, it is one of the most well-known buildings in Austria. A national library, meanwhile, is a repository of a nation's memories, including the darkest chapters of its history. The physical materiality of books in its collections is testament to this history, including the countless rare books that were "Aryanized" and thereby came into the library's collections during the period 1938–45. The Naming Memorial, on which the names of the 91,780 victims of National Socialism in Austria briefly appeared on the façades of the Austrian National Library became "the first national memorial in Europe to represent multiple victim groups of National Socialism, at the same moment, in a differentiated format."[85] All names were written in the same font, were the same color, were of the same size, and were projected for exactly the same length of time, thereby, as Frostig describes, "presenting each name as equal."[86]

In addition to the Naming Memorial, letters from victims of National Socialism were read out by actors on the Josefsplatz, while further readings took place within the walls of the Austrian National Library itself, both as part of the official closing ceremony with assembled dignitaries, and as part of reading circles consisting of the letter writers' family and friends.[87] On the day prior to the closing ceremony, letters were also read by school pupils and teachers at the thirty-eight memorial sites of *The Vienna Project* in a one-hour "reading marathon," with the aim of "infiltrat[ing] the city streets for a single hour with the voices of hundreds of victims of National Socialism."[88] The letters were collated following "a world-wide call for archival letters" written between 1938–45 by Austrian victims of National Socialist persecution, issued by *The Vienna Project* in the summer of 2014.[89] As part of this call for "archival" letters, people could upload letters from their relatives (which they could also volunteer to read at the closing ceremony), using a form on the project website.[90] In line with contemporary thinking on archives, particularly in the wake of ever-increasing digitalization, the reading out of "archival" letters (I purposely put the word archive in quotation marks, as, despite Karen Frostig's classification of the letters as such, the letters are held in what may be described as personal archives, rather than public repositories) constitutes a practice that has been termed "performing the archive" by Simone Osthoff and others.[91] This practice serves to bring neglected and underappreciated documents to public attention, in a creative and imaginative way. This performance, as any performance, gains a disruptive potential, destabilizing notions of the past and the present.

Performing the archives was an explicit aim of *The Vienna Project*,[92] which counts James E. Young, Heidemarie Uhl, and a number of other academics active in the field of memory studies, among its advisory board.[93] In being an impermanent memorial, subject to disappearance, this ephemeral performance follows the aesthetic of the countermonument, as outlined by Young. It must be noted that Karen Frostig herself, the initiator of *The Vienna Project*, who is an academic and educator in addition to being a practicing artist, has stated that she understands *The Vienna Project* in opposition to the "countermemorial" (like Young, Frostig seems to use the terms "countermonument" and "countermemorial" interchangeably), a type of memorial that she views as "essentially static, lacking the transformative element of dialogue."[94] She criticizes what she views as the "self-referential" nature of many contemporary memorials, their concerns with "memory of and about memory."[95] While *The Vienna Project*, in the multifaceted nature and educational scope of the project, more closely fits the description of the "combimemorial" as outlined by Niven,[96] rather than the countermonument, Frostig's criticism of the "countermemorial," as she understands it, seems unfair, considering that her own memorial project is also highly referential in its preoccupation with memory. Additionally, as Young persuasively shows, the precise aim of the countermonument is to disrupt fixity. However, Frostig is justified in asserting that her project is more dynamic than a static countermonument, and this is not least achieved through the performative aspects of the project. Akin to what Walter Benjamin termed a "flüchtiges Aufblitzen" (a momentary flickering up) or illuminating flash of recognition,[97] the performance of the archive brings light upon unjustly neglected artifacts, which are imprinted upon audience members' minds long enough for them to consider the documents' implications, while at the same time acknowledging the ephemerality of long-vanished voices, only reawakened through consciously invoking these in the present. The performative reading of letters becomes an act of "insightful remembrance" for the victims of National Socialism, serving to reawaken the voices of the past in the present.[98] However, like any memorial practice seeking to commemorate victims of mass murder, it cannot aim at any kind of totality or permanence.

While some aspects of *The Vienna Project* (which officially concluded with the closing ceremony on October 18, 2015) remain (most notably Gansterer's Memory Map in the Jewish Museum Vienna, as well as the substantial online presence of the project, including the mobile app), the majority have been temporary. *The Vienna Project* stencil sprays were already fading in the final months of the project, subject to the erasure and attrition caused by countless passersby walking over them in a busy capital city.[99] This fading is symptomatic also for the fading of memory, for the erasure to which memory becomes subject if it is not kept uppermost in our minds, through visual reminders or iterative performances. *The Vienna Project* acknowledges the impermanence of its own project, with the project's axiom, "What happens when we forget to remember?," foreshadowing the fading of the spray stencils at the thirty-eight sites, and with this, also the possible fading of memory, both of the project and of the events that it seeks to commemorate. The project succeeds in its endeavor to "make memory visible on the streets of Vienna,"[100] with the caveat that any such endeavor can only result in *temporary* visibility, as *The Vienna Project* self-reflectively acknowledges through its stencil sprays, with active remembrance necessitating a persistent engagement with the past.

Remembering Everyday Persecution: Catrin Bolt's *Alltagsskulpturen Mahnmal* (2014)

While *The Vienna Project* was certainly unique in its scope, the sheer geographical area that it covered, and the diversity of activities that the project encompassed, other memorial projects also share *The Vienna Project*'s ambitions to make memory topographically visible on the streets of Vienna. We have already examined this in the case of Elisabeth Ben David-Hindler's *Steine der Erinnerung* project and Julia Schulz's *Schlüssel gegen das Vergessen* memorial. A further recent topographical memorial project by artist Catrin Bolt, entitled *Alltagsskulpturen Mahnmal* (Everyday Sculptures Monument, 2014), is also worthy of attention in this context. The ten "sculptures" consist of text extracts traced in road marking paint for several meters in the pavement, which are taken from the memoirs of Holocaust survivors. In total, the markings span an area of one thousand meters.[101] These "everyday sculptures" are located in different locations across Vienna. Several are prominent locations; one *Alltagsskulptur* (everyday sculpture) is located outside the Vienna State Opera; another can be found in front of the planetarium in the Prater Park. Others are located at ostensibly more ordinary locations such as a small, neighborhood park, a promenade in front of the Danube canal, and a station platform at Vienna's *Westbahnhof* (West Station).

The ten text passages were chosen by Catrin Bolt because they specifically mention particular places in the Viennese topography, where an *Alltagsskulptur* was subsequently placed. For example, the *Alltagsskulptur* located in the Hermann-Gmeiner-Park, in the first district of Vienna, consists of a text passage by educator Minna Lachs (née Schiffmann),[102] which recalls an incident where, in the first days of the new regime following the Anschluss in March 1938, the author of the text, then a young girl, was walking through the park. Here she was told by one "Knirps" (young whippersnapper), of approximately eight years of age, who had noticed that the girl was not wearing a swastika, that Jews were not allowed to walk through the park, whereupon another boy, displaying a better knowledge of the new Nazi laws, corrects his friend in Viennese dialect: "Gehen darf s' schon, nur sitzen darf s' net" (She's allowed to walk through it, she's just not allowed to sit down; see fig. 7). The words "für die Arier" (for the Aryans) from the text extract are strategically made to curve in front of a park bench in the park (fig. 8).

The other nine *Alltagsskulpturen*, for the most part, similarly recall instances of persecution or thematize moments of resistance. One text passage by Margarete Lihotzky, painted onto the pavement in front of what is today the *Bundesamt für Eich- und Vermessungswesen* (Federal Office for Metrology and Surveying) in Vienna's Schiffamtsgasse, recalls how she and other Austrian communists who were incarcerated in the building (which, during the Nazi era, was a prison) celebrated May 1 (International Workers' Day) there in 1942.[103] In another text extract, stretching from the corner of Leopoldgasse/Malzgasse through the street Im Werd, again in Vienna's second district, the author Arno Getreider recalls the time when Jewish teachers at his school were beaten up in front of him and other school pupils, before Getreider himself was chased and beaten on the Im Werd street by a group of Hitler Youth.[104] The "sculpture" traces the route that Getreider took from the school through to the end of the Im Werd street. Another *Alltagsskulptur* in front of the Vienna State Opera recalls an anti-Semitic propaganda poster put up in front of the opera house in the spring of 1938 reading "Judentum ist Verbrechertum!" (Jewishness is criminality). Yet another *Alltagsskulptur* in front of the Vienna Planetarium in the Wiener Prater park describes a so-called *Praterfestsetzung* (Prater appointment) on April 24, 1938,

Fig. 7. Detail from Catrin Bolt's *Alltagsskulptur* in the Hermann-Gmeiner-Park in Vienna's first district. The text extract, taken from the memoirs of Minna Lachs (née Schiffmann), reads: "She's not allowed to sit down."

Fig. 8. Further detail from Catrin Bolt's *Alltagsskulptur* in the Hermann-Gmeiner-Park. The text extract in front of the park bench reads "For the Aryans."

in which Jews were marched through the Viennese park and humiliated, while an *Alltagsskulptur* on Vienna's Westbahnhof features the recollections of actor Otto Tausig, who was able to leave Vienna on the *Kindertransport*, about how he said goodbye to his parents at the station (figs. 9 and 10).[105]

The aim of the project was to draw the attention of inhabitants to the historic dimension of urban space and to one's own living environment:

> So kann der Stadtraum und das eigene Umfeld ganz anders wahrgenommen werden: nicht nur in der jetzigen Situation und Funktion, sondern die Orte in ihrer historischen Dimension und den hier stattgefundenen Handlungen.[106]

> [The urban space and one's own environment can thereby be perceived in a completely different manner: not only in their current situation and function, but in their historical dimension and through the actions that took place here.]

Similar to Frostig's *The Vienna Project*, Bolt's *Alltagsskulpturen Mahnmal* shares the aim of making memory visible in the cityscape: "das unsichtbar Gewordene [wird] wieder sichtbar gemacht" (that which has become invisible will once more be made visible).[107] The *Alltagsskulpturen Mahnmal* does not have the same international orientation as *The Vienna Project* does, with the text passages only being written in German. Putting the text passages in additional languages would not be practicable, in any case, given the particular form in which the text is inscribed in the ground, with the text passages stretching in large font over one line, often along whole streets, or curving around corners in some instances. A series of amateur videos give an indication of the time needed to walk from the beginning of a given *Alltagsskulptur* to the end, in order to read a particular text passage.[108]

There are also no explanatory plaques or references to where further information about the installations can be found, as in the case of *The Vienna Project*. However, nowadays, it is not difficult to find information online about any marking or intervention in public space, and the curious tourist or passerby may indeed turn to the Internet to do so. Nevertheless, it is clear that the *Alltagsskulpturen Mahnmal* is oriented largely toward German speakers—residents of Vienna, visitors from other parts of Austria, Germany, and Switzerland—rather than tourists from around the world. The project is localized in places that—the Vienna State Opera apart—tourists would not go out of their way to visit. The street markings are located in or recall everyday places—a park, a school, a bridge, a train station platform—and, for the most part, the street markings also draw attention to "everyday" persecution, persecution that

Fig. 9. Platform five on the Vienna West Station, with one of Catrin Bolt's *Alltagsskulpturen* (everyday sculptures) visible on the platform.

Fig. 10. Detail from Catrin Bolt's *Alltagsskulptur* (everyday sculpture) on platform five of the Vienna West Station. The text is taken from the memoirs of Austrian actor Otto Tausig. The text visible in the photo reads: "And then we were at the Vienna West Station."

became normalized under the Nazi regime, and that paved the way for the Holocaust. The street markings, by virtue of their design, force the viewer to walk along the very same places described in the text extracts. The viewer walking through the Hermann-Gmeiner-Park, for example (the *Alltagsskulptur* encourages the viewer to walk into, through, and out of the park), can thereby readily imagine the girl berated by Nazi youth for visiting the park. In a similar manner, we can imagine the mother and son escaping from a *Sammellager* (collection camp) in a school located in the second district, with the *Alltagsskulptur* stretching from the secluded entrance to the school, around the street corner, to the street outside. These street markings, imprinted upon the ground, draw attention to the multiple historical layers of these everyday places, to the traumatic events that have occurred there. The memorials are disruptive, disturbing our prior perception of hitherto innocuous-seeming places in the cityscape. They may also disrupt viewers in a more mundane way, perhaps forcing them to walk in an opposite direction from the one they had planned, in order to continue reading a given text extract and to take the time to reflect upon the story described in it.

It is important to note that a couple of the locations chosen for Bolt's memorial are already identified as memorial sites. For example, the school in Vienna's Kleine Sperlgasse has a commemorative plaque attesting to the fact that forty thousand Jews were interned in a part of the building between October 1941 and March 1943, from which they were deported to the death camps. At the Vienna Westbahnhof, a sculpture by Flor Kent, entitled *Für das Kind* (For the Child, part of a series of similar sculptures by the artist throughout Europe commemorating the Kindertransport), unveiled in 2008,[109] represents a boy sitting on a suitcase, attesting to the fact that ten thousand predominantly Jewish children were able to leave Vienna between 1938 and 1939 on the Kindertransport. What Bolt's *Alltagsskulpturen* add to these existing memorial plaques, which commemorate large groups of people, is an individualization, a focus on the fates of specific individuals, which representatively stand for thousands of others. A text marking that passengers can read while waiting for their westbound trains on platform five (figs. 9 and 10) of the Vienna Westbahnhof (the Kindertransporte also headed west on their way out of Austria), has a different effect upon the viewer than a sculpture and plaque placed in the middle of a train-station shopping center, as Kent's sculpture is.

The *Alltagsskulpturen* encourage one to walk through these historically freighted sites and thereby engage in a peripatetic mode that serves to imprint the texts and the places that one is walking through in our somatic memory. We are therefore encouraged to literally put ourselves in the place of the narrator of the text. The significance of place to memory has been highlighted since antiquity, when Greek lyric poet Simonides of Ceos, attending a banquet given by the nobleman Scopas, was famously able to identify the dead bodies of the guests by remembering where each had sat at the table, after the roof of the banqueting hall collapsed during his brief absence from the hall.[110] Thus the mnemonic process functions in a topographical fashion, with memory becoming fixed or arrested in space. Catrin Bolt's memorial project recognizes the inextricability of topography and memory, rendering her *Alltagsskulpturen* particularly effective "mnemorials" in Niven's terms. In a similar manner to *The Vienna Project* and the *Steine der Erinnerung* project, Bolt's decentralized memorial serves to draw our attention to the neglected history of the everyday places and streets that a Viennese resident may pass every day. Bolt's *Alltagsskulpturen* estrange these everyday places, forcing the viewer to regard them with their historical dimension in mind, and serve as reminders of the fact that these places were the sites of persecution that led to genocide.

The name for Bolt's interventions in public space, *Alltagsskulpturen*, deserves some attention. The name is certainly curious, as her memorials do not resemble sculptures in any way. Sculptures are typically three-dimensional representations of objects or figures, in stone, wood, or metal, Bolt's street markings remain flat on the ground. Arguably, they encourage us to create our own sculptures by activating our imaginative realm through the act of reading the stories, marked upon the ground, and to visualize the individuals described in them. It is the viewer who in fact adds the three-dimensional element, not the artist. The prefix *Alltags-* (everyday) emphasizes the antiheroic nature of these sculptures, the fact that these are sculptures dealing with ordinary individuals, places, and streets. At the same time, the prefix once again draws attention to the fact that acts of discrimination and persecution became "normalized" under the Nazi regime, becoming part of the everyday. Bolt's sculptures, traced in road-marking paint, are, similarly to the stencil sprays of *The Vienna Project*, subject to attrition and erasure. The markings on the ground are less than obvious; it took me some time to find the *Alltagskuptur* in front of the Vienna State Opera. As such, the casual passerby (who is not specifically searching for one of the *Alltagsskulpturen*) is likely to encounter the memorials by serendipity, with the *Alltagsskulpturen* disrupting the passerby's walk and prompting him or her to engage with the content of the text passage. Through concrete individual examples of historical persecution in the selfsame locations that the passerby has to walk through to read the "sculpture," the viewer is alerted to the historical legacies that the Viennese cityscape continues to be marked by, markings that through the road paint of the *Alltagsskulpturen* are temporarily made visible.

An Intervention in Existing Memorial Culture: Ruth Beckermann's *The Missing Image* (2015)

As described in chapter 4, the writer Robert Schindel, in his latest novel *Der Kalte*, offers a critique of Austria's insufficient confrontation with the past through his engagement with Alfred Hrdlicka's *Mahnmal gegen Krieg und Faschismus* (Monument against War and Fascism). His fictional amendment to Hrdlicka's controversial monument sees three further figures added to the figure of "the street-washing Jew," three Viennese who are humiliating the Jew and whose faces are marked by a "hehrer Fanatismus" (*DK*, 636; sublime fanaticism). As we have seen, Schindel here seems to enter into a fictional dialogue with his colleague Ruth Beckermann's 1989 book *Unzugehörig* where she severely criticizes Hrdlicka's monument and in particular his "street-washing Jew" figure, which lacks the perpetrators of anti-Semitic violence. In Schindel's novel, the temporary addition to Hrdlicka's monument, which serves as a reminder of Austrian complicity in the Holocaust, is removed four months following its installation. In 2015 a real-life corrective intervention by Ruth Beckermann in Hrdlicka's monument was installed for nine months. On March 12, 2015 (on the seventy-seventh anniversary of the Wehrmacht's crossing of the border into Austria, leading to the proclamation of Austria's de-facto Anschluss with Nazi Germany on March 13, 1938), an installation by Beckermann was put in front of the figure of "the street-washing Jew." This consisted of two three-meter-high LED screens placed on the back of the Tor der Gewalt (Gate of Violence) section of the walk-through sculpture, which is located directly opposite "the street-washing Jew" figure (fig. 11). On the screens a clip lasting ninety seconds showed a large group of people, smiling and clearly enjoying the occasion, surrounding two Jewish men being made to scrub the pavement. Men wearing swastika armbands, presumably members of the SA, are shown joining hands, pushing the crowd back behind them, so great is the enthusiasm of the crowd for "a Hetz" (a laugh), which is how the public humiliations of Jews were disparagingly described by the Viennese.[111] Further, we see a woman, at the foreground of the crowd, who is given a brush to hold up by a man standing next to her. We see his hand supporting the woman's hand as she holds up the brush, suggesting force and compulsion in the woman's actions. The woman has an ambiguous smile on her face as if she is unsure how to react to the situation unfolding around her. This is curious as, given that the broom has been placed into the woman's hand, we know that she must also be Jewish and that she has also therefore been singled out to clean the pavement. Ruth Beckermann reads the reaction of this female figure as symptomatic for that of Jews in Vienna at the time (particularly those belonging to the age group of the woman in the sequence); the woman's reaction is that

Fig. 11. Ruth Beckermann, *The Missing Image* installation positioned in front of Alfred Hrdlicka's figure of the "street-washing Jew," part of his *Mahnmal gegen Krieg und Faschismus* (Monument against War and Fascism).

of dazed disbelief, rather than any apprehension that these Reibpartien (scrubbing games) were "just the beginning" of a systematic process of persecution that would lead to the Holocaust.[112]

The ninety-second sequence was actually made from a five-second film clip, found in the archive of the Vienna Film Museum in 2013, the only known film recording of a so-called Reibpartie.[113] Beckermann worked with this film clip for several months, slowing it down and zooming in on particular sections (for example, of hands scrubbing the pavement), in order to bring out the detail in the clip.[114] The ninety-second sequence that resulted out of this work was played on a loop on the two screens placed in front of Hrdlicka's "street-washing Jew" statue. In addition to completing the figure of Hrdlicka's "street-washing Jew," the LED screens reflected the images of passersby, which intermeshed with that of the historical figures, prompting reflection on one's own role toward discrimination and suffering in the present day. Specially composed music by Olga Neuwirth was also added to the modified film clip as a soundtrack. Here a group of male voices repeatedly singing the same prolonged notes created a dissonant, eerie, and haunting effect. As Beckermann has stated, the music was meant to create "eine weitere Irritation" (a further irritation),[115] a Brechtian

Verfremdungseffekt (estrangement effect) perhaps, prompting reflection upon the installation.

Beckermann's installation was roundly praised for adding "the missing image" (to quote the title of her installation) to Hrdlicka's undifferentiated memorial to Nazi-era suffering. The missing images of the Viennese clearly enjoying and taking part in the spectacle of seeing their fellow citizens humiliated, reinstate the perpetrators into the picture. As Beckermann (for whom, as discussed in chapter 4, the inadequacy of Hrdlicka's monument has been a concern ever since its erection) describes: "Das Problem am [Hrdlickas] Mahnmal ist, dass die Zuschauer fehlen. Es hat ja jemand die Juden auf die Knie gezwungen, und das waren die Wiener Antisemiten." (The problem with the [Hrdlicka] monument is that the spectators are missing. Someone forced the Jews to their knees, and that was the Viennese anti-Semites.)[116] Beckermann was one of only a few critics of Hrdlicka's monument following its unveiling in 1988, in contrast to the majority of Austria's intellectuals, who felt that it was a positive step that a monument thematizing the Nazi era was constructed in Vienna at all.[117] Nearly three decades on from the unveiling of Hrdlicka's monument, Beckermann's intervention disrupted the easy narrative of Austrian victimhood presented by the monument. Instead, by reinstating the perpetrators into the picture, by adding "die Bilder der Täter, der Zuschauer, der Gaffer, der Grinser und der Mitläufer" (the images of the perpetrators, the spectators, the gawkers, the smirkers, and fellow travelers),[118] Beckermann's intervention serves to remind the viewer of Austrian complicity in the crimes of National Socialism.

Beckermann's temporary installation, which was originally planned to close on November 10, 2015 (to coincide with the anniversary of the November pogroms), was, in fact, dismantled on December 10, 2015.[119] It was initially hoped that the installation might be extended until April 30, 2016, with the Vienna City Council agreeing to pay for the heating costs associated with keeping the LED screens outside in winter.[120] Leading figures in Austrian cultural life also petitioned for the installation to become a permanent fixture on the Albertinaplatz, in an open letter written to Vienna's *Kulturstadtrat* (city councillor in charge of cultural affairs) Andreas Mailath-Pokorny. The letter's signatories included the Nobel laureate Elfriede Jelinek, writer Doron Rabinovici, artist André Heller, actress Elisabeth Orth, and actor and director Karl Markovics.[121] It was thought that, following the planned restoration of Hrdlicka's monument beginning in spring 2016, Beckermann's installation could be reinstalled on the Albertinaplatz permanently, subject to approval from Hrdlicka's widow.[122] In the end, the installation was dismantled in December 2015 due to lack of concrete support from Vienna's Kulturstadtrat for the heating fans that would enable the installation to remain in place during the winter period, and lack of authorization on the part of the *Bundesdenkmalamt* (Federal Monuments Office) and Hrdlicka's heirs.[123]

During the period of its installation, *The Missing Image* was certainly very well received in Vienna. Beckermann has pointed out that during the initial months of the installation's opening it was reported to her by Viennese tour guides that many tourists visiting Vienna for the first time had automatically assumed that the installation was part of Hrdlicka's original monument.[124] To correct this misapprehension, an explanatory plaque about Beckermann's installation was added to the side of one of the LED screens in spring 2015 (fig. 12). The fact that the memorial project was so readily regarded as a long-standing feature in Vienna's memorial landscape by tourists is testament to how little awareness there is internationally about Austria's true role in the Holocaust or, indeed, about Austria's evolving memory culture. The explanatory plaque offers a necessary corrective, showing the long progression in Austria's historical consciousness and, related to this, a progression in the memorial landscape reflecting this historical consciousness.

Ruth Beckermann is a filmmaker and intellectual who, as we have seen in chapter 1, constantly draws connections in her work between the past and the present. This is not least shown in the manner in which she supplanted her *Missing Image* installation for twenty-four hours on June 18–19, 2015,[125] with alternating close-ups from a photograph by Jürg Christandl (split between the two LED screens). The photograph shows Austrian Freedom Party led protests on June 3, 2015, against a refugee camp in Vienna, with three Syrian refugees (an adult male, followed by a small child and an older child) walking in front of the protesting group in the foreground. The temporary installation was entitled *Déjà-vu*. Christandl's photograph was the subject of political controversy,[126] after the Austrian Freedom Party accused the photographer of manipulation, while the photographer and the *Kurier* newspaper employing him in turn accused Austrian Freedom Party leader, Heinz-Christian Strache, of causing reputational damage to their publication.[127] Interestingly, although Christandl's photograph is in color, Beckermann used a black-and-white filter for the close-ups in the *Déjà-vu* installation, except for the figures of the Syrian refugees, which are left in color, serving as a reminder (along with the protestors' clothes and placards) that the images are taken from the present day.[128] In this manner, the anti-refugee-camp protesters are connected to the black-and-white figures in the "Reibpartie" film of *The Missing Image* installation. The use of the same color stock, and a similar use of close-ups as in *The Missing Image* film clip, to focus in on the facial expressions of the people in the photograph, creates a dialogue between *The Missing Image* and the *Déjà-vu* installation, serving to highlight the lack of progression that Beckermann sees in contemporary attitudes in Austria toward the foreign and other: "Déjà-vu spiegelt jenes Wien wider,

Fig. 12. An explanatory plaque, attached to the side of Ruth Beckermann's *The Missing Image* installation, reading: "In 2015 Austrian artist Ruth Beckermann recontextualized Alfred Hrdlicka's 1988 monument. The installation relates to the bronze figure depicting the Jews washing the streets after the so-called Anschluss in March 1938. Ruth Beckermann completes the scene by adding the missing images of laughing spectators."

das ein aufs andere Mal zur Hatz ruft. Damals wie heute." (Déjà-vu holds up a mirror to that Vienna, which time and again calls for persecution of the other).[129]

Beckermann's *Déjà-vu* installation was realized in conjunction with the *Republikanischer Club–Neues Österreich*,[130] of which Beckermann has been an active member since its foundation in 1986. For Beckermann, the parallels between the hate and prejudice of yesteryear and that of today are unmistakable: "da sind noch jene Wiener voller Ressentiments und selbstgerechtem Hass, die neuerlich die Vertriebenen zu Verfolgten macht." (there they are, those same Viennese full of resentment and self-righteous hate, which again makes the displaced into the persecuted.)[131] Her temporary supplanting of her own installation had the far-right supporters of the Austrian Freedom Party holding up their "Nein zum Asylantenheim" (No to the refugee center) posters in front of Hrdlicka's sculpture of "the street-washing Jew." The *Déjà-vu* installation is symptomatic for Beckermann's view that confronting the past is an ongoing process that informs the present, and that it is the job of cultural practitioners not to lose themselves in empty rituals of commemorating the past, but to draw attention to injustices in the present day: "Das 'Wie furchtbar war 38,' was ja inzwischen auch hier in Wien offiziell zugegeben wird und nun Thema von Gedenkveranstaltungen ist, halte ich für zu billig. Man muss heute darüber sprechen, was jetzt passiert und Bezüge herstellen." (I think the sentiment 'how terrible was 1938'—something that has now become officially acknowledged, and is the subject of memorial events even here in Vienna—is too easy. You have to speak about what is happening today and draw connections.)[132]

Through her interventions in Hrdlicka's monument, Beckermann has drawn attention to the inadequacy and telling absences that characterized Austria's memorial culture until relatively recently in its history. At the same time, the fact that it was possible to realize Beckermann's corrective addition to the monument in 2015, with the support of *Kunst im öffentlichen Raum Wien* (Art in Public Space Vienna) and other public bodies, on one of the most prominent places in central Vienna, is symptomatic of how much the nation has progressed vis-à-vis its remembrance culture since Hrdlicka's monument was unveiled in 1988. Beckermann's memorial has become the most successful initiative hitherto sponsored by *Kunst im öffentlichen Raum Wien*, in terms of visitor numbers and engagement.[133] Additionally, through the *Déjà-vu* installation, Beckermann drew attention to the need for alertness to injustices in the present, to prevent the repetition of the past.

Making Absence Visible: Iris Andraschek's and Hubert Lobnig's *Turnertempel Erinnerungsort* (2011)

If Ruth Beckermann's installation draws attention to the missing images in Vienna's memorial culture, Iris Andraschek's and Hubert Lobnig's *Turnertempel Erinnerungsort* (Turner Temple Memorial Site; see fig. 13) in Vienna's fifteenth district visibly makes present an absence from Vienna's cityscape, namely that of a synagogue, which was the third largest in Vienna, prior to its destruction on the night of November 9–10, 1938, during the November pogroms.[134] The memorial consists of a number of black concrete beams crisscrossing a small park, which are meant to represent the destroyed roof truss of the *Turnertempel* (Turner Temple), with the beams resembling "versteinertes Holz" (petrified wood).[135] In between the concrete beams and the linden trees (which were carefully removed, and later replanted, during the construction of the memorial in the park) we can see mosaics depicting fruits and plants that, as the artists describe, are mentioned in the Torah, and that have a particular significance in Judaism.[136] Previously, this area at the corner

Fig. 13. Iris Andraschek and Hubert Lobnig, *Turnertempel Erinnerungsort* (Turner Temple Memorial Site, 2011).

of two streets in Vienna's fifteenth district had been "eine nichtssagende Grünfläche" (a nondescript green area), where it was nearly impossible to tell that it was previously the site of one of the largest synagogues in Vienna.[137] In 1988 a small plaque, which could not be seen from the street, was erected on the side of a residential building bordering the public green area, testifying to the fact that a synagogue had stood there until the *Reichskristallnacht* (Reich Crystal Night) when it was "von fanatischen Anhängern des Hitlerregimes niedergebrannt u. zerstört. Niemals vergessen!" (burned down and destroyed by fanatical supporters of the Hitler regime. Never forget!)[138] The laconic imperative "Niemals vergessen!" (Never forget!), can be found on a number of postwar memorials in Vienna, yet its insistence upon remembering appears formulaic, an empty ritual of remembrance, and evokes James Young's statements about the imperative to remember springing "from an opposite and equal desire to forget."[139] Iris Andraschek's and Hubert Lobnig's Turnertempel memorial (realized by the studio of Maria Auböck and János Kárász), which was selected as the winner of a competition instigated in 2010 by *Kunst im öffentlichen Raum Wien*, turns the empty rhetoric of the commemorative plaque into a physical inscription of memory in this residential area of Vienna, which can no longer be ignored. In contrast to the former locations of other synagogues in Vienna destroyed in the November pogroms, the site of the former Turnertempel remained unbuilt upon, enabling the realization of the Turnertempel memorial project.[140]

Andraschek and Lobnig, the artists who were ultimately successful in the competition to design a suitable memorial on the site of the former Turnertempel, wished to create "einen benutzbaren Gedenkplatz . . ., der als ungewohnte, irritierende Gestaltung empfunden wird, durch den die Geschichte, die sich an dieser Stelle vor rund 73 Jahren abgespielt hat, wieder sichtbar und spürbar wird" (a usable memorial place . . ., that is perceived as an unfamiliar, irritating design, through which the history that played out here around seventy-three years ago, will once more be made visible and tangible).[141] The repeated emphasis, in the artists' description of the project, is upon creating a memorial that "irritates," disrupts, and disturbs the cityscape: "Ein Ort, der aus seiner Umgebung herausfällt" (a place that falls out of its environment); "Ein Platz, der sich deutlich vom städtischen Kontext abhebt" (a place that stands out significantly from the urban context).[142] As such, the memorial follows the logic of the countermonument, as defined by James E. Young, disturbing and disrupting public space.[143] The memorial's designers highlight how the memorial was constructed upon a "Nicht-Ort zwischen Straßen und Gemeindebau" (a nonplace between the streets and the municipal housing block),[144] an urban nonplace. The anthropologist Marc Augé coined the idea of the nonplace as a transient place unmarked by history, which is interchangeable from one location to the next, be it Berlin or New York, with airports, for example, being prototypical nonplaces.[145] Although Lobnig and architect Kárász use the term nonplace to connote an urban wasteland (the site was previously bordered off by hedges and a fence[146]), the former site of the Turnertempel can certainly not be described as an insignificant site, or as a place devoid of history. Further, the creation of the Turnertempel memorial in the Turnergasse has transformed the site into a place that, in its architectural design, stands outside of the architecture of the surrounding area. The designers were keen for the memorial site to become an "Ort der Begegnung" (a place of encounter), a "sozialer Treffpunkt" (a social meeting point), and a "benutzbare[r] Gedenkplatz" (usable memorial place),[147] and it is certainly used in this manner; an official guide to public art projects in Vienna produced by *Kunst im öffentlichen Raum Wien* includes a photograph showing people sitting on the concrete beams of the memorial.[148] However, it remains a place that stands apart, in that the dominating architecture of the memorial, crisscrossing the small park, precludes its use as, for example, a play area or football pitch. In this manner, through its "disruption" of space, the memorial invites the casual passerby to find out why the space is being disrupted in this way, to read the explanatory pillar erected on the site, or

132 ♦ Missing Images

the enamel panel erected on the wall of a house immediately adjacent to the site, giving information about the memorial.

The Turnertempel memorial, with its central design of the intersecting concrete beams, representing the roof of the destroyed temple, functions as a marker of absence in the cityscape. The memorial is essentially a making-present-of-absence, with the absence of the synagogue standing emblematically for the absence of a vibrant Austrian Jewish culture in post-Holocaust Austria. To paraphrase Karen Frostig's axiomatic project of "making memory visible," the Turnertempel memorial makes absence visible. This is particularly evident in winter, when the bare trees in among the black concrete beams of the memorial accentuate the absence at its heart, creating a desolate effect. Yet, the memorial is not meant to be wholly desolate, as can be seen from the vibrant mosaics in among the concrete beams, meant to recall the Pompeian-style wall decorations in the destroyed Turnertempel.[149] The artists working on the memorial conceived the project as one of symbolic reconstruction of "verlorene Schichten" (lost layers),[150] of "reflexive archaeology."[151] Archaeology is a practice that aims to uncover the past through the remains of material objects. Yet here, where the original building was burned to the ground, there can be no finding of remains, only reconstruction. However, the aesthetic presentation of the memorial does indeed look like an archaeological excavation, with the reconstructed roof truss lying upon the ground. The symbolic grounding of the roof truss (which is typically suspended high above a building structure) not only stands for the destruction of the same but also for the going-to-ground of the memorial project as a whole. The memorial encourages the viewer to look upon the ground and to reflect upon the destruction of the original Turnertempel, which once stood upon this ground. The roof truss encourages the viewer to imaginatively fill in the rest of the Turnertempel structure, to imagine what the temple must have looked like. As such it makes the absence of the Turnertempel tangible, drawing attention to the empty void in this residential area. Through making visible the absence of the Turnertempel, it is a memorial that draws attention to the broader absence in present-day Vienna of the vibrant Jewish culture of pre-Holocaust Austria. The erection of this memorial on the Turnertempel's former site ensures that the square is not built over (as was the case with most synagogues destroyed in the November pogroms in Vienna), but instead, that the memorial acts as a permanent marker of absence in the Viennese cityscape, drawing attention to the near-destruction of Austria's Jewish community.

As this chapter has shown, the memorial landscape in Vienna has been transformed in recent years from one of a lack of willingness to commemorate the Nazi past in Vienna's public space (or doing so inadequately, as in the case of Alfred Hrdlicka's *Mahnmal gegen Krieg und*

Faschismus [Monument against War and Fascism]) to one of a proliferation of memorials and memorial projects in public space. A number of these memorial projects have been rooted in grassroots initiatives (such as Ulrike Lienbacher's *Idylle* and Julia Schulz's *Schlüssel gegen das Vergessen*), while, at the same time, benefiting from municipal support, most notably through the organization *Kunst im öffentlichen Raum Wien*. Other projects such as the *Steine der Erinnerung*, are funded solely through private donations, while others, such as *The Vienna Project*, make use of innovative forms of crowd funding, while also drawing on wide-ranging municipal support. This grassroots support is indicative of a shift in public attitudes toward Austria's past that has occurred in the country with the political turning points of 1986 and 2000.

The eight memorial projects discussed in this chapter function in diverse ways, whether they seek to contextualize the remnants of a problematic history (as in the case of Lienbacher's and Litschauer's projects); raise awareness of Nazi-era persecution in the everyday spaces of Vienna and thereby, in Frostig's terms, "make memory visible" (Elisabeth Ben David-Hindler's *Steine der Erinnerung* project, Karen Frostig's *The Vienna Project*, and Catrin Bolt's *Alltagsskulpturen Mahnmal*); draw attention to the absence of Jewish culture in contemporary Vienna (Iris Andraschek's and Hubert Lobnig's *Turnertempel Erinnerungsort*); or, criticize an existing memorial culture and draw attention to "missing images" in the existing commemorative landscape (Ruth Beckermann's *The Missing Image*). While these memorials and memorial projects, in their disruption of public space, may be understood in the tradition of the countermonument, as we have seen, many of the memorial projects, and decentralized projects in particular (most notably *The Vienna Project*, but also the *Steine der Erinnerung*) incorporate practices more commonly associated with museums and other educational institutions, including outreach activities, readings and tours, making them into what Bill Niven terms "combimemorials." Not only do the different facets of these memorial projects allow the initiators to reach different audiences and thereby prolong engagement with the memorial, their use of multiple media to engage in a process of remembrance is symptomatic of the continual engagement with the past that these memorials advocate. Particularly through the impermanent nature of memorials such as *The Vienna Project* (that do, however, leave a significant digital legacy), attention is drawn to the impermanence of memory itself and to the need for a persistent engagement with the past.

Returning to the epigraph from Doron Rabinovici's 2004 novel *Ohnehin* (Anyway), which opened this chapter, it is clear that the memorial landscape in Vienna has undergone a significant shift since the beginning of the twenty-first century, from a culture in which monuments and memorials may indeed be described as "Instrumente . . . des Vergessens" (instruments of forgetting),[152] for which Hrdlicka's 1988 *Mahnmal gegen Krieg und Faschismus* is exemplary, to memorials that, far from constituting empty rituals of remembrance, invite us to a persistent and continual engagement with the past, and with the way that we remember and commemorate it.

Conclusion: Living with Shadows

> *I saw old Autumn in the misty morn*
> *Stand shadowless like Silence, listening*
> *To silence . . .*
>
> —Thomas Hood, "Ode: Autumn"

THIS BOOK HAS TREATED a number of case studies, taken from the past three decades of Austrian cultural production, to examine the diverse ways in which Austrian writers, filmmakers, and artists have treated Austria's multiple historical legacies, foremost among them the legacy of the Nazi past. At the same time, we have seen that the political changes, which have swept Austria since the mid-1980s, have not failed to leave their mark on the country's cultural production, with writers, filmmakers, and artists responding to such turning points as the Waldheim affair, and the 1999 elections, in their work. It is this dual concern of an intense preoccupation with the country's past, coupled with a keen focus on documenting and reflecting the present, that dominates the work of the writers, filmmakers, and artists explored in this study.

The early films of Ruth Beckermann, examined in chapter 1 of this study, continually oscillate between the present and the past. The melancholy journeys to the past, whether this be to interwar Vienna in *Wien retour*, the historical area of Bukovina in *Die papierene Brücke*, or Vienna's historical textile quarter in *Homemad(e)*, are always allied, in Beckermann's films, with explicit or oblique commentary on present-day Austria. Her films, while insistently concerned with the past, specifically with the legacy of the Holocaust in Austrian culture, are simultaneously a documentary chronicle of contemporary Austria, whether this be the culture of silence around Austria's Nazi past, which predominated up until the late 1980s (*Wien retour*); the Waldheim affair of the late 1980s (*Die papierene Brücke*); or the 1999 elections, which saw the Austrian Freedom Party enter the coalition government (*Homemad(e)*).

Similarly, Anna Mitgutsch's *Haus der Kindheit*, dealing with the topic of Nazi-era "Aryanization," continually reflects the legacy of this past in the present, indirectly commenting on political developments in Austria in the area of restitution, which became an increasingly prominent issue at the turn of the twenty-first century, when Mitgutsch's book was published. The novel, in its time span of the 1970s to the late 1990s, charts the progression of Austrian society vis-à-vis its attitude to the past, from one of silence and bureaucratic obfuscation, to an increased willingness to learn about the Holocaust and the country's Jewish heritage on the part of non-Jewish Austrians, albeit with this endeavor being fraught with difficulty.

Margareta Heinrich's and Eduard Erne's and, more recently, Elfriede Jelinek's, treatments of the Rechnitz massacre in film and drama respectively, explore the repercussions and legacy of the massacre in the present. Heinrich's and Erne's documentation of the search for the location of the possible mass grave in *Totschweigen* is set against the background of the rise of the Austrian Freedom Party, led by Jörg Haider, throughout the 1990s. Jelinek's play *Rechnitz (Der Würgeengel)* is concerned primarily with how the Nazi past is spoken about and commemorated today. Writing more than sixty years after the end of the Second World War, Jelinek severely criticizes a remembrance culture that is no longer marked by silence, but rather "garrulous silencing," a discourse about the past that Jelinek presents as formulaic, dominated by self-exculpation and relativizing of the past, and lacking true remorse, on the part of the perpetrators and their descendants, for crimes committed during the Second World War and the Holocaust.

As we have seen, Robert Schindel's novel about the Waldheim affair, *Der Kalte*, takes as its focus the Nazi past's long shadow and its manifestations in the Waldheim era. At the same time, Schindel's reflection on the Waldheim affair is written from the perspective of today, and his playful reinscription of historical events and personages highlights missed opportunities for reflecting on Austria's National Socialist legacy. The eight memorial projects discussed in chapter 5 are insistently concerned with drawing attention to the legacy of the Nazi past and to the Holocaust in contemporary Vienna, with "making memory visible," in Karen Frostig's formulation. At the same time, they draw attention to the absence of a vibrant Jewish community in contemporary Austria. Today's Jewish community in Austria barely numbers fifteen thousand, and that is largely due to immigration.[1] The artists responsible for the memorials seek innovative ways for residents and visitors to engage with the past in Vienna, while drawing attention to its resonances in the present. This is most notably evidenced in Ruth Beckermann's 2015 *Déjà-vu* installation, which drew parallels between the anti-refugee sentiments in today's Austria and the anti-Semitism of the 1930s.

This study has presented a plurality of different responses to the country's historical legacies and their resonances in the present. In film and literature, these range from the melancholy characterizing the early films of Ruth Beckermann, the nostalgia (both of the "restorative" and "reflective" type, in Boym's definition) in Anna Mitgutsch's *Haus der Kindheit*, to the radical satire of Jelinek's *Rechnitz* and the dark humor of Robert Schindel's *Der Kalte*. The films by Ruth Beckermann, Margareta

Heinrich, and Eduard Erne, explored in this study, are able to find a powerful visual language for the confrontations with Austria's past that they document. The use of nondiegetic music, authorial voice-over, and montage, all facilitate the drawing of connections between the past and the present, surface and reality. The artists responsible for the memorials and memorial projects, discussed in chapter 5, make use of a variety of media—whether this is video art, painting, or sculpture—to attract attention to neglected or forgotten aspects of the country's Nazi legacy, and to commemorate victims of racial persecution. To do so, many of these projects make use of innovative forms of public engagement, fully utilizing modern social media, mobile technology, and adopting educational practices commonly associated with museums and educational institutions.

In the chronological sweep examined in this study, we can observe a significant progression in the manner in which Austria's historical legacies are treated in Austrian literature, film, and culture, from the earliest case study examined here, Beckermann's *Wien retour*, to the most recent case study, *The Missing Image* memorial installation, by the same artist, from 2015. While in Beckermann's *Wien retour*, we can observe Franz West speaking against the, at the time, predominant silence on the country's Nazi past, the references to the resurfacing of populist right-wing politics remain tentative and oblique. The unexpected addendum of West's tape recording at the end of the film, where he details the fates of his family who perished in the Holocaust, is testament to the double difficulty for victims of Nazi persecution to speak about a traumatic past in a climate of silencing and forgetting. Beckermann's later film *Die papierene Brücke* constitutes a more explicit speaking against the resurfacing of Austria's unconfronted Nazi legacy at the height of the Waldheim affair. The places she visits in this travelogue, and the people that she gives voice to (from her parents to members of the Jewish community in northern Romania) serve to counter the narrative of Austria as "first victim" of fascism, and instead attest to the near extinction of a vibrant central European Jewish culture. *Homemad(e)*, a film made by the same filmmaker at the turn of the twenty-first century, more than a decade after *Die papierene Brücke* and nearly two decades after *Wien retour*, is characterized by a greater relaxation with regard to the Austrian present (the film captured the *politische Wende*[2] [political change], following the 1999 elections), albeit with the film protagonists' traumatic past never far from the surface. Thus, the progression in Austrian society with regard to its *Aufarbeitung* (working through) of the Nazi past can be observed even in the work of a single filmmaker.

Margareta Heinrich's and Eduard Erne's *Totschweigen*, documenting the futile search for the Rechnitz mass grave in the early 1990s, is set against the local background of silence and, often, open hostility, on the part of the war generation and its descendants, and the national background of rising far-right populism. Elfriede Jelinek's play *Rechnitz (Der Würgeengel)*, reflecting on the same massacre nearly fifteen years after the release of Heinrich's and Erne's *Totschweigen*, utilizes the power of fiction to juxtapose past and present, and through Jelinek's characteristic language play, to accentuate the failures of a remembrance culture that, in Jelinek's view, remains dominated by repression through ever-evolving strategies of self-exculpation and relativizing of the past. Thus we can see how works treating the same subject matter differ radically in their treatment of it, a difference that can be ascribed not only to the differences in genre and aesthetic approach, but also to the societal changes that the latter work by Jelinek mirrors.

Of course, fiction, by definition, allows for greater flexibility than documentary film, enabling Mitgutsch in her novel *Haus der Kindheit* to treat multiple time periods to show the progression in Austria's attitude vis-à-vis its Nazi past. Similarly, Schindel's panoramic novel *Der Kalte* imaginatively reinscribes the Waldheim affair, and the confrontations with the past that it unleashed, from the perspective of today, thereby juxtaposing multiple time periods, those of Austria in the 2010s, Waldheim-era Austria, and the Austria of the 1930s and 1940s. Schindel's reinscriptions of the Waldheim affair are symptomatic of a more distanced and measured attitude to the events of the late 1980s than was possible at the time (as can be seen in Beckermann's *Die papierene Brücke*). Concurrently, the traumatic nature of the events of the Waldheim affair, and the missed opportunities for remembrance and commemoration, remain palpable in Schindel's novel, published nearly three decades later.

As we have seen in chapter 5 of this study, in the area of visual art, the marked shift from a culture of repression of the Nazi past and the Holocaust to one of incremental remembrance, instituted on the national level (through, for example, revised citizenship laws and the creation of institutions to process restitution claims) throughout the 1990s and 2000s, has been reflected in a proliferation of memorials and memorial projects that would have been unimaginable just thirty years ago, when Waldheim described his participation in a genocidal regime as "doing one's duty." Now, it is possible to find a large number of both permanent and temporary interventions in Vienna's public spaces that attest to the racial persecution that took place not in distant concentration camps, but in streets and buildings in every corner of the city. The number of temporary memorials that can be found in Vienna at any given time serve as a reminder that memory cannot be outsourced to a memorial, that once erected, regards the particular historical event that it is commemorating as having been addressed. Instead, these temporary memorials attest to the impermanence of memory and to the need for a continual engagement with the past. Perhaps the best example of the marked shift that Austria's memorial culture has undergone is Ruth Beckermann's "installation as intervention,"[3] *The Missing Image*, in Alfred Hrdlicka's 1988 *Mahnmal gegen Krieg und Faschismus*. In 1989, Beckermann was one of only a few lone voices expressing her criticism of what many regarded as a long overdue anti-fascist monument; in 2015 she was able to realize a corrective to the monument that she could only dream of in the late 1980s, namely the symbolic addition of the perpetrators of anti-Semitic violence into the monument. The support both from municipal organizations, and through private donations and initiatives, for these wide-ranging memorial projects, is testament to backing both at the grassroots and institutional level for projects, which certainly could not have been realized thirty years ago.

One could be forgiven therefore for thinking that Austria has finally stepped out of the long shadow of its Nazi past, that the shifts in representation of the Nazi past that we can observe in Austrian literature, film, and culture over the last thirty years are testament to the great progress that has been made in the area of working through the country's historical legacy of National Socialism. While this is undoubtedly true to some extent—today's Austria is a very different country from the one that it was in 1986—Austrian artists remind us that there is no room for complacency in endeavors to confront the Austrian past (Jelinek's *Rechnitz*), and draw attention to resurgent racism and intolerance in the present (Beckermann's *Déjà-vu installation*). To return to the discussion of the concept of the shadow, elaborated in the introduction to this study, Aleida Assmann notably posited that it will not be possible to "step out" of the shadow of the Nazi past and the Holocaust: "Verstehen wir unter 'Schatten' die nachwirkende Präsenz der traumatischen Vergangenheit, so werden wir mit ihm leben müssen." (If, by shadow, we understand the lasting presence of the traumatic past, we will have to live with it.)[4]

As we have seen, the legacy of the Nazi past, and its repercussions in the present, have been and will continue to be (judging by planned future projects[5]), a key concern for the writers and artists belonging to the second postwar generation, who have been the predominant focus of this investigation. Nevertheless, members belonging to the third postwar generation, represented in this study by the visual artists Catrin Bolt (1979–) and Julia Schulz (1979–), are still very much concerned and engaged with this time period, utilizing innovative forms of artistic and memorial practice to engage the public with the legacy of the Nazi past in the everyday spaces and places of Vienna. However, this is not only true for visual artists; the third postwar generation of writers and filmmakers remains insistently concerned with the long shadow of Austria's Nazi past, as can be seen in the work of authors such as Vladimir Vertlib (1966–), Eva Menasse (1970–), and Julya Rabinowich (1970–), and in the work of filmmakers such as Anja Salomonowitz (1976–) and Elisabeth Scharang (1969–). It will be interesting to see how the legacy of the Nazi past will continue to be represented in Austrian literature, film, and visual art, as this period recedes further from living memory, and in the context of a continually evolving political climate. As we have seen in the introduction to this study, Austria's political climate remains precarious, where progressive politics are pitted against an ahistorical wish to return to a purportedly simpler past. It will be interesting to see also, how discussions and plans for the Haus der Geschichte (House of History) on Austria's Heldenplatz continue to evolve, with its opening originally scheduled to coincide with the Gedenkjahr 1918 (commemorative year 1918), marking the end of the First World War, the fall of the Habsburg monarchy, one hundred years of the Austrian Republic, and eighty years since the Anschluss. The completion of the large-scale Haus der Geschichte project is currently scheduled for 2019.[6] One thing remains certain, however; regardless of what happens in the political arena, Austrian writers, filmmakers, and artists will continue to hold up a mirror to the country's present and draw attention to a still disturbing past.

In a study in which memorials and memorial projects have formed a key focus, it would perhaps be worth mentioning one final memorial, to illustrate the evolving confrontations with the past in the Austrian context, which have been examined in the preceding five chapters. On October 24, 2014, on the Ballhausplatz in central Vienna, the *Denkmal für die Verfolgten der NS-Militärjustiz* (Memorial for the Victims of Nazi Military Justice), designed by German artist Olaf Nicolai (1962–), was ceremonially unveiled. It is located opposite the office of the Austrian president and the Austrian chancellery, and just meters away from the historically freighted Heldenplatz, where Hitler proclaimed the entry of his native Austria *heim ins Reich* (home into the Reich) on March 15, 1938. The memorial takes the shape of a three-step concrete plinth bearing the words "all alone" on top of it (fig. 14). The citation is taken from a poem by Scottish poet Ian Hamilton Finlay (1925–2006), and represents the isolation "des Enzelnen . . . gegenüber gesellschaftlichen Ordnungs- und Machtverhältnissen." (the individual . . . against social structures and power relations.)[7] Approximately fifteen hundred Austrians were executed for deserting the Wehrmacht during the Second World War.[8] Meanwhile, deserters who survived the war faced discrimination in postwar Austria, and were only formally rehabilitated by the Austrian government in 2009.[9] This paved the way for the realization of Nicolai's memorial, following lengthy discussion about the memorial's possible location, and the advertising of a competition to design the memorial in 2012.[10]

The memorial honors those who refused to follow orders in a murderous regime, less than thirty years after Kurt Waldheim famously boasted of only having done his duty in the service of the Wehrmacht. The erection of the memorial and its unveiling were plagued by controversy, not least by groups representing former Wehrmacht veterans.[11] However, in general, the memorial has been positively received, and heralded as long

Fig. 14. Detail from Olaf Nicolai, *Denkmal für die Verfolgten der NS-Militärjustiz* (Memorial for the Victims of Nazi Military Justice, 2014).

overdue by former Wehrmacht deserters, who had campaigned for years for the erection of a memorial through the organization *Gerechtigkeit für die Opfer der NS-Militärjustiz* (Justice for the Victims of National Socialist Military Justice), founded in 2002.[12] The aesthetic design of a memorial on one of the most prominent public spaces in Vienna will naturally be controversial. One flaw of the aesthetic design is that, in order to read the writing on the uppermost level of the memorial, one needs to climb the two steps, which poses difficulty to the elderly and anyone with mobility problems. Even then, the memorial is not fully visible; the best "bird's-eye view" is arguably afforded to the Austrian president and chancellor, who can look down upon the memorial from their office windows. Nevertheless, at any time of day or evening, one can observe Viennese and tourists alike sitting on all three levels of the memorial, talking or eating sandwiches, with the Heldenplatz behind them in the background (fig. 15). A sign of a more relaxed attitude toward Austria's historical legacy or a demonstration of oblivious forgetting? As one sits upon the conceptual memorial commemorating military victims of the Nazi regime, one can look upon the Hofburg Palace, now partly housing the Austrian Republic's presidential and chancellor's offices, and the Austrian National Library, largely filled with young people studiously reading and intermittently stepping outside into the old imperial garden

Fig. 15. Olaf Nicolai, *Denkmal für die Verfolgten der NS-Militärjustiz* (Memorial for the Victims of Nazi Military Justice, 2014), with the Heldenplatz and the Austrian National Library in the background.

or onto the Heldenplatz for a break. Past and present coexist in Vienna like in few other cities on earth; the Hofburg Palace with its tainted Führerbalkon (Führer balcony) casts a shadow, as does Nicolai's memorial in turn. Not casting a shadow has traditionally been associated with something uncanny, with devilry, or vampirism.[13] Dark shadows can be made less frightening by illuminating and casting light upon them, as the writers, filmmakers, and artists discussed in this study do so ably. The aim, however, is not to stand "shadowless, like Silence" as the epigraph to this chapter would have it, with the simile attesting to an equation of a lack of shadows to the process of silencing something, such as the past. This leads, if we take the poem's metaphor of "old Autumn," a season traditionally associated with decay and death, to mortality. Living means to accept and coexist with the shadows around us.

Notes

Introduction

[1] Charles Bremner, "Biggest Vote for Far Right since 1945 in Austria poll," *Times*, May 24, 2016; Kate Connoly, Philip Oltermann, Jon Henley, "Far Right Is Edged Out in Knife-Edge Austrian poll," *Guardian*, May 24, 2016.

[2] See N. N., "Bundespräsidentenwahl 2016: Österreich, endgültiges Endergebnis," *Bundesministerium für Inneres*, http://wahl16.bmi.gv.at/ (accessed August 8, 2016).

[3] N. N., "Bundespräsidentenwahl 2016: Österreich Briefwahl," Bundesministerium für Inneres, http://wahl16.bmi.gv.at/1605-bw_ov_0.html (accessed August 7, 2016).

[4] N. N., "Entscheidung vertagt," *news.orf.at*, May 22, 2016, http://orf.at/stories/2340500/2340505/.

[5] Ibid.

[6] Ibid.

[7] N. N., "Bundespräsidentenwahl 2016: Österreich, 1. Wahlgang," Bundesministerium für Inneres, http://wahl16.bmi.gv.at/1604-0.html (accessed August 8, 2016).

[8] See Katharina Mittelstaedt, "'Aufgeheizte Stimmung' in zweigeteilten Gemeinden," *Der Standard*, May 24, 2016.

[9] Connoly, Oltermann, Henley, "Far Right Is Edged Out in Knife-Edge Austrian Poll."

[10] Christiane Amanpour, Twitter post, *@camanpour*, May 24, 2016, 10:20 a.m., https://twitter.com/camanpour/status/735158583310979072.

[11] See N. N., "Die 8 Wahlanfechtungen der Bundespräsidentenwahl 2016," www.bundespraesidentschaftswahl.at, http://www.bundespraesidentschaftswahl.at/wahlanfechtung.html (accessed August 7, 2016).

[12] See N. N., "Bundespräsidenten-Stichwahl muss in ganz Österreich und komplett wiederholt werden," Presseinformation Verfassungsgerichtshof, July 1, 2016, https://www.vfgh.gv.at/cms/vfgh-site/attachments/8/0/4/CH0003/CMS1467363234408/verkuendung_w_presseinformation.pdf.

[13] Ibid.

[14] APA, "Ministerrat fixiert 2. Oktober als Stichwahl-Termin," *Der Standard*, July 5, 2016.

15 Hellin Sapinski, "'Klebergate': Sobotka lässt gegen Hotline-Mitarbeiter ermitteln," *Die Presse*, September 12, 2016.

16 The religious affirmation is by no means compulsory. See N. N., "Amtsantritt und Amtsende," *Österreichische Präsidentschaftskanzlei*, 2013, http://www.bundespraesident.at/aufgaben/wahl-und-amtszeit/amtsantritt-und-amtsende/.

17 See Cathrin Kahlweit, "Der Hofer und der Herrgott," *Süddeutsche Zeitung*, October 25, 2016.

18 APA, "Holocaust-Überlebende warnt vor rechter Rhetorik bei Bundespräsidentenwahlkampf," *Der Standard*, November 26, 2016.

19 See APA, "Mitterlehner, Karmasin offen für Van der Bellen—Lopatka für Hofer," *Der Standard*, November 24, 2016.

20 N. N., "Österreich, vorläufiges Endergebnis inklusive Briefwahlstimmen," http://wahl16.bmi.gv.at/ (accessed December 9, 2016).

21 Simon Tisdall, "Victory for Van Der Bellen and the Left Is a Sigh of Relief for Europe," *Guardian*, December 4, 2016.

22 Allyson Fiddler, "Why Did Many More Austrians Vote against the Far Right than in the First Head-to-Head? Brexit and Trump Were Strong Factors," *Independent*, December 5, 2016.

23 "Die Waldheim-Affäre hat Österreich verändert, und zwar von Grund auf"; Christa Zöchling speaking in Christian Rainer and Christa Zöchling, "Videoblog: Die Affäre Waldheim hat eine ganze Generation geprägt," *profil.at*, March 19, 2016, http://www.profil.at/videos/videoblog-kurt-waldheim-6276119.

24 "Österreich zuerst" is an established slogan of the Austrian Freedom Party, most notably associated with a *Volksbegehren* (petition), initiated by the Austrian Freedom Party in 1992, calling for a freeze on immigration and other restrictions on immigrants residing in Austria. The slogan was most recently used in the 2016 presidential election to reflect the party's anti-EU stance.

25 Hans Rauscher, "'Ich habe im Krieg nichts anderes getan als meine Pflicht erfüllt'," *Der Standard*, February 27, 2016.

26 Kuno Knöbl, "Die Geschichte des Waldheim-Holzpferdes," *Republikanischer Club–Neues Österreich: Geschichte*, http://www.repclub.at/geschichte/ (accessed August 7, 2016). Ellipses in original, my emphases in English translation.

27 Ibid.

28 See Richard Mitten, "Bitburg, Waldheim, and the Politics of Remembering and Forgetting," in *From World War to Waldheim: Culture and Politics in Austria and the United States*, ed. David F. Wood and Ruth Wodak (New York, Oxford: Berghahn, 1999), 68.

29 *Neue Kronenzeitung*, 12.3.1986, 3, as cited in Cornelius Lehnguth, *Waldheim und die Folgen: Der parteipolitische Umgang mit dem Nationalsozialismus in Österreich* (Frankfurt am Main, New York: Campus, 2013), 99.

30 Knöbl, "Die Geschichte des Waldheim-Holzpferdes."

[31] During the "Gedenkjahr" (commemorative year) 2005, it was exhibited in the Jewish Museum Vienna as part of an exhibition on the history of anti-Semitism in Austria. See Martin Staudinger, "Der Super-Gaul," in *1986: Das Jahr, das Österreich veränderte*, ed. Barbara Tóth and Hubertus Czernin (Vienna: Czernin, 2006), 139.

[32] See N. N., "30 Jahre Waldheim-Affäre," Wien Museum, http://www.wienmuseum.at/index.php?id=917 (accessed August 7, 2016).

[33] See Steven Beller, *A Concise History of Austria* (Cambridge: Cambridge University Press, 2006), 291.

[34] Czernin was the journalist who published an exposé of Waldheim's past in the Austrian weekly *profil* in March 1986.

[35] Barbara Tóth and Hubertus Czernin, "Vorwort der Herausgeber," in Tóth and Czernin, *1986*, 11.

[36] Hubertus Czernin, "Einleitung," in Tóth and Czernin, *1986*, 19.

[37] Christa Zöchling, "Der gewisse Jargon," in Tóth and Czernin, *1986*, 172.

[38] Rauscher, "'Ich habe im Krieg nichts anderes getan als meine Pflicht erfüllt.'"

[39] Walter Manoschek, "Die Generation Waldheim," in Tóth and Czernin, *1986*, 127.

[40] Wolfgang Paterno, "Robert Schindel: Erst als Toter pflegt man Gleichmut," *profil.at*, February 9, 2013, http://www.profil.at/home/robert-schindel-erst-toter-gleichmut-352177.

[41] The exact wording is "the first free country to fall a victim to Hitlerite aggression." N. N., "The Moscow Declaration; October 1943. Joint Four-Nation Declaration," The Avalon Project: Documents in Law, History and Diplomacy, Yale Lillian Goldmann Law Library, http://avalon.law.yale.edu/wwii/moscow.asp (accessed August 7, 2016).

[42] Manoschek, "Die Generation Waldheim," 130.

[43] Zöchling, "Als Österreich erwachsen wurde," *profil* 47, no. 12 (March 21, 2016): 18–25.

[44] Walter Manoschek, for example, views the *Wehrmachtsausstellung* (German Army Exhibition) as more important in ultimately destroying the myth of the so-called clean Wehrmacht; Manoschek, "Die Generation Waldheim," 130–31. By contrast, Gerhard Botz ascribes "länger wirkende Folgen" (long-lasting consequences) to the Waldheim affair; Gerhard Botz, "Die 'Waldheim-Affäre' als Widerstreit kollektiver Erinnerungen," in Tóth and Czernin, *1986*, 75. Richard Mitten similarly views the Waldheim affair as having left a lasting legacy on Austria's political landscape; Richard Mitten, "Der kurze Schatten der Vergangenheit," in Tóth and Czernin, *1986*, 110–11.

[45] See Tóth and Czernin, *1986: Das Jahr, das Österreich veränderte*; "30 Jahre danach: Wie Waldheim Österreich veränderte," was the cover headline of *profil*'s title story by Christa Zöchling, "Als Österreich erwachsen wurde," March 21, 2016.

[46] "Für sie sei damals die Republik 'ein zweites Mal gegründet worden,' sagt Beckermann." As cited in Zöchling, "Als Österreich erwachsen wurde," 25.

[47] Zöchling, "Als Österreich erwachsen wurde," 18.

[48] See Tóth and Czernin, "Vorwort der Herausgeber," 11.

[49] Dagmar C. G. Lorenz, "The Struggle for a Civil Society and Beyond: Austrian Writers and Intellectuals Confronting the Political Right," *New German Critique*, no. 93 (2004): 25.

[50] See Staudinger, "Der Super-Gaul," 139–40.

[51] See N. N., "Waldheim oder THE ART OF FORGETTING," Filmfonds Wien, http://www.filmfonds-wien.at/filme/waldheim-oder-the-art-of-forgetting (accessed August 11, 2016).

[52] Both Gerhard Botz and Richard Mitten argue that the Waldheim affair paved the way for the rise of the Austrian Freedom Party under Haider. See Botz, "Die 'Waldheim-Affäre' als Widerstreit kollektiver Erinnerungen," 75; Mitten, "Der kurze Schatten der Vergangenheit," 110–11.

[53] See Oliver Das Gupta, "Wie rechts Norbert Hofer wirklich ist," *Süddeutsche Zeitung*, May 20, 2016.

[54] Ibid.

[55] Ibid.

[56] See APA, "Fischer: 500.000 Flüchtlinge durch Österreich bis Jahresende," October 26, 2015, http://derstandard.at/2000024534991/Fischer-wirbt-fuer-Verstaendnis-fuer-Fluechtlinge.

[57] See N. N., "Bundespräsidentenwahl 2016: Österreich, 1. Wahlgang."

[58] See Cathrin Kahlweit, "Der Rechtspopulismus ist in Österreich endgültig salonfähig," *Süddeutsche Zeitung*, April 24, 2016.

[59] See N. N., "Österreichische Staatsbürgerschaft," *Israelitische Kultusgemeinde Wien: Abteilung für Restitutionsangelegenheiten*, http://www.restitution.or.at/schwerpunkte/s-anliegen-staatsbuergerschaft.html (accessed August 7, 2016).

[60] See Beller, *A Concise History of Austria*, 296.

[61] See N. N., "5. Mai-Gedenktag gegen Gewalt und Rassismus im Gedenken an die Opfer des Nationalsozialismus," *erinnern.at*, http://www.erinnern.at/bundeslaender/oesterreich/gedenktage/5.-mai-gedenktag-gegen-gewalt-und-rassismus-im-gedenken-an-die-opfer-des-nationalsozialismus (accessed August 7, 2016).

[62] See Magdalena Neumüller, "Erinnerung in Rechnitz: Microstudie über den Umgang mit Toten," in *Der Fall Rechnitz: Das Massaker an Juden im März 1945*, ed. Walter Manoschek (Vienna: Braumüller, 2009), 212.

[63] Bruno Simma and Hans-Peter Folz, *Restitution und Entschädigung im Völkerrecht: Die Verpflichtungen der Republik Österreich nach 1945 im Lichte ihrer außenpolitischen Praxis* (Vienna, Munich: Veröffentlichungen der

Österreichischen Historikerkommission, 2004), as cited in Neumüller, "Erinnerung in Rechnitz," 216.

64 Heidemarie Uhl, "Die Wiederentdeckung der Orte," in *Architektur: Vergessen: Jüdische Architekten in Graz*, ed. Antje Senarclens de Grancy and Hudrun Zettelbauer (Vienna: Böhlau, 2011), 52.

65 Simon Curtis, *Woman in Gold* (London: BBC Films/Origin Pictures, 2015).

66 See Olga Kronsteiner, "'Die Frau in Gold': Faktentreue ist eine schlechte Dramaturgin," *Der Standard*, May 29, 2015; Barbara Petsch, "'Die Frau in Gold': Klimts goldene Adele als Kino-Saga," *Die Presse*, June 2, 2015; Thomas Trenkler, "Der Fall 'Goldene Adele,' tendenziös erzählt," *Kurier*, June 2, 2015.

67 Deborah Ross, "Woman in Gold Review: Even Helen Mirren Is Weighed Down by the Script's Banalities," *Spectator*, April 11, 2015. See also Stephen Holden, "Review: 'Woman in Gold' Stars Helen Mirren in Tug of War over Artwork," *New York Times*, March 31, 2015; Tim Robey, "Woman in Gold Review: 'Distinctly Ordinary,'" *Telegraph*, April 9, 2015.

68 See Alexander Pollak, "Nenn sie nicht 'Wehrmachtsausstellung'!" in *Zeitgeschichte ausstellen in Österreich: Museen—Gedenkstätte—Ausstellungen*, ed. Dirk Rupnow and Heidemarie Uhl (Vienna: Böhlau, 2011), 246.

69 See Walter Manoschek, "Wehrmachtsausstellung: Verbrechen erinnern," *Neue Kriminalpolitik* 10, no. 1 (1998): 15.

70 See Pollak, "Nenn sie nicht 'Wehrmachtsausstellung'!" 246.

71 See Benedikt Erenz, "Verbrechen der Wehrmacht: Vor 20 Jahren wurde die Hamburger Ausstellung eröffnet—sogar der Bundestag diskutierte über sie," *Die Zeit*, March 23, 2015.

72 Manoschek, "Die Generation Waldheim," 125.

73 Ibid., 130.

74 Ibid., 131.

75 Beckermann, *Jenseits des Krieges* (Vienna: Aichholzer Filmproduktion, 1996).

76 See Beckermann, "Oktober bis November 1995: Das Drehtagebuch," in *Jenseits des Krieges: Ehemalige Wehrmachtsoldaten erinnern sich*, by Ruth Beckermann (Vienna: Döcker, 1998), 85–98.

77 Ibid., 89.

78 See "Flüchtlingsland Österreich," *UNHCR The UN Refugee Agency*, http://www.unhcr.at/unhcr/in-oesterreich/fluechtlingsland-oesterreich.html (accessed August 7, 2016).

79 See Beller, *A Concise History of Austria*, 298–99.

80 See Andrea Götzelmann, *Wer macht Asylpolitik? AkteurInnen und ihre Strategien in der österreichischen Asylgesetzgebung* (Berlin: Lit Verlag, 2010), 49.

81 Ibid., 49.

[82] See N. N., "20 Jahre Lichtermeer," *orf.at*, January 20, 2013, http://oesterreich.orf.at/stories/2567688.

[83] Ibid.

[84] See Beller, *A Concise History of Austria*, 302.

[85] Geoff Winestock, "EU Countries Drop Sanctions against Austria after Report," *Wall Street Journal*, September 13, 2000.

[86] See Dagmar C. G. Lorenz, "The Struggle for a Civil Society and Beyond"; Robert Misik, "Kein Heldenplatz ohne Waldheim," in Tóth and Czernin, *1986*, 141–47.

[87] Misik, "Kein Heldenplatz ohne Waldheim," 141.

[88] The emblematic function of the Heldenplatz can be gleaned from the title of Thomas Bernhard's eponymous play and Ernst Jandl's poem "wien: Heldenplatz"; Thomas Bernhard, *Heldenplatz* (Frankfurt am Main: Suhrkamp, 1988), Ernst Jandl, "wien: heldenplatz," in *Gedichte*, ed. Klaus Siblewski, vol. 1 of *Gesammelte Werke*, ed. Klaus Siblewski (Frankfurt am Main: Luchterhand, 1990), 124.

[89] See Bernard Henri Lévy, "Die Stimmen des Anderen Österreich," in *Österreich: Berichte aus Quarantanien*, ed. Isolde Charim and Doron Rabinovici (Frankfurt am Main: Suhrkamp, 2000), 160.

[90] See Frederick Baker and Elisabeth Boyer, "Statistiken," in *Wiener Wandertage: Die Demonstrationskultur gegen die Haider-Schüssel-Koalition; Reden, Texte, Berichte (2000–2002)*, ed. Frederick Baker and Elisabeth Boyer, 2nd ed. (Klagenfurt: Wieser, 2010), 503.

[91] See interview with Doron Rabinovici in Frederick Baker, *Widerstand in Haiderland—Masse ohne Macht?* (Vienna: Filmbäckerei Wien, 2010).

[92] Frederick Baker, "Der 19. Februar 2000: Die Geburt eines Widerstands-Oratoriums," in Baker and Boyer, *Wiener Wandertage*, 172.

[93] See Frederick Baker and Elisabeth Boyer, "Chronologie der Ereignisse," in Baker and Boyer, *Wiener Wandertage*, 494.

[94] Baker and Boyer, "Statistiken," 504.

[95] See Frederick Baker and Elisabeth Boyer, "Vorbemerkung," in Baker and Boyer, *Wiener Wandertage*, 7.

[96] Frederick Baker speaking at a screening of his film *Widerstand in Haiderland* at the Contemporary Austrian Literature, Film and Culture: International Conference, University of Nottingham, UK, April 13–15, 2015.

[97] Baker and Boyer, "Vorbemerkung," 7.

[98] See Charim and Rabinovici, *Österreich*; Baker and Boyer, *Wiener Wandertage*; Frederick Baker and Petra Herczeg, *Die beschämte Republik: 10 Jahre nach Schwarz-Blau in Österreich* (Vienna: Czernin, 2010).

[99] Baker, *Widerstand in Haiderland*; Allyson Fiddler, "Points of Departure in Austria 2000: Street Protest and Performance" (paper presented at the

Contemporary Austrian Literature, Film and Culture: International Conference, University of Nottingham, UK, April 13–15, 2015).

[100] Beller, *A Concise History of Austria*, 303.

[101] Ibid., 303.

[102] Ibid., 305.

[103] Ibid.

[104] Elfriede Jelinek, "Das Kommen," www.elfriedejelinek.com, April 26, 2016, http://www.elfriedejelinek.com/.

[105] Ibid.

[106] Jelinek, *Das Lebewohl: Drei kleine Dramen* (Berlin: Berlin Verlag, 2000). The text is also available on Elfriede Jelinek Homepage Wien under "Theatertexte," http://www.elfriedejelinek.com/ (accessed August 30, 2016). See also Karin Cerny's report on the premiere, "Elfriede Jelinek: Das Lebewohl," *Literaturhaus Wien*, February 2, 2002, http://www.literaturhaus.at/index.php?id=4355, and extract of the performance in Frederick Baker's *Widerstand in Haiderland*. For an analysis of Jelinek's *Das Lebewohl* in the context of resistance to Haider's FPÖ see Allyson Fiddler, "Staging Jörg Haider: Protest and Resignation in Elfriede Jelinek's *Das Lebewohl* and Other Recent Texts for the Theatre," *Modern Language Review* 97, no. 2 (2002): 353–64.

[107] Carl Merz and Helmut Qualtinger, *Der Herr Karl*, ed. Traugott Krischke (Vienna: Deuticke, 1996).

[108] See Georg Biron, "Vom Herrn Karl . . .: Vor 50 Jahren empörte Helmut Qualtinger mit dem Monolog eines Opportunisten die Nation," *Die Zeit*, November 11, 2011.

[109] Merz and Qualtinger, *Der Herr Karl*, 22. Ellipses in original.

[110] See, for example, this image of Norbert Hofer: "Wer ist wer: Biografie von Ing. Norbert Hofer," Republik Österreich Parlament, https://www.parlament.gv.at/WWER/PAD_35521/ (accessed August 7, 2016).

[111] Otto Back et al., eds., *Österreichisches Wörterbuch: Schulausgabe*, 41st ed. (Vienna: ÖBV, 2009), 122.

[112] See "ORF | Willkommen Österreich—Herr Karl (03.05.2016)," YouTube video, 2:39, posted by der fenstergucker, May 15, 2016, https://www.youtube.com/watch?v=dyekFiRqmUc.

[113] See Aleida Assmann, *Der lange Schatten der Vergangenheit: Erinnerungskultur und Geschichtspolitik* (Munich: Beck, 2006), 278.

[114] Ibid.

[115] Ibid., 279.

[116] Ibid., 278.

[117] Ibid.

[118] William Faulkner, *Requiem for a Nun* (London: Vintage, 2015), 85.

[119] Doron Rabinovici speaking in Frederick Baker's documentary *Widerstand in Haiderland*.

[120] Ibid.

[121] Sigmund Freud, *Der Mann Moses und die monotheistische Religion*, in *Fragen der Gesellschaft: Ursprünge der Religion*, vol. 9 of *Sigmund Freud: Studienausgabe*, Alexander Mitscherlich, Angela Richards, and James Strachey (Frankfurt am Main: Fischer, 1972), 459–581.

[122] For a summary of the concept of trauma, see Assmann, *Der lange Schatten der Vergangenheit*, 93.

[123] Ibid.

[124] Theodor W. Adorno, "Was bedeutet: Aufarbeitung der Vergangenheit," in *Kulturkritik und Gesellschaft II: Eingriffe; Stichworte; Anhang*, vol. 10.2 of *Theodor W. Adorno: Gesammelte Schriften*, ed. Rolf Tiedemann (Frankfurt am Main: Suhrkamp, 1977), 557.

[125] See APA, "Nicht nur Opfer, auch Täter," *Kurier*, March 12, 2013.

[126] See Helmut König, Michael Kohlstruck, and Andreas Wöll, "Einleitung der Herausgeber," in *Vergangenheitsbewältigung am Ende des zwanzigsten Jahrhunderts*, ed. Helmut König, Michael Kohlstruck, and Andreas Wöll (Opladen: Westdeutscher Verlag, 1998), 8.

[127] Adorno, "Was bedeutet," 555–72.

[128] Ibid., 555.

[129] Ibid., 571.

[130] Sigmund Freud, "Erinnern, Wiederholen und Durcharbeiten," in *Ergänzungsband*, vol. 11 of *Sigmund Freud: Studienausgabe*, ed. Alexander Mitscherlich, Angela Richards, and James Strachey (Frankfurt am Main: Fischer, 1975).

[131] *Merriam Webster Dictionary*, s.v. "confrontation," accessed August 9, 2016, http://www.merriam-webster.com/dictionary/confrontation.

[132] Marianne Hirsch, *Family Frames: Photography, Narrative and Postmemory* (Cambridge, MA: Harvard University Press, 1997), 22.

[133] Ibid.

[134] Ibid.

[135] Ibid.

[136] Sigmund Freud, "Trauer und Melancholie," in *Psychologie des Unbewußten*, vol. 3 of *Sigmund Freud: Studienausgabe*, ed. Alexander Mitscherlich, Angela Richards, and James Strachey (Frankfurt am Main: Fischer, 1975), 193–213.

[137] Svetlana Boym, *The Future of Nostalgia* (New York: Basic Books, 2001), xiii.

[138] Ibid., 41.

[139] Ibid., 49.

140 Ibid., 351.

141 Linda Hutcheon, "Irony, Nostalgia, and the Postmodern," in *Methods for the Study of Literature as Cultural Memory*, ed. Raymond Vervliet and Annemarie Estor (Amsterdam, Atlanta: Rodopi, 2000), 198.

142 Dirk Moses and Michael Rothberg, "A Dialogue on the Ethics and Politics of Transcultural Memory," in *The Transcultural Turn: Interrogating Memory Between and Beyond Borders*, ed. Lucy Bond and Jessica Rapson (Berlin: De Gruyter, 2014), 29.

143 Michael Rothberg, *Multidirectional Memory: Remembering the Holocaust in the Age of Decolonization* (Stanford, CA: Stanford University Press, 2009).

144 Peter Carrier and Kobi Kabalek, "Cultural Memory and Transcultural Memory—A Conceptual Analysis," in *The Transcultural Turn: Interrogating Memory Between and Beyond Borders*, ed. Lucy Bond and Jessica Rapson (Berlin: De Gruyter, 2014), 56.

145 See APA, "Ein Drittel der Österreicher sehnt sich nach 'starkem Führer,'" *Der Standard*, May 7, 2014.

146 Matthias Beilein, *86 und die Folgen: Robert Schindel, Robert Menasse und Doron Rabinovici im literarischen Feld Österreichs* (Berlin: Schmidt, 2008).

147 Andrea Reiter, *Contemporary Jewish Writing: Austria after Waldheim* (New York: Routledge, 2013).

148 Ibid., 4.

149 Ibid., 6.

150 Hillary Hope Herzog, *"Vienna is Different": Jewish Writers in Austria from the Fin de Siècle to the Present* (New York, Oxford: Berghahn, 2011).

151 Boym, *The Future of Nostalgia*, 49.

Chapter One

Epigraph. Franz West speaking in *Wien Retour* [Return to Vienna], dir. Ruth Beckermann and Josef Aichholzer, DVD Ruth Beckermann-Filmproduktion 2007 (Vienna: Filmladen, 1983).

1 Freud, "Trauer und Melancholie," *193–213*.

2 Dagmar C. G. Lorenz, "Discovering and Making Memory: Jewish Cultural Expression in Contemporary Europe," *German Quarterly* 73, no. 2 (2000): 177.

3 These three films have commonly been described as a "trilogy" of films treating Jewish identity. See Hillary Hope Herzog, "The Global and the Local in Ruth Beckermann's Films and Writings," in *Rebirth of a Culture: Jewish Identity and Jewish Writing in Germany and Austria Today*, ed. Hillary Hope Herzog, Todd Herzog, and Benjamin Lapp (New York, Oxford: Berghahn, 2008), 106; Andrea Reiter, *Contemporary Jewish Writing*, 5.

⁴ See Renate S. Posthofen, "Ruth Beckermann: Re-activating Memory—In Search of Time Lost," in *Out from the Shadows: Essays on Contemporary Austrian Women Writers and Filmmakers*, ed. Margarete Lamb-Faffelberger (Riverside, CA: Ariadne Press, 1997), 264–76; Christina E. Guenther, "Cartographies of Identity: Memory and History in Ruth Beckermann's Documentary Films," in *New Austrian Film*, ed. Robert von Dassanowsky and Oliver C. Speck (New York, Oxford: Berghahn, 2011), 64–78.

⁵ See Herzog, "The Global and the Local," 100–109.

⁶ See Lorenz, "Discovering and Making Memory"; Lorenz, "Post-Shoah Positions of Displacement in the Films of Ruth Beckermann," *Austrian Studies* 11 (2003): 154–70; Lorenz, "The Struggle for a Civil Society and Beyond"; Herzog, "Vienna is Different," (section on Beckermann, 229–37); Reiter, *Contemporary Jewish Writing*. See also Alisa S. Lebow's brief discussion of Beckermann's *Die papierene Brücke*, in *First Person Jewish* (Minneapolis: University of Minnesota Press, 2008), 27–29.

⁷ Christina Guenther, "The Politics of Location in Ruth Beckermann's 'Vienna Films,'" *Modern Austrian Literature* 37, no. 3–4 (2004): 33.

⁸ Boym, *The Future of Nostalgia*, 351.

⁹ Christina Guenther, "Cartographies of Identity," 65.

¹⁰ The music for the song was originally written in 1920 in the Soviet Union in the context of the Russian Civil War by Samuil Pokrass and set to words by Petr Grigoriev as "Belaia armiia, chernyi baron" (White Army, Black Baron); see Edith W. Clowes, *Russia on the Edge: Imagined Geographies and Post-Soviet Identities* (Ithaca, NY: Cornell University Press), 87. Pokrass's melody was then set to Fritz Brügel's song text "Die Arbeiter von Wien"; see N. N., "Fritz Brügel," *Wien Geschichte Wiki*, July 20, 2016, https://www.wien.gv.at/wiki/index.php?title=Fritz_Br%C3%BCgel.

¹¹ See Beckermann, *Die Mazzesinsel: Juden in der Wiener Leopoldstadt 1918–1938* (Vienna: Löcker, 1984), 19.

¹² Boym, *The Future of Nostalgia*, xiii.

¹³ This is something that Beckermann herself has highlighted in a video interview accompanying the *Wien retour* film DVD; Ruth Beckermann, interview by Bert Rebhandl, August 9, 2007, on *Wien retour* DVD.

¹⁴ Beckermann, *Die Mazzesinsel*.

¹⁵ Hirsch, *Family Frames*, 20.

¹⁶ Ibid., 21.

¹⁷ Beller, *A Concise History of Austria*, 207.

¹⁸ For a discussion of this see Heidemarie Uhl, "The Politics of Memory: Austria's Perception of the Second World War and the National Socialist Period," in *Austrian Historical Memory and National Identity*, ed. Anton Pelinka and Günter Bischof (New Brunswick, NJ: Transaction, 1997), 64–94.

¹⁹ Posthofen, "Ruth Beckermann," 265.

[20] Dagmar C. G. Lorenz, *Keepers of the Motherland: German Texts by Jewish Women Writers* (Lincoln: University of Nebraska Press, 1997), 236.

[21] Beckermann speaking in interview by Bert Rebhandl.

[22] Beckermann, *Unzugehörig: Österreicher und Juden nach 1945* (Vienna: Löcker, 1989).

[23] See Hella Pick, *Guilty Victim: Austria from the Holocaust to Haider* (London: I. B. Tauris, 2000), 206–7.

[24] Ruth Beckermann, interview by Bert Rebhandl.

[25] Beckermann, as cited in *Wien retour* DVD booklet, 5.

[26] Peter Turrini, as cited in *Wien retour* DVD booklet, 2.

[27] Guenther, "Cartographies of Identity," 65.

[28] Boym, *The Future of Nostalgia*, 351.

[29] Manès Sperber, *Die Wasserträger Gottes* (Vienna: Europaverlag, 1983), 60, as cited in Beckermann, "Auf der Brücke: Rede zur Verleihung des Manès Sperber-Preises, Wien, 16/10/2000," *German Quarterly* 74, no. 1 (2001): 2.

[30] Beckermann, "Auf der Brücke," 2.

[31] Guenther, "Cartographies of Identity," 68–69.

[32] Hirsch, *Family Frames*, 6.

[33] Ingeborg Bachmann, "Der Umgang mit Namen," in *Essays, Reden, Vermischte Schriften, Anhang*, vol. 4 of *Ingeborg Bachmann: Werke*, ed. Christine Koschel, Inge von Weidenbaum, and Clemens Münster (Munich: Piper, 1978), 239.

[34] Walter Benjamin, "Das Kunstwerk im Zeitalter seiner technischen Reproduzierbarkeit," in *Aufsätze, Essays, Vorträge*, vol. 2.2 of *Walter Benjamin: Gesammelte Schriften*, ed. Rolf Tiedemann and Hermann Schweppenhäuser (Frankfurt am Main: Suhrkamp, 1974), 475–79.

[35] Marianne Hirsch, *Family Frames*, 13.

[36] Marianne Hirsch and Leo Spitzer, *Ghosts of Home: The Afterlife of Czernowitz in Jewish Memory* (Berkeley: University of California Press, 2010), xxv.

[37] Ibid., xv.

[38] Reiter, *Contemporary Jewish Writing*, 115.

[39] In *Ursprung des deutschen Trauerspiels* Benjamin reads Albrecht Dürer's engraving *Melencolia I* (1514), showing the allegorical figure of winged Melancholia, as emblematic for a conception of melancholy as connected to the experience of landscape. Walter Benjamin, *Ursprung des deutschen Trauerspiels*, in *Abhandlungen*, vol. 1.1 of *Walter Benjamin: Gesammelte Schriften*, ed. Rolf Tiedemann and Hermann Schweppenhäuser (Frankfurt am Main: Suhrkamp, 1974), 353.

[40] Ibid.

⁴¹ Roland Barthes, *Camera Lucida: Reflections on Photography* (London: Vintage, 1993), 14.

⁴² Sigmund Freud, "Das Unheimliche," in *Psychologische Schriften*, vol. 4 of *Sigmund Freud: Studienausgabe*, ed. Alexander Mitscherlich, Angela Richards, and James Strachey (Frankfurt am Main: Fischer, 1972), 250.

⁴³ Reiter, *Contemporary Jewish Writing*, 114.

⁴⁴ Ibid., 115.

⁴⁵ Ruth Beckermann and Elfriede Jelinek, "Ein Gespräch," in *Stadtkino Programm 110: Ruth Beckermann, Die papierene Brücke* (Vienna: Stadtkino, 1987), 2–4.

⁴⁶ Ruth Beckermann, "Die Verhaftung: Vier Tage in Czernowitz, das einmal eine österreichische Stadt war," *profil* 15, no. 34 (August 19, 1985), 50–54.

⁴⁷ Benjamin, "Das Kunstwerk," 479.

⁴⁸ Ruth Beckermann's later film *Ein flüchtiger Zug nach dem Orient* (1999) is dedicated to the memory of her father, whose birth date is given as 1911.

⁴⁹ Wilfried Geldner, "Für Kaiser und Land: Die papierene Brücke," *Süddeutsche Zeitung*, September 20, 1988.

⁵⁰ Beckermann describes the postwar Jewish community in Vienna as being made up of "polnische, rumänische und ungarische Juden, die auch als Flüchtlinge vor dem Stalinismus in Österreich geblieben waren" (Polish, Rumanian and Hungarian Jews, that had also remained in Austria as refugees from Stalinism), in *Unzugehörig*, 99.

⁵¹ Ibid., 101.

⁵² Ibid., 109.

⁵³ Beckermann, interview by Bert Rebhandl, August 9, 2007.

⁵⁴ Herzog, "The Global and the Local," 108.

⁵⁵ Ruth Beckermann, as cited in Erika Wantoch, "'Seit Waldheim weiß ich, wo die Grenzen sind': Erika Wantoch sprach mit der Filmautorin Ruth Beckermann," *profil* 17, no. 14 (April 6, 1987), 62.

⁵⁶ Dagmar C. G. Lorenz, "Austrian Responses to National Socialism and the Holocaust," in *A History of Austrian Literature 1918–2000*, ed. Katrin Kohl and Ritchie Robertson (Rochester, NY: Camden House, 2006), 193.

⁵⁷ Beckermann, *Unzugehörig*, 10.

⁵⁸ "Heute stirbt das Textilviertel aus," *PB*.

⁵⁹ Guenther, "The Politics of Location," 33.

⁶⁰ Doron Rabinovici, "'Tina, ruf die Polizei!'" *Die Presse*, September 8, 2001.

⁶¹ Herzog, "The Global and the Local," 106.

⁶² Beckermann, "*Homemad(e)*," *ruthbeckermann.com*, accessed August 10, 2016, http://www.ruthbeckermann.com/home.php?il=14&l=eng.

⁶³ Walter Benjamin, "Über den Begriff der Geschichte," in *Abhandlungen*, vol 1.2 of *Walter Benjamin: Gesammelte Schriften*, ed. Rolf Tiedemann and Hermann Schweppenhäuser (Frankfurt am Main: Suhrkamp, 1974), 704.

⁶⁴ Doron Rabinovici, *Papirnik: Stories* (Frankfurt am Main: Suhrkamp, 1994), 61.

⁶⁵ Beckermann, "Ich nenne es 'Austronazismus,'" *Der Standard*, November 1, 1999.

⁶⁶ Lorenz, "Austrian Responses to National Socialism and the Holocaust," 193.

⁶⁷ Ibid.

⁶⁸ Beckermann, *Unzugehörig*, 121.

⁶⁹ Ibid.

⁷⁰ Lorenz, "Austrian Responses to National Socialism and the Holocaust," 195.

⁷¹ Beckermann, *Unzugehörig*, 65.

⁷² Herzog, "The Global and the Local," 107.

⁷³ Ibid.

Chapter Two

Epigraph. Vladimir Nabokov, *Speak, Memory: An Autobiography Revisited* (London: Penguin, 2000), 91.

¹ Anna Mitgutsch, *Haus der Kindheit*, 4th ed. (2000; Munich: Deutscher Taschenbuch Verlag, 2008); hereafter cited in text as *HdK*. English translations are taken from David Dollenmayer's published translation, *House of Childhood* (New York: Other Press, 2006); hereafter cited in text as *HoC*.

² Karl-Markus Gauss, "Photographierte Sehnsucht. Anna Mitgutschs grosser Roman 'Haus der Kindheit,'" *Neue Zürcher Zeitung*, May 31, 2000.

³ Ibid.

⁴ Anthony Bushell, "Facts, Fiction, and Friction in a Difficult Relationship: Vienna and Provincial Austria," *German Life and Letters* 65, no. 2 (2012): 239.

⁵ Bruno Lässer, "Die Ungnade der später Angekommenen. 'Haus der Kindheit' von Mitgutsch, eine Neuerscheinung, der man eine große Leserschaft wünscht," *Vorarlberger Nachrichten*, May 13, 2000, D8.

⁶ Kristin Teuchtmann, "Haus der Kindheit," *Austrian Studies Newsletter* 12, no. 3 (2000): 14.

⁷ Ibid.

⁸ Katherine Elizabeth Evans, "'Das Politische ist nicht anders erlebbar als privat': A Study of Anna Mitgutsch's Fiction and its Portrayal of Austrian Society" (PhD diss., University of Wales, Bangor, 2003), 116.

⁹ See Reinhold Tauber, "Vom Wandern zwischen den Welten. Anna Mitgutschs neue Prosa ist das bisher reifste Buch der Autorin," *Oberösterreichische Nachrichten*, March 8, 2000, 7; Lässer, "Die Ungnade der später Angekommenen," D8; Walter Hinck, "Im verlorenen Paradies. Heimkehrversuch: Anna Mitgutschs Roman 'Haus der Kindheit,'" *Frankfurter Allgemeine Zeitung*, April 28, 2000; SAS, "Anna Mitgutsch," *Die Presse*, March 10, 2000.

¹⁰ Lässer, "Die Ungnade der später Angekommenen," D8.

¹¹ SAS, "Anna Mitgutsch," 41.

¹² Kirstin Breitenfellner, "Exilroman remixed," *Falter*, February 25, 2000.

¹³ Evans, "'Das Politische ist nicht anders erlebbar als privat,'" 78.

¹⁴ See Kristin Teuchtmann, "Zur Darstellbarkeit der Zeit: Erinnerung und Erfindung in Anna Mitgutschs 'Die Züchtigung' und 'Haus der Kindheit,'" *Modern Austrian Literature* 35, no. 1–2 (2002): 43–61; Kristin Teuchtmann, *Über die Faszination des Unsagbaren: Anna Mitgutsch, eine Monografie* (Frankfurt am Main, Oxford: Peter Lang, 2003); Monika Shafi, "'Enteignung' und 'Behaustheit': Zu Anna Mitgutschs Roman 'Haus der Kindheit,'" *Modern Austrian Literature* 36, no. 1–2 (2003): 33–51; Christa Gürtler, "Abschied von einem fremden Haus," in *Anna Mitgutsch*, ed. Heide Stockinger and Kristin Teuchtmann (Linz: Rampe, 2004), 73–76; Wolfgang Hackl, "Erzählendes Erinnern: Bemerkungen zu einem poetologischen Aspekt in Anna Mitgutschs Romanen," in *Anna Mitgutsch*, ed. Heide Stockinger and Kristin Teuchtmann (Linz: Rampe, 2004), 39–44; Maria-Regina Kecht, "Traditionen des Gedenkens: Anna Mitgutsch, *Haus der Kindheit*," *Chilufim*, no. 6 (2009): 17–74; Eva Steindorfer, "Narrative der Erinnerung: Funktionen—Formen—Fallstricke des Erinnerns in 'Familienfest', 'Haus der Kindheit' und 'Zwei Leben und ein Tag,'" ed. Kurt Bartsch and Günther A. Höfler (Graz: Droschl, 2009), 73–86.

¹⁵ See Teuchtmann, "Zur Darstellbarkeit der Zeit"; Shafi, "'Enteignung' und 'Behaustheit,'"; Hackl, "Erzählendes Erinnern"; Gürtler, "Abschied von einem fremden Haus"; Kecht, "Traditionen des Gedenkens."

¹⁶ See Teuchtmann, "Zur Darstellbarkeit der Zeit"; Shafi, "'Enteignung' und 'Behaustheit'"; Kecht, "Traditionen des Gedenkens."

¹⁷ See Teuchtmann, *Über die Faszination des Unsagbaren*; Kecht, "Traditionen des Gedenkens."

¹⁸ See Evans, "'Das Politische ist nicht anders erlebbar als privat'"; Kecht, "Traditionen des Gedenkens."

¹⁹ See Erica Carter, James Donald, and Judith Squires, eds., *Space and Place: Theories of Identity and Location* (London: Lawrence & Wishart, 1993), xii.

20 Katya Krylova, *Walking through History: Topography and Identity in the Works of Ingeborg Bachmann and Thomas Bernhard* (Oxford: Peter Lang, 2013), 25.

21 Benjamin, *Ursprung des deutschen Trauerspiels*, 226.

22 Boym, *The Future of Nostalgia*, 41.

23 Ibid., 49.

24 See Teuchtmann, "Zur Darstellbarkeit der Zeit"; Shafi, "'Enteignung' und 'Behaustheit'"; Kecht, "Traditionen des Gedenkens."

25 Susan Sontag, *On Photography* (New York: Farrar, Strauss and Giroux, 2001), 15, as cited in Shafi, "'Enteignung' und 'Behaustheit,'" 38.

26 Shafi, "'Enteignung' und 'Behaustheit,'" 38.

27 Kecht, "Traditionen des Gedenkens," 55.

28 Boym, *The Future of Nostalgia*, 49.

29 Ibid.

30 N. N., "The Moscow Declaration; October 1943. Joint Four-Nation Declaration."

31 Gerhard Roth, as cited in Annette Meyhöfer, "Im Land des Schweigens," *Der Spiegel*, April 13, 1992.

32 Boym, *The Future of Nostalgia*, 49.

33 Ibid.

34 Freud, "Das Unheimliche," 241–74.

35 Shafi, "'Enteignung' und 'Behaustheit,'" 39.

36 Ibid.

37 Boym, *The Future of Nostalgia*, 49.

38 Ibid., 351.

39 See Benjamin, "Über den Begriff der Geschichte," 694.

40 Boym, *The Future of Nostalgia*, 41.

41 Katrien Vloeberghs, "Architektur der Unbehaustheit in Anna Mitgutschs Roman *Haus der Kindheit*," in *Anna Mitgutsch*, ed. Kurt Bartsch and Günther A. Höfler (Graz: Droschl, 2009), 119.

42 Boym, *The Future of Nostalgia*, 49.

43 Ibid., 41.

Chapter Three

Epigraph. Ingeborg Bachmann, "Das Buch Franza (Todesarten), Textstufe III, Vorreden," in *"Todesarten"-Projekt: Kritische Ausgabe*, ed. Monika Albrecht and Dirk Göttsche (Munich: Piper, 1995), 2:77.

[1] Walter Manoschek, "Nationalsozialistische Moral, situativer Rahmen und individuelle Handlungsspielräume als konstitutive Elemente bei der Vernichtung der Juden," in *Der Fall Rechnitz: Das Massaker an Juden im März 1945*, ed. Walter Manoschek (Vienna: Braumüller, 2009), 5–26.

[2] Rüter, as cited in Manoschek, "Nationalsozialistische Moral," 5.

[3] Manoschek, "Nationalsozialistische Moral," 13–14.

[4] See Teresa Kovacs, "Chronik der Ereignisse," in *"Die endlose Unschuldigkeit": Elfriede Jelineks Rechnitz (Der Würgeengel)*, ed. Pia Janke, Teresa Kovacs, and Christian Schenkermayr (Vienna: Praesens, 2010), 31–32.

[5] Ibid., 33.

[6] Manoschek, "Nationalsozialistische Moral," 14.

[7] Ibid., 6.

[8] Kovacs, "Chronik der Ereignisse," 37.

[9] Manoschek, "Nationalsozialistische Moral," 6.

[10] David R. L. Litchfield, *The Thyssen Art Macabre* (London: Quartet Books, 2006).

[11] Litchfield, "The Killer Countess: The Dark Past of Baron Heinrich Thyssen's Daughter," *Independent*, October 6, 2007.

[12] David R. L. Litchfield, "Die Gastgeberin der Hölle," *Frankfurter Allgemeine Zeitung*, October 18, 2007.

[13] Sacha Batthyany, "Ein schreckliches Geheimnis," *Das Magazin*, December 12, 2009, 14.

[14] Manoschek, "Nationalsozialistische Moral," 6.

[15] Jossi Wieler, "Hinter den Sprachmasken," interview by Christine Diller, *Merkur*, November 26, 2008, http://www.merkur.de/kultur/hinter-sprachmasken-22478.html.

[16] See Bettina Wörgötter, "Ein erschütterndes Dokument gegen das Verdrängen," *Tiroler Tageszeitung*, March 23, 1995, 6.

[17] See N. N., "Massengrab und Grabesstille," *Kurier*, May 26, 1994.

[18] See Michael Omasta, "Stimmen des Schweigens," *Falter*, May 27, 1994, 20.

[19] Ibid.

[20] Eduard Erne, as cited in Barbara Freitag, "Vom Sterben der Erinnerung: Ein Gespräch mit Eduard Erne über seinen Film 'Totschweigen,'" *Wiener Zeitung*, September 9, 1994, 10.

[21] Bill Nichols, *Introduction to Documentary* (Bloomington: Indiana University Press, 2001), 21.

[22] Patricia Aufderheide, *Documentary Film: A Very Short Introduction* (Oxford: Oxford University Press, 2007), 2.

[23] See ibid., 10–11.

24 Ibid., 12–13.

25 Johanna Jiranek and Maria Scheucher, "Darstellungen von Endphasenverbrechen in der österreichischen Kunst am Beispiel Rechnitz," in *Der Fall Rechnitz: Das Massaker an Juden im März 1945*, ed. Walter Manoschek (Vienna: Braumüller, 2009), 185.

26 This is the English translation of "Die waren sehr arm" given in the Totschweigen DVD by translators Eyal Bazelet et al., with which I agree fully; Margareta Heinrich and Eduard Erne, Totschweigen (Vienna: Extrafilm, 1994). In Margareta Heinrich, ed. Vrääth Öhner (Vienna: Verlag Filmarchiv Austria, 2011).

27 As elaborated in the introduction to this book, the phrase "open wound" is frequently used with reference to Austria's National Socialist past. With reference to *Rechnitz*, the theater director Michael Simon, who staged the 2012 Graz production, commented that the particularity of the play for him constituted: "Der Schrecken, der auch heute immer noch da drin steckt, die Vergangenheitsbewältigung, die schlussendlich immer noch eine offene Wunde ist" (The horror that continues to dominate, the confrontation with the past that is ultimately an open wound). Michael Simon, as cited in N. N., "Jelinek als Mittel gegen das Vergessen," *orf.at*, May 16, 2012, http://steiermark.orf.at/tv/stories/2525044/.

28 Eduard Erne, as cited in Elke Schüttelkopf, "An der Grenze zum Vergessen," *Volksstimme*, March 23, 1995, 18.

29 See Krylova, "'Eine den Menschen zerzausende Landschaft': Psychotopography and the Alpine Landscape in Thomas Bernhard's 'Frost,'" *Austrian Studies* 18 (2010): 74–88.

30 Bert Rebhandl, "Unumgängliches Kino gegen falschen Frieden: 'Totschweigen,'" *Der Standard*, May 25, 1994.

31 Robert Buchschwenter, "Das Schweigen gegen die Angst," *Die Presse*, May 26, 1994.

32 Neumüller, "Erinnerung in Rechnitz," 200–202.

33 Translation from the Hungarian as given in Totschweigen DVD; Heinrich and Erne, Totschweigen (Vienna: Extrafilm, 1994).

34 Schüttelkopf, "An der Grenze zum Vergessen," 18.

35 Wieler, as cited in interview by Diller, "Hinter den Sprachmasken."

36 See Elfriede Jelinek, "'Diese falsche und verlogene Unschuldigkeit Österreichs ist wirklich immer mein Thema gewesen': Elfriede Jelinek im Gespräch mit Pia Janke," in Janke, Kovacs, and Schenkermayr, *"Die endlose Unschuldigkeit,"* 23.

37 For a comprehensive discussion of this British production (which used an English translation of *Rechnitz* by Gitta Honegger, published in 2015) in the context of cultural transfer and mediation, see Allyson Fiddler, "Reckoning

with Rechnitz: On Elfriede Jelinek, Translation and Cultural Reproduction," *Austrian Studies* 22 (2014): 199–214.

[38] Jelinek, "'Diese falsche und verlogene Unschuldigkeit,'" 17.

[39] Jelinek, *Rechnitz (Der Würgeengel)*, in *Die Kontrakte des Kaufmanns; Rechnitz (Der Würgeengel); Über Tiere* (Reinbeck: Rowohlt, 2009), 56 (hereafter cited in text as *R*). English translations are my own.

[40] See Kovacs, "Chronik der Ereignisse," 33.

[41] Pia Janke, "'Herrschsucht, ja, haben wir': Die Täter in Elfriede Jelineks *Rechnitz (Der Würgeengel)*," in Janke, Kovacs, and Schenkermayr, *"Die endlose Unschuldigkeit,"* 243.

[42] Gerhard Scheit, "*Stecken, Stab und Stangl*; *Rechnitz (Der Würgeengel)*," in *Jelinek Handbuch*, ed. Pia Janke (Stuttgart: Metzler, 2013), 159.

[43] Elfriede Jelinek, as cited in N. N., "Sieben Fragen an Elfriede Jelinek: 'Ich bin eine Autorin der Axt,'" *Nachtkritik*, 2009, http://nachtkritik-stuecke09.de/elfriede-jelinek/sieben-fragen.

[44] Julia Lochte, "Totschweigen oder die Kunst des Berichtens," in Janke, Kovacs, and Schenkermayr, *"Die endlose Unschuldigkeit,"* 412.

[45] See ibid., 413.

[46] Ibid., 412.

[47] Hans-Thies Lehmann, *Postdramatisches Theater* (Frankfurt am Main: Verlag der Autoren, 1999).

[48] See Juliane Vogel, "Drama in Austria, 1945–2000," in *A History of Austrian Literature 1918–2000*, ed. Katrin Kohl and Ritchie Robertson (Rochester, NY: Camden House, 2006), 213.

[49] Elfriede Jelinek, "Gesprochen und beglaubigt: Dankesrede zur Verleihung des Mühlheimer Dramatikerpreises 2009," in Janke, Kovacs, and Schenkermayr, *"Die endlose Unschuldigkeit,"* 454.

[50] Jelinek, "'Diese falsche und verlogene Unschuldigkeit,'" 20.

[51] Vogel, "Drama in Austria, 1945–2000," 213.

[52] Norbert Mayer, "Elfriede Jelinek lässt die Mörder unter uns sein," *Die Presse*, March 18, 2012.

[53] Fiddler, "Reckoning with Rechnitz," 208.

[54] Jelinek, "'Diese falsche und verlogene Unschuldigkeit,'" 20.

[55] See Peter Terrell, Veronika Schnorr, Wendy V. A. Morris, and Roland Breitsprecher, *Collins German Dictionary: German-English, English-German*, 4th ed. (Glasgow: HarperCollins, 1999), 733.

[56] André Jung, "'Die Sprache ist die Figur': André Jung im Gespräch mit Christian Schenkermayr," in Janke, Kovacs, and Schenkermayr, *"Die endlose Unschuldigkeit,"* 441.

[57] Jelinek, "'Diese falsche und verlogene Unschuldigkeit,'" 22.

58 Fiddler, "Reckoning with Rechnitz," 202.

59 Hannah Arendt, *Eichmann in Jerusalem: A Report on the Banality of Evil* (London: Faber, 1963).

60 Fiddler, "Reckoning with Rechnitz," 209.

61 Hermann Schmidt-Rahmer, Katrin Nottrodt, and Stephan Wetzel, "Rechnitz verstehen? Der Regisseur Hermann Schmidt-Rahmer und die Bühnenbildnerin Katrin Nottrodt im Gespräch mit dem Dramaturgen Stephan Wetzel," in *Rechnitz (Der Würgeengel) von Elfriede Jelinek* (theater program) (Düsseldorf: Düsseldorfer Schauspielhaus, 2010), 21–22.

62 See Christopher Browning, "Raul Hilberg," *Yad Vashem Studies* 35, no. 2 (2007): 11.

63 "Das sprengt jede Vorstellungskraft" (It exceeds all comprehension); Jelinek, "'Diese falsche und verlogene Unschuldigkeit,'" 17.

Chapter Four

Epigraph. Robert Schindel, interview with Robert Schindel, interview by Katya Krylova, August 18, 2015.

1 Schindel, as cited in Paterno, "Robert Schindel."

2 Robert Schindel, *Der Kalte* (Frankfurt am Main: Suhrkamp, 2013); hereafter cited in text as *DK*. Translations from the German are my own.

3 Wolfgang Paterno asserts that *Der Kalte* is a novel "in dem die Waldheim-Affäre erstmals literarisch aufbereitet wird" (in which the Waldheim affair undergoes a literary treatment for the first time), in "Robert Schindel." This is not the case. Earlier literary treatments of the Waldheim affair include Elfriede Jelinek's 1987 dramolet *Präsident Abendwind* (President Abendwind), available at http://www.elfriedejelinek.com/fabendwn.htm (accessed December 12, 2016). For a discussion of this, see Fiddler, "Staging Jörg Haider," 357–58. Thomas Bernhard's *Heldenplatz* (1988) also makes oblique references to the Waldheim affair, at the height of which the play was written, as do novels, such as, for example, Doron Rabinovici's *Ohnehin* (2004), which centers on a younger generation's confrontation with a former SS-man, who, in his old age, begins to recollect his war years with acute clarity.

4 Schindel, Interview with Robert Schindel by Krylova.

5 Schindel, *Gebürtig*, 9th ed. (Frankfurt am Main: Suhrkamp, 2012); Schindel, *Born-Where*, trans. Michael Roloff (Riverside, CA: Ariadne Press, 1995); Robert Schindel and Lukas Stepanik, *Gebürtig* (Vienna: Cult Film/Extra Film, 2002).

6 Schindel, "Der Kalte: Erstes Kapital (Als ob)," *Manuskripte* 38, no. 141 (1998). A longer version of the chapter draft was published in a special issue of *Text + Kritik* in April 2007: Schindel, "Beginn des Romans 'Der Kalte': Erstes Kapitel (Als ob)," *Text + Kritik* 174 (2007): 52–68.

[7] Schindel, Interview with Robert Schindel by Krylova.

[8] See Robert Schindel and Martin Pollack, "'Wir kannten unsere Väter nicht.' Hat Pollacks Vater Schindels Mutter verhört? Ein Gespräch," in *Linz, Randgeschichten*, ed. Alfred Pittertschatscher (Vienna: Picus, 2009), 291.

[9] Ibid., 296–97.

[10] Ibid., 297.

[11] Ibid.

[12] Ibid.

[13] Ibid.

[14] Schindel, Interview with Robert Schindel by Krylova.

[15] Matti Bunzl, "Political Inscription, Artistic Reflection: A Recontextualization of Contemporary Viennese-Jewish Literature," *German Quarterly* 73, no. 2 (2000): 168.

[16] The last date in the novel (in the epilogue) is given as February 26, 1986, in Schindel, *Gebürtig*, 341.

[17] These include images of Waldheim used in a protagonist's cabaret program, a news bulletin playing on the TV screen in the background of a scene, with an item about the unfolding scandal, and a reference to Waldheim's election slogans deterring the exiled Hermann Gebirtig from returning to Vienna.

[18] Reiter, *Contemporary Jewish Writing*, 23.

[19] Lorenz, "The Struggle for a Civil Society and Beyond," 37–38.

[20] Robert Schindel, as cited in Paterno, "Robert Schindel."

[21] See Tobias Lindemann, "Robert Schindel-Interview zu seinem Roman 'Der Kalte' über die Waldheim-Jahre in Österreich," *Stoffwechsel* (freie-radios.net), http://www.freie-radios.net/56812 (accessed August 14, 2016); Paterno, "Robert Schindel"; Beilein, *86 und die Folgen*, 311–12.

[22] Beller, *A Concise History of Austria*, 287.

[23] Ibid.

[24] See N. N., "Mann ohne Eigenschaften," *Der Spiegel*, March 10, 1986.

[25] See Jacob Heilbrunn, "Waldheim and His Protectors," review of *Betrayal: The Untold Story of the Kurt Waldheim Investigation and Cover-Up*, by Eli M. Rosenbaum with William Hoffer, *New York Times*, October 10, 1993.

[26] Hubertus Czernin, "Waldheim und die SA," *profil*, March 3, 1986, 16–20, as cited in Cornelius Lehnguth, *Waldheim und die Folgen: Der parteipolitische Umgang mit dem Nationalsozialismus in Österreich* (Frankfurt am Main: Campus Verlag, 2013), 93.

[27] See Lehnguth, *Waldheim und die Folgen*, 93.

[28] See Beller, *A Concise History of Austria*, 288.

[29] Ibid.

[30] Ibid.

[31] See N. N., "'Wir Österreicher wählen, wen wir wollen,'" *Der Spiegel*, April 14, 1986.
[32] Beller, *A Concise History of Austria*, 290.
[33] Ibid., 291.
[34] See Pick, *Guilty Victim*, 162.
[35] *Kurier*, November 18, 1987, as cited in Lehnguth, *Waldheim und die Folgen*, 115.
[36] N. N., "The Moscow Declaration."
[37] See Tony Judt, *Postwar: A History of Europe since 1945* (London: Pimlico, 2007), 808.
[38] See Lindemann, "Robert Schindel-Interview zu seinem Roman 'Der Kalte'"
[39] As Stefan Zweig asserted, the first pages that a Viennese would turn to in his morning newspaper would inevitably be the theater listings, as opposed to the national or international news, in *Die Welt von Gestern: Erinnerungen eines Europäers* (Frankfurt am Main: Fischer, 2001), 30.
[40] See Cornelius Hell, "Der Kalte: Roman von Robert Schindel," *oe1.orf.at*, February 14, 2013, http://oe1.orf.at/artikel/331361.
[41] See Thomas E. Schmidt, "Wien, die Skandalmaschine," *Die Zeit*, April 11, 2013.
[42] See ibid.; Franz Haas, "Zeitgeschichte als Wiener Melange," *Neue Zürcher Zeitung*, April 13, 2013; Wolf Scheller, "Wiener Walzer rechtsherum," *Jüdische Allgemeine*, March 21, 2013.
[43] Schindel, as cited in Stefan Gmunder, "Wenn Fragen vor Selbstgerechtigkeit schützen," *Der Standard*, February 21, 2013.
[44] See Klara Obermüller, "Nachrichten aus dem Operettenland," *Die Welt*, April 20, 2013.
[45] Schindel, Interview with Robert Schindel by Krylova.
[46] Manoschek, "Die Generation Waldheim," 128–29.
[47] Freud, *Der Mann Moses*, 459–581.
[48] Ibid., 493.
[49] James E. Young, *The Texture of Memory: Holocaust Memorials and Meaning* (New Haven, CT: Yale University Press, 1993), 105.
[50] See N. N., "Mahnmal gegen Krieg und Faschismus," *Zentrale Österreichische Forschungsstelle Nachkriegsjustiz*, http://www.nachkriegsjustiz.at/vgew/1010_alb.php (accessed August 14, 2016).
[51] Young, *The Texture of Memory*, 105.
[52] See ibid., 105–6.
[53] Pierre Nora, "Between Memory and History: Les Lieux de Mémoire," *Representations* 26 (1989): 7–24.

⁵⁴ Aleida Assmann, *Erinnerungsräume: Formen und Wandlungen des kulturellen Gedächtnisses* (Munich: Beck, 1999).

⁵⁵ Eva Kuttenberg, "Austria's Topography of Memory: Heldenplatz, Albertinaplatz, Judenplatz, and Beyond," *German Quarterly* 80, no. 4 (2007): 469.

⁵⁶ Young, *The Texture of Memory*, 112.

⁵⁷ See Erich Klein, *Denkwürdiges Wien: Gehen & Sehen: 3 Routen zu Mahnmalen,Gedenkstätten und Orten der Erinnerung der Ersten und Zweiten Republik* (Vienna: Falter, 2004), 103.

⁵⁸ David Art, *The Politics of the Nazi Past in Germany and Austria* (Cambridge: Cambridge University Press, 2006), 125.

⁵⁹ Beckermann, *Unzugehörig*, 14.

⁶⁰ Heidemarie Uhl, "Renaissance des Denkmals in der Postmoderne: Kunst als Medium der neuen Erinnerungskultur," in *Denk!mal Zukunft: Der Umgang mit historischem Kulturgut im Spannungsfeld von Gesellschaft, Forschung und Praxis*, ed. Eva Klein, Rosemarie Schiestl, and Margit Stadlober (Graz, 2012), 123–24.

⁶¹ Beckermann, *Unzugehörig*, 15.

⁶² Title of chapter in G. E. R. Gedye, *Fallen Bastions: The Central European Tragedy* (London: Victor Gollancz, 1939).

⁶³ Beckermann, *Unzugehörig*, 15.

⁶⁴ See Matti Bunzl, "On the Politics and Semantics of Austrian Memory: Vienna's Monument against War and Fascism," *History and Memory* 7, no. 2 (1995): 28–29.

⁶⁵ See Lorenz, "The Struggle for a Civil Society and Beyond," 26.

⁶⁶ Ibid., 26.

⁶⁷ Lorenz, "Austrian Responses to National Socialism and the Holocaust," 193.

Chapter Five

Epigraph. Doron Rabinovici, *Ohnehin* (Frankfurt am Main: Suhrkamp, 2004), 92.

¹ Heidemarie Uhl, "Die Wiederentdeckung der Orte."

² Ibid., 52.

³ Ibid.

⁴ Heidemarie Uhl, "Denkmäler als Symbole des Geschichtsbewußtseins in der Zweiten Republik," in *Grenzenloses Österreich. Dokumentation 5* (Vienna: Bundesministerium für Wissenschaft und Verkehr, 1997), 109–28.

⁵ Ibid., 109.

⁶ Ibid.

[7] See Heidemarie Uhl, "Renaissance des Denkmals in der Postmoderne," 123.

[8] Ibid., 123–24.

[9] Uhl, "Denkmäler als Symbole des Geschichtsbewußtseins in der Zweiten Republik."

[10] See N. N., "porem-Politics of Remembrance and the Transition of Public Spaces. A Political and Social Analysis of Vienna, 1995–2015," *Politics of Remembrance*, http://porem.univie.ac.at/ (accessed August 16, 2016).

[11] Peter Pirker, "Time, Space, Meaning and Actors: Reflections on the Study of Politics of Remembrance" (German Studies Association Thirty-Ninth Annual Conference, Washington, DC, 2015).

[12] Daniel Benyes, *Erinnern für die Zukunft: Wien und seine Gedächtniskultur/Remembrance for the Future: Vienna's Culture of Remembrance* (Vienna: Stadt Wien, 2014).

[13] Ibid., 3.

[14] Ibid., 8.

[15] See N. N., "Best of 2013–15: Das Fest zum Tag der Befreiung," *Fest der Freude*, http://www.festderfreude.at/de/das-fest/best-2013-15 (accessed August 16, 2016).

[16] Magnus Koch, "Conflicting Memories: Commemorating World War II at Heldenplatz/ Ballhausplatz" (German Studies Association Thirty-Ninth Annual Conference, Washington, DC, 2015).

[17] See N. N., "HistorikerInnen-Bericht über Wiens Straßennamen," *wien.at*, https://www.wien.gv.at/kultur/strassennamen/strassennamenpruefung.html (accessed August 16, 2016).

[18] Benyes, *Erinnern für die Zukunft*, 38.

[19] Peter Autengruber, Birgit Nemec, Oliver Rathkolb, and Florian Wenninger, *Umstrittene Wiener Straßennamen: Ein kritisches Lesebuch* (Vienna: Pichler, 2014).

[20] N. N., "Unsere Stadt! Jüdisches Wien bis heute," *Jüdisches Museum Wien*, http://www.jmw.at/de/exhibitions/unsere-stadt-juedisches-wien-bis-heute (accessed August 19, 2016).

[21] As city of Vienna authorities are keen to stress, sometimes it is "more effective to draw attention to this facet and thus to add plaques with biographical information alongside the respective street signs, as simply exchanging one name for another would merely mean consigning controversial personalities to oblivion," in Benyes, *Erinnern für die Zukunft*, 38.

[22] See "Gedenkbuch für die Opfer des Nationalsozialismus an der Universität Wien 1938," *Universität Wien*, March 5, 2013, http://medienportal.univie.ac.at/uniview/forschung/detailansicht/artikel/gedenkbuch-fuer-die-opfer-das-nationalsozialismus-an-der-universitaet-wien-1938/.

23 See Herbert Posch, "DENK-MAL Marpe Lanefesch: Ehemaliges jüdisches Bethaus im Alten Allgemeinen Krankenhaus 1903–2015," *Universität Wien*, last modified December 21, 2015, http://geschichte.univie.ac.at/de/artikel/denk-mal-marpe-lanefesch.

24 See APA, "NS-Aufarbeitung: Wiener Philharmoniker präsentieren Ergebnisse," *Kurier*, March 10, 2013.

25 Michael Wurmitzer, "Haus der Geschichte: Vorstudie präsentiert, Eröffnung doch erst 2019," *Der Standard*, May 4, 2016.

26 Young, *The Texture of Memory*, 8.

27 Ibid., 30.

28 Ibid., 5.

29 Ibid.

30 Ibid., 30.

31 Ibid., 3.

32 Bill Niven, "From Countermonument to Combimemorial: Developments in German Memorialisation," in *"Holocaust"-Fiktion: Kunst jenseits der Authentizität*, ed. Iris Roebling-Grau and Dirk Rupnow (Paderborn: Fink, 2015), 183–97.

33 Ibid., 189.

34 Ibid.

35 "The Missing Image" is the name of Ruth Beckermann's 2015 installation on Vienna's Albertinaplatz.

36 Karen Frostig, "Project Description," *The Vienna Project*, http://theviennaproject.org/project-details/ (accessed August 16, 2016).

37 Niven, "From Countermonument to Combimemorial," 191.

38 See APA, "'Vorgehaltener Filter' für NS-Wandbild," *Der Standard*, May 8, 2002.

39 See Nora Höglinger, ed., *Kunst im Öffentlichen Raum* (leaflet), 3rd ed. (Vienna: Kunst im öffentichen Raum GmbH, 2015).

40 See APA, "'Vorgehaltener Filter' für NS-Wandbild."

41 Maria Theresa Litschauer, "Text der Schrifttafel: [transkription]," *Kunst im öffentlichen Raum Wien*, 2009, http://www.koer.or.at/cgi-bin/page.pl?id=202&lang=de.

42 Ibid.

43 Ibid.

44 Ibid.

45 Ibid.

46 Oliver Rathkolb, "Permanente Intervention: Maria Theresia Litschauer," *Kunst im öffentlichen Raum Wien*, accessed August 16, 2016, http://www.koer.or.at/cgi-bin/page.pl?id=129;lang=de.

⁴⁷ See John McHardy Sinclair, ed., *Collins Concise Dictionary*, 4th ed. (Glasgow: HarperCollins Publishers, 1999), 1580.

⁴⁸ Rathkolb, "Permanente Intervention."

⁴⁹ Uhl, "Die Wiederentdeckung der Orte."

⁵⁰ See N. N., "Gedenksymbol Servitengasse. Schlüssel gegen das Vergessen," accessed August 16, 2016, http://www.koer.or.at/cgi-bin/page.pl?id=39;lang=de.

⁵¹ Niven, "From Countermonument to Combimemorial," 189.

⁵² See Oona Kroisleitner and Maria von Usslar, "Ein Andenken an Leid und Unrecht am Alsergrund," *Der Standard*, August 22, 2016.

⁵³ A stele is defined as "an upright stone slab or column decorated with figures or inscriptions" and as "a prepared vertical surface that has a commemorative inscription or design, esp. one on the face of a building." See Sinclair, ed., *Collins Concise Dictionary*, 1456.

⁵⁴ N. N., "Enthüllung der Gedenkstele in der Fluchtgasse 7," *Gedenkprojekt Volksopernviertel 1938*, accessed August 23, 2016, http://www.volksopernviertel1938.at/. Incidentally, the Fluchtgasse (literally: Exodus Street) was given its name in 1862, after the nearby house sign, erected in circa 1808, "Zur Flucht nach Ägypten" (At the Flight to Egypt). See N. N., "Fluchtgasse," *Wien Geschichte Wiki*, May 23, 2016, https://www.wien.gv.at/wiki/index.php/Fluchtgasse.

⁵⁵ See Stolpersteine, Twitter post, @_Stolpersteine_, November 6, 2015, 2:35 a.m., https://twitter.com/_Stolpersteine_/status/662579004831105024.

⁵⁶ See N. N., "Ich möchte einen Stein," *Steine der Erinnerung*, accessed August 16, 2016, http://steinedererinnerung.net/mein-beitrag/mein-stein/.

⁵⁷ Sidney Rosenfeld, *Understanding Joseph Roth* (Columbia: University of South Carolina Press, 2001), 9.

⁵⁸ See N. N., "Projekte," *Steine der Erinnerung*, http://steinedererinnerung.net/projekte/ (accessed August 16, 2016).

⁵⁹ N. N., "Vermittlung," *Steine der Erinnerung*, http://steinedererinnerung.net/vermittlung/ (accessed August 23, 2016).

⁶⁰ See Andrea Strutz, "Split Lives: Memories and Narratives of Austrian Jewish Refugees," in *New Perspectives on Austrians and World War II*, ed. Gunter Bischof, Fritz Plasser, and Barbara Stelzl-Marx (New Brunswick, NJ: Transaction Publishers, 2009), 182–99.

⁶¹ Frostig, "Project Description."

⁶² Ibid.

⁶³ Frostig, "Mapping 1938 Vienna." Kickstarter video, 2:51. Posted April 2013. https://www.kickstarter.com/projects/130272597/mapping-1938-vienna/description.

64 Frostig, "Project Description."

65 Frostig, "The Vienna Project: From Opening to Close (English)," YouTube video, 9:59, posted by The Vienna Project, October 18, 2015, https://www.youtube.com/watch?v=035ILIa2n9Y.

66 Frostig, "Project Description."

67 Frostig, "Home," *The Vienna Project*, http://theviennaproject.org/ (accessed August 17, 2016).

68 See this Kickstarter video and web page: Frostig, "Mapping 1938 Vienna."

69 Karen Frostig, "Research," *The Vienna Project*, http://theviennaproject.org/research/ (accessed August 17, 2016).

70 Frostig, "Project Description."

71 Frostig, "Mapping 1938 Vienna."

72 Ibid.

73 Niven, "From Countermonument to Combimemorial," 189.

74 CSS Gmbh, "The Vienna Project," Google Play, Vers. 1.0 (2013), https://play.google.com/store/apps/details?id=at.roommint.theviennaproject (accessed August 17, 2016).

75 Wiener Digital Manufaktur, "Jewish Vienna: Between the Museums," Google Play, Vers. 2.1.0 (2015), https://play.google.com/store/apps/details?id=at.jmw.betweenthemuseums (accessed August 17, 2016).

76 Niven, "From Countermonument to Combimemorial," 191.

77 Edmund de Waal, *The Hare with Amber Eyes* (London: Vintage, 2011).

78 Frostig, "Research."

79 See Frostig, "Public Programs 2013–2014," *The Vienna Project*, http://theviennaproject.org/installations/ (accessed August 17, 2016).

80 See Frostig, "Memory Map," *The Vienna Project*, http://theviennaproject.org/memory-map/ (accessed August 17, 2016).

81 Ibid.

82 Ibid.

83 See N. N., "The Memory Map," *Jüdisches Museum Wien*, http://www.jmw.at/de/exhibitions/memory-map-eine-topologie-des-gedenkens-0 (accessed August 17, 2016).

84 Frostig, "Closing Events," *The Vienna Project*, http://theviennaproject.org/closing-events/ (accessed August 17, 2016).

85 Frostig, "The Vienna Project: From Opening to Close (English)," YouTube video.

86 Frostig, "Closing Speeches from the National Library" YouTube video, 6:11, posted by The Vienna Project, October 18, 2015, https://www.youtube.com/watch?v=XGPPoa-NryM.

87 Frostig, "Closing Events."

⁸⁸ Frostig, "Collecting Archival Letters for Closing Ceremony," *The Vienna Project*, http://theviennaproject.org/call-for-archival-letters-for-the-vienna-projects-closing-ceremony/ (accessed August 17, 2016).

⁸⁹ Ibid.

⁹⁰ See N. N., "The Vienna Project Archival Letters Submission," *The Vienna Project*, http://www.jotform.us/form/41144022369144 (accessed August 17, 2016).

⁹¹ Simone Osthoff, *Performing the Archive: The Transformation of the Archive in Contemporary Art from Repository of Documents to Art Medium* (New York: Atropos Press, 2009).

⁹² Frostig, "Project Details."

⁹³ See Frostig, "Board," *The Vienna Project*, http://theviennaproject.org/advisory-board/ (accessed August 17, 2016).

⁹⁴ Frostig, "Citizenship after Genocide: Materializing Memory Through Art Activism," in *Beyond Citizenship? Feminism and the Transformation of Belonging*, ed. Sasha Roseneil (Basingstoke: Palgrave Macmillan, 2013), 217.

⁹⁵ Ibid.

⁹⁶ Niven, "From Countermonument to Combimemorial," 189.

⁹⁷ Benjamin, "Über den Begriff der Geschichte," 697.

⁹⁸ Ibid., 704.

⁹⁹ During a research visit to Vienna in August 2014, I observed that, due to attrition, a number of the stencils were no longer visible in the places where they should be.

¹⁰⁰ Frostig, "Mapping 1938 Vienna."

¹⁰¹ See N. N., "Presseaussendung: Alltagsskulpturen Mahnmal," *Kunst im öffentlichen Raum Wien*, http://www.koer.or.at/cgi-bin/file.pl?id=1487 (accessed August 17, 2016).

¹⁰² The texts and authors' biographies are reproduced in an accompanying booklet to the memorial project: Catrin Bolt, *Alltagsskulpturen Mahnmal* (Vienna: REMAprint, 2014). Here, 34.

¹⁰³ Bolt, *Alltagsskulpturen Mahnmal*, 35.

¹⁰⁴ Ibid., 36.

¹⁰⁵ Ibid., 42.

¹⁰⁶ N. N., "Presseaussendung: Alltagsskulpturen Mahnmal."

¹⁰⁷ Ibid.

¹⁰⁸ See, for example, "Alltagsskulpturen Mahnmal (Franzensbrücke)," YouTube video, 1:59, posted by myllernet, May 10, 2015, https://www.youtube.com/watch?v=MPnBdlK9MX4.

109 See APA, "Mahnmal für 'Kindertransporte': Skulptur am Westbahnhof," *Vienna.at*, March 14, 2008, http://www.vienna.at/mahnmal-fr-kindertransporte-skulptur-am-westbahnhof/news-20080314-04005592.

110 See Frances A. Yates, *The Art of Memory* (London: Routledge and K. Paul, 1966), 1–2.

111 See Margaretha Kopeinig, "Eine 'Hetz' bei der 'Reibpartie,'" *Kurier*, March 11, 2015.

112 Ruth Beckermann, "The Missing Image: An Installation as Intervention" (Contemporary Austrian Literature, Film and Culture: International Conference, University of Nottingham, UK, 2015).

113 See N. N., "Installation zeigt Erniedrigung bei 'Reibpartie,'" *orf.at*, March 12, 2015, http://wien.orf.at/news/stories/2699168/.

114 Beckermann, as cited in N. N., "Installation zeigt Erniedrigung bei 'Reibpartie.'"

115 Ibid.

116 Ibid.

117 Beckermann, "The Missing Image: An Installation as Intervention."

118 Beckermann, as cited in Margaretha Kopeinig, "Eine 'Hetz' bei der 'Reibpartie.'"

119 See Thomas Trenkler, "Beckermann-Installation 'The Missing Image' in Wien abgebaut," *Kurier*, January 4, 2016.

120 See APA, "Beckermann-Installation 'The Missing Image' kann vorerst bleiben," *Der Standard*, November 19, 2015.

121 See APA, "Kulturschaffende fordern Verbleib von Gedenkinstallation 'The Missing Image,'" *Der Standard*, September 24, 2015; APA, "Beckermann-Installation 'The Missing Image' kann vorerst bleiben."

122 See N. N., "Filmemacherin Ruth Beckermann mit Ehrenkreuz ausgezeichnet," *Kleine Zeitung*, October 9, 2015.

123 See Trenkler, "Beckermann-Installation 'The Missing Image' in Wien abgebaut."

124 Beckermann, "The Missing Image: An Installation as Intervention."

125 See Ruth Beckermann, "Déjà-vu," *ruthbeckermann.com*, http://www.ruthbeckermann.com/home.php?il=103&l=deu (accessed August 17, 2016).

126 See Nihad Amara, "Zwei Welten prallten bei Demos vor Asylwerberheim aufeinander," *Kurier*, June 3, 2015.

127 See red., APA., "Foto von FPÖ-Protest: 'Kurier' klagt Strache," *Der Standard*, June 11, 2015.

128 See images at Beckermann, "Déjà-vu."

129 Ibid.

[130] See Johanna Hager, "Kurier-Foto künstlerisch verfremdet: 'Déjà-vu' statt 'Reibpartie,'" *Kurier*, June 19, 2015.

[131] Ruth Beckermann, "Déjà-vu."

[132] See Karin Schiefer, "'Der Film ist für mich auch ein Ausdruck einer Ratlosigkeit über den Zustand Europas und seiner Umgebung.' Ruth Beckermann über *Those Who Go Those Who Stay*," *ruthbeckermann.com*, October 2013, http://www.ruthbeckermann.com/aduploads/93.02.ma,austrianfilmcommission-interviews.pdf.

[133] Ruth Beckermann in a conversation with the author, August 11, 2015.

[134] See Stefan Musil, "Ein neuer Erinnerungsort in der Wiener Gedächtnislandschaft," in *Turnertempel Erinnerungsort: Suche nach einer reflexiven Archäologie*, ed. Sonja Huber and Stefan Musil (Nuremberg: Verlag für Moderne Kunst, 2012), 14.

[135] See Hubert Lobnig and János Kárász, "Der Turnertempel: Auf der Suche nach einer reflexiven Archäologie," in Huber and Musil, *Turnertempel Erinnerungsort*, 35.

[136] See ibid., 36.

[137] Musil, "Ein neuer Erinnerungsort in der Wiener Gedächtnislandschaft," 14.

[138] Ibid.

[139] Young, *The Texture of Memory*, 5.

[140] See Bettina Leidl, "Vorwort," in Huber and Musil, *Turnertempel Erinnerungsort*, 7.

[141] Lobnig and Kárász, "Der Turnertempel," 34.

[142] Ibid.

[143] Young, *The Texture of Memory*, 30.

[144] Lobnig and Kárász, "Der Turnertempel," 34.

[145] Marc Augé, *Non-Places: Introduction to an Anthropology of Supermodernity*, trans. John Howe (London: Verso, 1995), 96.

[146] See Musil, "Ein neuer Erinnerungsort in der Wiener Gedächtnislandschaft," 16.

[147] Ibid., 14.

[148] See Höglinger, ed., *Kunst im öffentlichen Raum*.

[149] See Lobnig and Kárász, "Der Turnertempel," 36.

[150] Ibid., 37.

[151] Ibid., 34.

[152] Rabinovici, *Ohnehin*, 92.

Conclusion

Epigraph. Thomas Hood, "Ode: Autumn," *Poems* (London: E. Moxon, 1857), 344.

[1] See N. N., "Über uns," *Israelitische Kultusgemeinde Wien*, http://www.ikg-wien.at/?page_id=304 (accessed August 25, 2016).

[2] "Politische Wende" is a term that is frequently used in connection with the 1999 general election in Austria leading to the formation of the ÖVP-FPÖ coalition government in February 2000. See, for example: Anita Moser, *Die Kunst der Grenzüberschreitung: Postkoloniale Kritik im Spannungsfeld von Ästhetik und Politik* (Bielefeld: transcript, 2011), 105.

[3] Beckermann, "*The Missing Image*: An Installation as Intervention" (Contemporary Austrian Literature, Film and Culture: International Conference, University of Nottingham, UK, 2015).

[4] Assmann, *Der lange Schatten der Vergangenheit*, 278.

[5] Robert Schindel's third volume in his planned trilogy on the legacy of National Socialism in Austria, and Ruth Beckermann's forthcoming film about the Waldheim affair are both cases in point here.

[6] See Michael Wurmitzer, "Haus der Geschichte: Vorstudie präsentiert, Eröffnung doch erst 2019," *Der Standard*, May 4, 2016.

[7] Kunst im öffentlichen Raum GmbH, *Denkmal für die Verfolgten der NS-Militärjustiz: Olaf Nicolai 2014* (Vienna: Kunst im öffentichen Raum GmbH, 2014).

[8] See Peter Mayr, "Denkmal für Wehrmachtsdeserteure: Anfang, nicht Ende," *Der Standard*, October 24, 2014.

[9] See chronology in Peter Mayr, "Ein Denkmal für die Opfer der NS-Militärjustiz," *Der Standard*, October 20, 2014.

[10] Ibid.

[11] See Bethany Bell, "Austria Unveils World War Two Deserters' Memorial," *BBC News*, October 24, 2014, http://www.bbc.com/news/world-europe-29754386.

[12] See N. N., "Späte Rehabilitation: Deserteursdenkmal enthüllt," *orf.at*, October 24, 2014, http://wien.orf.at/news/stories/2675377/.

[13] See Elizabeth Miller, "Getting to Know the Un-Dead: Bram Stoker, Vampires and Dracula," in *Vampires: Myths and Metaphors of Enduring Evil*, ed. Peter Day (Amsterdam, NY: Rodopi, 2006), 16.

Bibliography

Adorno, Theodor W. "Was bedeutet: Aufarbeitung der Vergangenheit." In *Kulturkritik und Gesellschaft II: Eingriffe; Stichworte; Anhang.* Vol. 10.2 of *Theodor W. Adorno: Gesammelte Schriften*, edited by Rolf Tiedemann, 555–72. Frankfurt am Main: Suhrkamp, 1977.

Amara, Nihad. "Zwei Welten prallten bei Demos vor Asylwerberheim aufeinander." *Kurier*, June 3, 2015.

APA. "Beckermann-Installation 'The Missing Image' kann vorerst bleiben." *Der Standard*, November 19, 2015.

———. "Ein Drittel der Österreicher sehnt sich nach 'starkem Führer.'" *Der Standard*, May 7, 2014.

———."Fischer: 500.000 Flüchtlinge durch Österreich bis Jahresende." *Der Standard*, October 26, 2015.

———. "Holocaust-Überlebende warnt vor rechter Rhetorik bei Bundespräsidentenwahlkampf." *Der Standard*, November 26, 2016.

———. "Kulturschaffende fordern Verbleib von Gedenkinstallation 'The Missing Image.'" *Der Standard*, September 24, 2015.

———. "Mahnmal für 'Kindertransporte': Skulptur am Westbahnhof." *Vienna.at*, March 14, 2008. http://www.vienna.at/mahnmal-fr-kindertransporte-skulptur-am-westbahnhof/news-20080314-04005592.

———. "Ministerrat fixiert 2. Oktober als Stichwahl-Termin." *Der Standard*, July 5, 2016.

———. "Mitterlehner, Karmasin offen für Van der Bellen—Lopatka für Hofer." *Der Standard*, November 24, 2016.

———. "Nicht nur Opfer, auch Täter." *Kurier*, March 12, 2013.

———. "NS-Aufarbeitung: Wiener Philharmoniker präsentieren Ergebnisse." *Kurier*, March 10, 2013.

———. "'Vorgehaltener Filter' für NS-Wandbild." *Der Standard*, May 8, 2002.

Arendt, Hannah. *Eichmann in Jerusalem: A Report on the Banality of Evil.* London: Faber, 1963.

Art, David. *The Politics of the Nazi Past in Germany and Austria.* Cambridge: Cambridge University Press, 2006.

Assmann, Aleida. *Der lange Schatten der Vergangenheit: Erinnerungskultur und Geschichtspolitik.* Munich: Beck, 2006.

———. *Erinnerungsräume: Formen und Wandlungen des kulturellen Gedächtnisses.* Munich: Beck, 1999.

Aufderheide, Patricia. *Documentary Film: A Very Short Introduction.* Oxford: Oxford University Press, 2007.

Augé, Marc. *Non-Places: Introduction to an Anthropology of Supermodernity*. Translated by John Howe. London: Verso, 1995.
Autengruber, Peter, Birgit Nemec, Oliver Rathkolb, and Florian Wenninger. *Umstrittene Wiener Straßennamen: Ein kritisches Lesebuch*. Vienna: Pichler, 2014.
Bachmann, Ingeborg. "Das Buch Franza (Todesarten), Textstufe III, Vorreden." In *"Todesarten"-Projekt: Kritische Ausgabe*, edited by Monika Albrecht and Dirk Göttsche, 2:71–78. Munich: Piper, 1995.
———. "Der Umgang mit Namen." In *Essays, Reden, Vermischte Schriften, Anhang*. Vol. 4 of *Ingeborg Bachmann: Werke*, edited by Christine Koschel, Inge von Weidenbaum, and Clemens Münster, 238–55. Munich: Piper, 1978.
Back, Otto, et al. *Österreichisches Wörterbuch: Schulausgabe*. 41st ed. Vienna: ÖBV, 2009.
Baker, Frederick. "Der 19. Februar 2000: Die Geburt eines Widerstands-Oratoriums." In Baker and Boyer, *Wiener Wandertage*, 171–77.
———. "Widerstand in Haiderland: Masse ohne Macht?" Film screening introduced by the director, Frederick Baker, at the Contemporary Austrian Literature, Film and Culture: International Conference, University of Nottingham, UK, April 13–15, 2015.
———. *Widerstand in Haiderland—Masse ohne Macht?* Vienna: Filmbäckerei, 2010.
Baker, Frederick, and Elisabeth Boyer. "Chronologie der Ereignisse." In Baker and Boyer, *Wiener Wandertage*, 491–501.
———. "Statistiken." In Baker and Boyer, *Wiener Wandertage*, 503–5.
———. "Vorbemerkung." In Baker and Boyer, *Wiener Wandertage*, 7–8.
———, eds. *Wiener Wandertage: Die Demonstrationskultur gegen die Haider-Schüssel-Koalition; Reden, Texte, Berichte (2000–2002)*. 2nd ed. Klagenfurt: Wieser, 2010.
Baker, Frederick, and Petra Herczeg, eds. *Die beschämte Republik: 10 Jahre nach Schwarz-Blau in Österreich*. Vienna: Czernin, 2010.
Barthes, Roland. *Camera Lucida: Reflections on Photography*. London: Vintage, 2000.
Batthyany, Sacha. "Ein schreckliches Geheimnis." *Das Magazin*, December 12, 2009, 13–27.
Beckermann, Ruth. "Auf der Brücke: Rede zur Verleihung des Manès Sperber-Preises, Wien, 16/10/2000." *German Quarterly* 74, no. 1 (2001): 1–7.
———. "Déjà-vu." *ruthbeckermann.com*. Accessed August 17, 2016. http://www.ruthbeckermann.com/home.php?il=103&l=deu.
———. *Die Mazzesinsel: Juden in der Wiener Leopoldstadt 1918–1938*. Vienna: Löcker, 1984.
———. *Die papierene Brücke*. Vienna: Filmladen/Ruth Beckermann, 1987.
———. "Die Verhaftung: Vier Tage in Czernowitz, das einmal eine österreichische Stadt war." *profil* 15, no. 34 (August 19, 1985): 44–56.

———. *Ein flüchtiger Zug nach dem Orient*. Vienna: Aichholzer Filmproduktion, 1999.
———. *Homemad(e)*. Vienna: Ruth Beckermann Filmproduktion, 2001.
———. "Homemad(e)." *ruthbeckermann.com*. Accessed August 10, 2016. http://www.ruthbeckermann.com/home.php?il=14&l=eng.
———. "Ich nenne es 'Austronazismus.'" *Der Standard*, November 1, 1999.
———. "Interview Bert Rebhandl/ Ruth Beckermann, August 9, 2007." *Wien retour* (Vienna: Filmladen, 1983). DVD Ruth Beckermann-Filmproduktion 2007.
———. *Jenseits des Krieges (East of War)*. Vienna: Aichholzer Filmproduktion, 1996.
———. "The Missing Image: An Installation as Intervention." Paper presented at the Contemporary Austrian Literature, Film and Culture: International Conference, University of Nottingham, UK, April 13–15, 2015.
———. "Oktober bis November 1995: Das Drehtagebuch." In *Jenseits des Krieges: ehemalige Wehrmachtssoldaten erinnern sich*, 85–98. Vienna: Döcker, 1998.
———. *Unzugehörig: Österreicher und Juden nach 1945*. Vienna: Löcker, 1989.
Beckermann, Ruth, and Josef Aichholzer. *Wien retour*. Vienna: Filmladen, 1983.
Beckermann, Ruth, and Elfriede Jelinek. "Ein Gespräch." In *Stadtkino Programm 110: Ruth Beckermann, Die papierene Brücke*, 2–4. Vienna: Stadtkino, 1987.
Beilein, Matthias. *86 und die Folgen: Robert Schindel, Robert Menasse und Doron Rabinovici im literarischen Feld Österreichs*. Berlin: Schmidt, 2008.
Bell, Bethany. "Austria Unveils World War Two Deserters' Memorial." *BBC News*, October 24, 2014. http://www.bbc.com/news/world-europe-29754386.
Beller, Steven. *A Concise History of Austria*. Cambridge: Cambridge University Press, 2006.
Benjamin, Walter. "Das Kunstwerk im Zeitalter seiner technischen Reproduzierbarkeit." In *Aufsätze, Essays, Vorträge*. Vol. 2.2 of *Walter Benjamin: Gesammelte Schriften*, edited by Rolf Tiedemann and Hermann Schweppenhäuser, 431–509. Frankfurt am Main: Suhrkamp, 1974.
———. "Über den Begriff der Geschichte." In *Abhandlungen*. Vol. 1.2 of *Walter Benjamin: Gesammelte Schriften*, edited by Rolf Tiedemann and Hermann Schweppenhäuser, 691–704. Frankfurt am Main: Suhrkamp, 1974.
———. *Ursprung des deutschen Trauerspiels*. In *Abhandlungen*. Vol. 1.1 of *Walter Benjamin: Gesammelte Schriften*, edited by Rolf Tiedemann and Hermann Schweppenhäuser, 203–431. Frankfurt am Main: Suhrkamp, 1974.
Benyes, Daniel. *Erinnern für die Zukunft: Wien und seine Gedächtniskultur/ Remembrance for the Future: Vienna's Culture of Remembrance*. Vienna: Stadt Wien, 2014.

Bernhard, Thomas. *Heldenplatz*. Frankfurt am Main: Suhrkamp, 1988.
Biron, Georg. "Vom Herrn Karl . . .: Vor 50 Jahren empörte Helmut Qualtinger mit dem Monolog eines Opportunisten die Nation." *Die Zeit*, November 11, 2011.
Bolt, Catrin. *Alltagsskulpturen Mahnmal*. Vienna: REMAprint, 2014.
Botz, Gerhard. "Die 'Waldheim-Affäre' als Widerstreit kollektiver Erinnerungen." In Tóth and Czernin, *1986*, 74–95.
Boym, Svetlana. *The Future of Nostalgia*. New York: Basic Books, 2001.
Breitenfellner, Kirstin. "Exilroman remixed." *Falter*, February 25, 2000.
Bremner, Charles. "Biggest Vote for Far Right since 1945 in Austria Poll." *Times*, May 24, 2016.
Browning, Christopher. "Raul Hilberg." *Yad Vashem Studies* 35, no. 2 (2007): 7–20.
Buchschwenter, Robert. "Das Schweigen gegen die Angst." *Die Presse*, May 26, 1994.
Bunzl, Matti. "On the Politics and Semantics of Austrian Memory: Vienna's Monument against War and Fascism." *History and Memory* 7, no. 2 (1995): 7–40.
———. "Political Inscription, Artistic Reflection: A Recontextualization of Contemporary Viennese-Jewish Literature." *German Quarterly* 73, no. 2 (2000): 163–70.
Bushell, Anthony. "Facts, Fiction, and Friction in a Difficult Relationship: Vienna and Provincial Austria." *German Life and Letters* 65, no. 2 (2012): 237–52.
Carrier, Peter, and Kobi Kabalek. "Cultural Memory and Transcultural Memory—A Conceptual Analysis." In *The Transcultural Turn: Interrogating Memory Between and Beyond Borders*, edited by Lucy Bond and Jessica Rapson, 39–60. Berlin: De Gruyter, 2014.
Carter, Erica, James Donald, and Judith Squires, eds. *Space and Place: Theories of Identity and Location*. London: Lawrence & Wishart, 1993.
Cerny, Karin. "Elfriede Jelinek: Das Lebewohl." *Literaturhaus Wien*, February 2, 2002. http://www.literaturhaus.at/index.php?id=4355.
Charim, Isolde, and Doron Rabinovici, eds. *Österreich: Berichte aus Quarantanien*. Frankfurt am Main: Suhrkamp, 2000.
Clowes, Edith W. *Russia on the Edge: Imagined Geographies and Post-Soviet Identity*. Ithaca, NY: Cornell University Press, 2011.
Connoly, Kate, Philip Oltermann, and Jon Henley. "Far Right Is Edged Out in Knife-Edge Austrian Poll." *Guardian*, May 24, 2016.
CSS Gmbh, "The Vienna Project," Google Play, Vers. 1.0 (2013). Accessed August 17, 2016. https://play.google.com/store/apps/details?id=at.roommint.theviennaproject.
Curtis, Simon. *Woman in Gold*. UK/US: BBC Films/Origin Pictures, 2015.
Czernin, Hubertus. "Einleitung." In Tóth and Czernin, *1986*, 15–24.
Das Gupta, Oliver. "Wie rechts Norbert Hofer wirklich ist." *Süddeutsche Zeitung*, May 20, 2016.
de Waal, Edmund. *The Hare with Amber Eyes*. London: Vintage, 2011.

Erenz, Benedikt. "Verbrechen der Wehrmacht: Vor 20 Jahren wurde die Hamburger Ausstellung eröffnet—sogar der Bundestag diskutierte über sie." *Die Zeit*, March 23, 2015.

Erne, Eduard, and Margareta Heinrich. *Totschweigen* (Vienna: Extrafilm, 1994). In *Margareta Heinrich*, edited by Vrääth Öhner. Vienna: Verlag Filmarchiv Austria, 2011.

Evans, Katherine Elizabeth. "'Das Politische ist nicht anders erlebbar als privat': A Study of Anna Mitgutsch's Fiction and Its Portrayal of Austrian Society." PhD diss., University of Wales, Bangor, 2003.

Faulkner, William. *Requiem for a Nun*. London: Vintage Classics, 2015.

Fiddler, Allyson. "Points of Departure in Austria 2000: Street Protest and Performance." Paper presented at the Contemporary Austrian Literature, Film and Culture: International Conference, University of Nottingham, UK, April 13–15, 2015.

———. "Reckoning with Rechnitz: On Elfriede Jelinek, Translation and Cultural Reproduction." *Austrian Studies* 22 (2014): 199–214.

———. "Staging Jörg Haider: Protest and Resignation in Elfriede Jelinek's *Das Lebewohl* and Other Recent Texts for the Theatre." *Modern Language Review* 97, no. 2 (2002): 353–64.

———. "Why Did Many More Austrians Vote against the Far Right than in the First Head-to-Head? Brexit and Trump Were Strong Factors." *Independent*, December 5, 2016.

Freitag, Barbara. "Vom Sterben der Erinnerung: Ein Gespräch mit Eduard Erne über seinen Film 'Totschweigen.'" *Wiener Zeitung*, September 9, 1994.

Freud, Sigmund. "Das Unheimliche." In *Psychologische Schriften*. Vol. 4 of *Sigmund Freud: Studienausgabe*, edited by Alexander Mitscherlich, Angela Richards, and James Strachey, 241–74. Frankfurt am Main: Fischer, 1972.

———. *Der Mann Moses und die monotheistische Religion*. In *Fragen der Gesellschaft: Ursprünge der Religion*. Vol. 9 of *Sigmund Freud: Studienausgabe*, edited by Alexander Mitscherlich, Angela Richards, and James Strachey, 459–581. Frankfurt am Main: Fischer, 1972.

———. "Erinnern, Wiederholen und Durcharbeiten." In *Ergänzungsband*. Vol. 11 of *Sigmund Freud: Studienausgabe*, edited by Alexander Mitscherlich, Angela Richards, and James Strachey, 205–15. Frankfurt am Main: Fischer, 1975.

———. "Trauer und Melancholie." In *Psychologie des Unbewußten*. Vol. 3 of *Sigmund Freud: Studienausgabe*, edited by Alexander Mitscherlich, Angela Richards, and James Strachey, 193–213. Frankfurt am Main: Fischer, 1975.

Frostig, Karen. "Board." *The Vienna Project*. Accessed August 17, 2016. http://theviennaproject.org/advisory-board/.

———. "Citizenship After Genocide: Materializing Memory Through Art Activism." In *Beyond Citizenship? Feminism and the Transformation of Belonging*, edited by Sasha Roseneil, 211–30. Basingstoke: Palgrave Macmillan, 2013.

———. "Closing Events." *The Vienna Project*. Accessed August 17, 2016. http://theviennaproject.org/closing-events/.

———. "Collecting Archival Letters for Closing Ceremony." *The Vienna Project*. Accessed August 17, 2016. http://theviennaproject.org/call-for-archival-letters-for-the-vienna-projects-closing-ceremony/.

———. "Home." *The Vienna Project*. Accessed August 17, 2016. http://theviennaproject.org/.

———. *Mapping 1938 Vienna*. Kickstarter, 2013. https://www.kickstarter.com/projects/130272597/mapping-1938-vienna.

———. "Memory Map." *The Vienna Project*. Accessed August 17, 2016. http://theviennaproject.org/memory-map/.

———. "Project Description." *The Vienna Project*. Accessed August 16, 2016. http://theviennaproject.org/project-details/.

———. "Public Programs 2013–2014." *The Vienna Project*. Accessed August 17, 2016. http://theviennaproject.org/installations/.

———. "Research." *The Vienna Project*. Accessed August 17, 2016. http://theviennaproject.org/research/.

Gauss, Karl-Markus. "Photographierte Sehnsucht. Anna Mitgutschs grosser Roman 'Haus der Kindheit.'" *Neue Zürcher Zeitung*, May 31, 2000.

Gedye, G. E. R. *Fallen Bastions: The Central European Tragedy*. London: Victor Gollancz, 1939.

Geldner, Wilfried. "Für Kaiser und Land: Die papierene Brücke." *Süddeutsche Zeitung*, September 20, 1988.

Gmunder, Stefan. "Wenn Fragen vor Selbstgerechtigkeit schützen." *Der Standard*, February 21, 2013.

Götzelmann, Andrea. *Wer macht Asylpolitik?: AkteurInnen und ihre Strategien in der österreichischen Asylgesetzgebung*. Berlin: Lit Verlag, 2010.

Guenther, Christina. "Cartographies of Identity: Memory and History in Ruth Beckermann's Documentary Films." In *New Austrian Film*, edited by Robert von Dassanowsky and Oliver C. Speck, 64–78. New York, Oxford: Berghahn Books, 2011.

———. "The Politics of Location in Ruth Beckermann's 'Vienna Films.'" *Modern Austrian Literature* 37, no. 3–4 (2004): 33–46.

Gürtler, Christa. "Abschied von einem fremden Haus." In *Anna Mitgutsch*, edited by Heide Stockinger and Kristin Teuchtmann, 73–76. Linz: Rampe, 2004.

Haas, Franz. "Zeitgeschichte als Wiener Melange." *Neue Zürcher Zeitung*, April 13, 2013.

Hackl, Wolfgang. "Erzählendes Erinnern: Bemerkungen zu einem poetologischen Aspekt in Anna Mitgutschs Romanen." In *Anna Mitgutsch*, edited by Heide Stockinger and Kristin Teuchtmann, 39–44. Linz: Rampe, 2004.

Hager, Johanna. "Kurier-Foto künstlerisch verfremdet: 'Déjà-vu' statt 'Reibpartie.'" *Kurier*, June 19, 2015.

Heilbrunn, Jacob. "Waldheim and His Protectors." Review of *Betrayal: The Untold Story of the Kurt Waldheim Investigation and Cover-Up*, by Eli M. Rosenbaum with William Hoffer. *New York Times*, October 10, 1993.
Hell, Cornelius. "Der Kalte: Roman von Robert Schindel." *oe1.orf.at*, February 14, 2013. http://oe1.orf.at/artikel/331361.
Herzog, Hillary Hope. "The Global and the Local in Ruth Beckermann's Films and Writings." In *Rebirth of a Culture: Jewish Identity and Jewish Writing in Germany and Austria Today*, edited by Hillary Hope Herzog, Todd Herzog, and Benjamin Lapp, 100–109. New York, Oxford: Berghahn, 2008.
——. *"Vienna Is Different": Jewish Writers in Austria from the Fin de Siècle to the Present*. New York, Oxford: Berghahn Books, 2011.
Hinck, Walter. "Im verlorenen Paradies. Heimkehrversuch: Anna Mitgutschs Roman 'Haus der Kindheit.'" *Frankfurter Allgemeine Zeitung*, April 28, 2000.
Hirsch, Marianne. *Family Frames: Photography, Narrative, and Postmemory*. Cambridge, MA: Harvard University Press, 1997.
Hirsch, Marianne, and Leo Spitzer. *Ghosts of Home: The Afterlife of Czernowitz in Jewish Memory*. Berkeley: University of California Press, 2010.
Höglinger, Nora, ed. *Kunst im öffentlichen Raum* (leaflet). 3rd ed. Vienna: Kunst im öffentichen Raum GmbH, 2015.
Holden, Stephen. "Review: 'Woman in Gold' Stars Helen Mirren in Tug of War over Artwork." *New York Times*, March 31, 2015.
Hood, Thomas. "Ode: Autumn." In *Poems*, 344–46. London: E. Moxon, 1857.
Huber, Sonja, and Stefan Musil, eds. *Turnertempel Erinnerungsort: Suche nach einer reflexiven Archäologie*. Nuremberg: Verlag für Moderne Kunst, 2012.
Hutcheon, Linda. "Irony, Nostalgia, and the Postmodern." In *Methods for the Study of Literature as Cultural Memory*, edited by Raymond Vervliet and Annemarie Estor, 189–207. Amsterdam, Atlanta: Rodopi, 2000.
Jandl, Ernst. *Gesammelte Werke. Band 1: Gedichte*, edited by Klaus Siblewski. Darmstadt: Luchterhand, 1990.
Janke, Pia. "'Herrschsucht, ja, haben wir': Die Täter in Elfriede Jelineks *Rechnitz (Der Würgeengel)*." In Janke, Kovacs, and Schenkermayr, *"Die endlose Unschuldigkeit,"* 239–54.
Janke, Pia, Teresa Kovacs, and Christian Schenkermayr, eds. *"Die endlose Unschuldigkeit": Elfriede Jelineks Rechnitz (Der Würgeengel)*. Vienna: Praesens, 2010.
Jelinek, Elfriede. "Das Kommen." *www.elfriedejelinek.com*, April 26, 2016. http://www.elfriedejelinek.com/.
——. *Das Lebewohl : Drei kleine Dramen*. Berlin: Berlin Verlag, 2000.
——. "'Diese falsche und verlogene Unschuldigkeit Österreichs ist wirklich immer mein Thema gewesen': Elfriede Jelinek im Gespräch mit Pia Janke." In Janke, Kovacs, and Schenkermayr, *"Die endlose Unschuldigkeit,"* 17–23.

———. "Elfriede Jelinek Homepage Wien." *www.elfriedejelinek.com*. Accessed August 11, 2016. http://www.elfriedejelinek.com/.
———. "Gesprochen und beglaubigt: Dankesrede zur Verleihung des Mühlheimer Dramatikerpreises 2009." In Janke, Kovacs, and Schenkermayr, *"Die endlose Unschuldigkeit,"* 453–57.
———. "Präsident Abendwind." *elfriedejelinek.com*. Accessed December 13, 2016. http://www.elfriedejelinek.com/fabendwn.htm.
———. *Rechnitz (Der Würgeengel)*. In *Die Kontrakte des Kaufmanns; Rechnitz (Der Würgeengel); Über Tiere*, 53–205. Reinbeck: Rowohlt, 2009.
Jiranek, Johanna, and Maria Scheucher. "Darstellungen von Endphasenverbrechen in der österreichischen Kunst am Beispiel Rechnitz." In *Der Fall Rechnitz: Das Massaker an Juden im März 1945*, edited by Walter Manoschek, 165–97. Vienna: Braumüller, 2009.
Judt, Tony. *Postwar: A History of Europe since 1945*. London: Pimlico, 2007.
Jung, André. "'Die Sprache ist die Figur': André Jung im Gespräch mit Christian Schenkermayr." In Janke, Kovacs, and Schenkermayr, *"Die endlose Unschuldigkeit,"* 440–41.
Kahlweit, Cathrin. "Der Hofer und der Herrgott." *Süddeutsche Zeitung*, October 25, 2016.
———. "Der Rechtspopulismus ist in Österreich endgültig salonfähig." *Süddeutsche Zeitung*, April 24, 2016.
Kecht, Maria-Regina. "Traditionen des Gedenkens: Anna Mitgutsch, *Haus der Kindheit*." *Chilufim*, no. 6 (2009): 17–74.
Klein, Erich. *Denkwürdiges Wien: Gehen & Sehen: 3 Routen zu Mahnmalen, Gedenkstätten und Orten der Erinnerung der Ersten und Zweiten Republik*. Vienna: Falter, 2004.
Knöbl, Kuno. "Die Geschichte des Waldheim-Holzpferdes." *Republikanischer Club–Neues Österreich: Geschichte*. Accessed August 7, 2016. http://www.repclub.at/geschichte/.
Koch, Magnus. "Conflicting Memories: Commemorating World War II at Heldenplatz/ Ballhausplatz." Paper presented at the *German Studies Association Thirty-Ninth Annual Conference*, Washington, DC, October 1–4, 2015.
König, Helmut, Michael Kohlstruck, and Andreas Wöll. "Einleitung der Herausgeber." In *Vergangenheitsbewältigung am Ende des zwanzigsten Jahrhunderts*, edited by Helmut König, Michael Kohlstruck, and Andreas Wöll, 7–14. Opladen: Westdeutscher Verlag, 1998.
Kopeinig, Margaretha. "Eine 'Hetz' bei der 'Reibpartie.'" *Kurier*, March 11, 2015.
Kovacs, Teresa. "Chronik der Ereignisse." In Janke, Kovacs, and Schenkermayr, *"Die endlose Unschuldigkeit,"* 28–50.
Kroisleitner, Oona, and Maria von Usslar. "Ein Andenken an Leid und Unrecht am Alsergrund." *Der Standard*, August 22, 2016.
Kronsteiner, Olga. "'Die Frau in Gold': Faktentreue ist eine schlechte Dramaturgin." *Der Standard*, May 29, 2015.

Krylova, Katya. "'Eine den Menschen zerzausende Landschaft': Psychotopography and the Alpine Landscape in Thomas Bernhard's 'Frost.'" *Austrian Studies* 18 (2010): 74–88.

———. *Walking through History: Topography and Identity in the Works of Ingeborg Bachmann and Thomas Bernhard*. Oxford: Peter Lang, 2013.

Kunst im öffentlichen Raum GmbH. *Denkmal für die Verfolgten der NS-Militärjustiz: Olaf Nicolai 2014*. Vienna: Kunst im öffentichen Raum GmbH, 2014.

Kuttenberg, Eva. "Austria's Topography of Memory: Heldenplatz, Albertinaplatz, Judenplatz, and Beyond." *German Quarterly* 80, no. 4 (2007): 468–91.

Lässer, Bruno. "Die Ungnade der später Angekommenen. 'Haus der Kindheit' von Mitgutsch, eine Neuerscheinung, der man eine große Leserschaft wünscht." *Vorarlberger Nachrichten*, May 13, 2000.

Lebow, Alisa S. *First Person Jewish*. Minneapolis: University of Minnesota Press, 2008.

Lehmann, Hans-Thies. *Postdramatisches Theater*. Frankfurt am Main: Verlag der Autoren, 1999.

Lehnguth, Cornelius. *Waldheim und die Folgen: der parteipolitische Umgang mit dem Nationalsozialismus in Österreich*. Frankfurt am Main: Campus, 2013.

Leidl, Bettina. "Vorwort." In Huber and Musil, *Turnertempel Erinnerungsort*, 7.

Lévy, Bernard Henri. "Die Stimmen des Anderen Österreich." In *Österreich: Berichte aus Quarantanien*, edited by Isolde Charim and Doron Rabinovici, 156–71. Frankfurt am Main: Suhrkamp, 2000.

Lindemann, Tobias. "Robert Schindel-Interview zu seinem Roman 'Der Kalte' über die Waldheim-Jahre in Österreich." *Stoffwechsel*. freie-radios. net. Accessed August 14, 2016. http://www.freie-radios.net/56812.

Litchfield, David R. L. "Die Gastgeberin der Hölle." *Frankfurter Allgemeine Zeitung*, October 18, 2007.

———. "The Killer Countess: The Dark Past of Baron Heinrich Thyssen's Daughter." *Independent*, October 6, 2007.

———. *The Thyssen Art Macabre*. London: Quartet Books, 2006.

Litschauer, Maria Theresa. "Text der Schrifttafel: [transkription]." *Kunst im öffentlichen Raum Wien*. 2009. http://www.koer.or.at/cgi-bin/page.pl?id=202&lang=de.

Lobnig, Hubert, and János Kárász. "Der Turnertempel: Auf der Suche nach einer reflexiven Archäologie." In Huber and Musil, *Turnertempel Erinnerungsort*, 34–39.

Lochte, Julia. "Totschweigen oder die Kunst des Berichtens." In Janke, Kovacs, and Schenkermayr, *"Die endlose Unschuldigkeit,"* 411–25.

Lorenz, Dagmar C. G. "Austrian Responses to National Socialism and the Holocaust." In *A History of Austrian Literature 1918–2000*, edited by Katrin Kohl and Ritchie Robertson, 181–200. Rochester, NY: Camden House, 2006.

———. "Discovering and Making Memory: Jewish Cultural Expression in Contemporary Europe." *German Quarterly* 73, no. 2 (2000): 175–78.

———. *Keepers of the Motherland: German Texts by Jewish Women Writers.* Lincoln: University of Nebraska Press, 1997.

———. "Post-Shoah Positions of Displacement in the Films of Ruth Beckermann." *Austrian Studies* 11 (2003): 154–70.

———. "The Struggle for a Civil Society and Beyond: Austrian Writers and Intellectuals Confronting the Political Right." *New German Critique*, no. 93 (2004): 19–41.

Manoschek, Walter, ed. *Der Fall Rechnitz: Das Massaker an Juden im März 1945.* Vienna: Braumüller, 2010.

———. "Die Generation Waldheim." In Tóth and Czernin, *1986*, 124–31.

———. "Nationalsozialistische Moral, situativer Rahmen und individuelle Handlungsspielräume als konstitutive Elemente bei der Vernichtung der Juden." In *Der Fall Rechnitz: Das Massaker an Juden im März 1945*, edited by Walter Manoschek, 5–26. Vienna: Braumüller, 2009.

———. "Wehrmachtsausstellung: Verbrechen erinnern." *Neue Kriminalpolitik* 10, no. 1 (1998): 15–19.

Mayer, Norbert. "Elfriede Jelinek lässt die Mörder unter uns sein." *Die Presse*, March 18, 2012.

Mayr, Peter. "Denkmal für Wehrmachtsdeserteure: Anfang, nicht Ende." *Der Standard*, October 24, 2014.

———. "Ein Denkmal für die Opfer der NS-Militärjustiz." *Der Standard*, October 20, 2014.

Merz, Carl, and Helmut Qualtinger. *Der Herr Karl.* Edited by Traugott Krischke. Vienna: Deuticke, 1996.

Meyhöfer, Annette. "Im Land des Schweigens." *Der Spiegel*, April 13, 1992.

Miller, Elizabeth. "Getting to Know the Un-Dead: Bram Stoker, Vampires and Dracula." In *Vampires: Myths and Metaphors of Enduring Evil*, edited by Peter Day, 3–19. Amsterdam, New York: Rodopi, 2006.

Misik, Robert. "Kein Heldenplatz ohne Waldheim." In Tóth and Czernin, *1986*, 141–47.

Mitgutsch, [Waltraud] Anna. *Abschied von Jerusalem.* 2nd ed. Munich: Deutscher Taschenbuch Verlag, 2005.

———. *Haus der Kindheit.* 4th ed. Munich: Deutscher Taschenbuch Verlag, 2008.

———. *House of Childhood.* Translated by David Dollenmayer. New York: Other Press, 2006.

———. *In fremden Städten.* Munich: Deutscher Taschenbuch Verlag, 1994.

Mittelstaedt, Katharina. "'Aufgeheizte Stimmung' in zweigeteilten Gemeinden." *Der Standard*, May 24, 2016.

Mitten, Richard. "Bitburg, Waldheim, and the Politics of Remembering and Forgetting." In *From World War to Waldheim: Culture and Politics in Austria and the United States*, edited by David F. Good and Ruth Wodak, 51–84. New York, Oxford: Berghahn, 1999.

———. "Der kurze Schatten der Vergangenheit." In Tóth and Czernin, *1986*, 109–23.

Moser, Anita. *Die Kunst der Grenzüberschreitung: Postkoloniale Kritik im Spannungsfeld von Ästhetik und Politik*. Bielefeld: transcript, 2011.

Moses, A. Dirk, and Michael Rothberg. "A Dialogue on the Ethics and Politics of Transcultural Memory." In *The Transcultural Turn: Interrogating Memory Between and Beyond Borders*, edited by Lucy Bond and Jessica Rapson, 29–38. Berlin: De Gruyter, 2014.

Musil, Stefan. "Ein neuer Erinnerungsort in der Wiener Gedächtnislandschaft." In Huber and Musil, *Turnertempel Erinnerungsort*, 14–17.

N., N. "5. Mai-Gedenktag gegen Gewalt und Rassismus im Gedenken an die Opfer des Nationalsozialismus." *erinnern.at*. Accessed August 7, 2016. http://www.erinnern.at/bundeslaender/oesterreich/gedenktage/5.-mai-gedenktag-gegen-gewalt-und-rassismus-im-gedenken-an-die-opfer-des-nationalsozialismus.

———. "20 Jahre Lichtermeer." *orf.at*, January 20, 2013. http://oesterreich.orf.at/stories/2567688.

———. "30 Jahre Waldheim-Affäre." *Wien Museum*. Accessed August 7, 2016. http://www.wienmuseum.at/index.php?id=917.

———. "Amtsantritt und Amtsende." *Österreichische Präsidentschaftskanzlei*, 2013. http://www.bundespraesident.at/aufgaben/wahl-und-amtszeit/amtsantritt-und-amtsende/.

———. "Best of 2013–15: Das Fest zum Tag der Befreiung." *Fest der Freude*. Accessed August 16, 2016. http://www.festderfreude.at/de/das-fest/best-2013-15.

———."Bundespräsidenten-Stichwahl muss in ganz Österreich und komplett wiederholt werden." Presseinformation Verfassungsgerichtshof, July 1, 2016, https://www.vfgh.gv.at/cms/vfgh-site/attachments/8/0/4/CH0003/CMS1467363234408/verkuendung_w_presseinformation.pdf.

———. "Bundespräsidentenwahl 2016: Österreich, 1. Wahlgang." *Bundesministerium für Inneres*. Accessed August 8, 2016. http://wahl16.bmi.gv.at/1604-0.html.

———. "Bundespräsidentenwahl 2016: Österreich, endgültiges Endergebnis." *Bundesministerium für Inneres*. Accessed August 8, 2016. http://wahl16.bmi.gv.at/.

———. "Bundespräsidentenwahl 2016: Österreich Briefwahl." *Bundesministerium für Inneres*. Accessed August 7, 2016. http://wahl16.bmi.gv.at/1605-bw_ov_0.html.

———. "Die 8 Wahlanfechtungen der Bundespräsidentenwahl 2016." www.bundespraesidentschaftswahl.at. Accessed August 7, 2016. http://www.bundespraesidentschaftswahl.at/wahlanfechtung.html.

———. "Enthüllung der Gedenkstele in der Fluchtgasse 7." *Gedenkprojekt Volksopernviertel 1938*. Accessed August 23, 2016. http://www.volksopernviertel1938.at/.

———. "Entscheidung vertagt." *news.orf.at*, May 22, 2016. http://orf.at/stories/2340500/2340505/.
———. "Filmemacherin Ruth Beckermann mit Ehrenkreuz ausgezeichnet." *Kleine Zeitung*, October 9, 2015.
———. "Fluchtgasse." *Wien Geschichte Wiki*, May 23, 2016. https://www.wien.gv.at/wiki/index.php/Fluchtgasse.
———. "Flüchtlingsland Österreich." *UNHCR The UN Refugee Agency*. Accessed August 7, 2016. http://www.unhcr.at/unhcr/in-oesterreich/fluechtlingsland-oesterreich.html.
———. "Fritz Brügel." *Wien Geschichte Wiki*, July 20, 2016. https://www.wien.gv.at/wiki/index.php?title=Fritz_Br%C3%BCgel.
———. "Gedenkbuch für die Opfer des Nationalsozialismus an der Universität Wien 1938." *Universität Wien*, March 5, 2013. http://medienportal.univie.ac.at/uniview/forschung/detailansicht/artikel/gedenkbuch-fuer-die-opfer-des-nationalsozialismus-an-der-universitaet-wien-1938/.
———. "Gedenksymbol Servitengasse. Schlüssel gegen das Vergessen." Accessed August 16, 2016. http://www.koer.or.at/cgi-bin/page.pl?id=39;lang=de.
———. "HistorikerInnen-Bericht über Wiens Straßennamen." *wien.at*. Accessed August 16, 2016. https://www.wien.gv.at/kultur/strassennamen/strassennamenpruefung.html.
———. "Ich möchte einen Stein." *Steine der Erinnerung*. Accessed August 16, 2016. http://steinedererinnerung.net/mein-beitrag/mein-stein/.
———. "Installation zeigt Erniedrigung bei 'Reibpartie.'" *orf.at*, March 12, 2015. http://wien.orf.at/news/stories/2699168/.
———. "Jelinek als Mittel gegen das Vergessen." *orf.at*, May 16, 2012. http://steiermark.orf.at/tv/stories/2525044/.
———. "Mahnmal gegen Krieg und Faschismus." *Zentrale österreichische Forschungsstelle Nachkriegsjustiz*. Accessed August 14, 2016. http://www.nachkriegsjustiz.at/vgew/1010_alb.php.
———. "Mann ohne Eigenschaften." *Der Spiegel*, March 10, 1986.
———. "Massengrab und Grabesstille." *Kurier*, May 26, 1994.
———. "The Memory Map." *Jüdisches Museum Wien*. Accessed August 17, 2016. http://www.jmw.at/de/exhibitions/memory-map-eine-topologie-des-gedenkens-0.
———. "The Moscow Declaration; October 1943. Joint Four-Nation Declaration." *The Avalon Project: Documents in Law, History and Diplomacy, Yale Lillian Goldmann Law Library*. Accessed August 7, 2016. http://avalon.law.yale.edu/wwii/moscow.asp.
———. "Österreich, vorläufiges Endergebnis inklusive Briefwahlstimmen." Accessed December 9, 2016. http://wahl16.bmi.gv.at/.
———. "Österreichische Staatsbürgerschaft." *Israelitische Kultusgemeinde Wien: Abteilung für Restitutionsangelegenheiten*. Accessed August 7, 2016. http://www.restitution.or.at/schwerpunkte/s-anliegen-staatsbuergerschaft.html.

———. "porem-Politics of Remembrance and the Transition of Public Spaces. A Political and Social Analysis of Vienna, 1995–2015." *Politics of Remembrance*. Accessed August 16, 2016. http://porem.univie.ac.at/.

———. "Presseaussendung: Alltagsskulpturen Mahnmal," *Kunst im öffentlichen Raum Wien*. Accessed August 17, 2016. http://www.koer.or.at/cgi-bin/file.pl?id=1487.

———. "Projekte." *Steine der Erinnerung*. Accessed August 16, 2016. http://steinedererinnerung.net/projekte/.

———. "Sieben Fragen an Elfriede Jelinek: 'Ich bin eine Autorin der Axt.'" *Nachtkritik*, 2009. http://nachtkritik-stuecke09.de/elfriede-jelinek/sieben-fragen.

———. "Späte Rehabilitation: Deserteursdenkmal enthüllt." *orf.at*, October 24, 2014. http://wien.orf.at/news/stories/2675377/.

———. "Über uns." *Israelitische Kultusgemeinde Wien*. Accessed August 25, 2016. http://www.ikg-wien.at/?page_id=304.

———. "Unsere Stadt! Jüdisches Wien bis heute." *Jüdisches Museum Wien*. Accessed August 19, 2016. http://www.jmw.at/de/exhibitions/unsere-stadt-juedisches-wien-bis-heute.

———. "Vermittlung." *Steine der Erinnerung*. Accessed August 23, 2016. http://steinedererinnerung.net/vermittlung/.

———. "The Vienna Project Archival Letters Submission." *The Vienna Project*. Accessed August 17, 2016. http://www.jotform.us/form/41144022369144.

———. "Waldheim oder THE ART OF FORGETTING." *Filmfonds Wien*. Accessed August 11, 2016. http://www.filmfonds-wien.at/filme/waldheim-oder-the-art-of-forgetting.

———. "Wer ist wer: Biografie von Ing. Norbert Hofer." *Republik Österreich Parlament*. Accessed August 7, 2016. https://www.parlament.gv.at/WWER/PAD_35521/.

———. "'Wir Österreicher wählen, wen wir wollen.'" *Der Spiegel*, April 14, 1986.

Nabokov, Vladimir. *Speak, Memory: An Autobiography Revisited*. 1967. London: Penguin, 2000.

Neumüller, Magdalena. "Erinnerung in Rechnitz: Microstudie über den Umgang mit Toten." In *Der Fall Rechnitz: Das Massaker an Juden im März 1945*, edited by Walter Manoschek, 199–219. Vienna: Braumüller, 2009.

Nichols, Bill. *Introduction to Documentary*. Bloomington: Indiana University Press, 2001.

Niven, Bill. "From Countermonument to Combimemorial: Developments in German Memorialisation." In *"Holocaust"-Fiktion: Kunst jenseits der Authentizität*, edited by Iris Roebling-Grau and Dirk Rupnow, 183–97. Paderborn: Fink, 2015.

Nora, Pierre. "Between Memory and History: Les Lieux de Mémoire." *Representations* 26 (1989): 7–24.

Obermüller, Klara. "Nachrichten aus dem Operettenland." *Die Welt*, April 20, 2013.
Omasta, Michael. "Stimmen des Schweigens." *Falter*, May 27, 1994.
Osthoff, Simone. *Performing the Archive: The Transformation of the Archive in Contemporary Art from Repository of Documents to Art Medium.* New York: Atropos Press, 2009.
Paterno, Wolfgang. "Robert Schindel: Erst als Toter pflegt man Gleichmut." *profil.at*, February 9, 2013. http://www.profil.at/home/robert-schindel-erst-toter-gleichmut-352177.
Petsch, Barbara. "'Die Frau in Gold': Klimts goldene Adele als Kino-Saga." *Die Presse*, June 2, 2015.
Pick, Hella. *Guilty Victim: Austria from the Holocaust to Haider.* London: I. B. Tauris, 2000.
Pirker, Peter. "Time, Space, Meaning and Actors: Reflections on the Study of Politics of Remembrance." Paper presented at the *German Studies Association Thirty-Ninth Annual Conference*, Washington, DC, October 1–4, 2015.
Pollak, Alexander. "Nenn sie nicht 'Wehrmachtsausstellung'!" In *Zeitgeschichte ausstellen in Österreich: Museen—Gedenkstätten—Ausstellungen*, edited by Dirk Rupnow and Heidemarie Uhl, 237–54. Vienna: Böhlau, 2011.
Posch, Herbert. "DENK-MAL Marpe Lanefesch: Ehemaliges jüdisches Bethaus im Alten Allgemeinen Krankenhaus 1903–2015." *Universität Wien*. Last modified December 21, 2015. http://geschichte.univie.ac.at/de/artikel/denk-mal-marpe-lanefesch.
Posthofen, Renate S. "Ruth Beckermann: Re-activating Memory—In Search of Time Lost." In *Out from the Shadows: Essays on Contemporary Austrian Women Writers and Filmmakers*, edited by Margarete Lamb-Faffelberger, 264–76. Riverside, CA: Ariadne Press, 1997.
Rabinovici, Doron. *Ohnehin*. Frankfurt am Main: Suhrkamp, 2004.
———. *Papirnik*. Frankfurt am Main: Suhrkamp, 1994.
———. "'Tina, ruf die Polizei!'" *Die Presse*, September 8, 2001.
Rainer, Christian, and Christa Zöchling. "Videoblog: Die Affäre Waldheim hat eine ganze Generation geprägt." *profil.at*, March 19, 2016. http://www.profil.at/videos/videoblog-kurt-waldheim-6276119.
Rathkolb, Oliver. "Permanente Intervention: Maria Theresia Litschauer." *Kunst im öffentlichen Raum Wien*. Accessed August 16, 2016. http://www.koer.or.at/cgi-bin/page.pl?id=129;lang=de.
Rauscher, Hans. "'Ich habe im Krieg nichts anderes getan als meine Pflicht erfüllt.'" *Der Standard*, February 27, 2016.
Rebhandl, Bert. "Unumgängliches Kino gegen falschen Frieden: 'Totschweigen.'" *Der Standard*, May 25, 1994.
red., APA. "Foto von FPÖ-Protest: 'Kurier' klagt Strache." *Der Standard*, June 11, 2015.
Reiter, Andrea. *Contemporary Jewish Writing: Austria after Waldheim.* New York: Routledge, 2013.

Robey, Tim. "Woman in Gold Review: 'Distinctly Ordinary.'" *Telegraph*, April 9, 2015.
Rosenfeld, Sidney. *Understanding Joseph Roth*. Columbia: University of South Carolina Press, 2001.
Ross, Deborah. "Woman in Gold Review: Even Helen Mirren Is Weighed Down by the Script's Banalities." *Spectator*, April 11, 2015.
Rothberg, Michael. *Multidirectional Memory: Remembering the Holocaust in the Age of Decolonization*. Stanford, CA: Stanford University Press, 2009.
Sapinski, Hellin. "'Klebergate': Sobotka lässt gegen Hotline-Mitarbeiter ermitteln." *Die Presse*, September 12, 2016.
SAS. "Anna Mitgutsch." *Die Presse*, March 10, 2000.
Scheit, Gerhard. "*Stecken, Stab und Stangl*; *Rechnitz (Der Würgeengel)*." In *Jelinek Handbuch*, edited by Pia Janke, 156–62. Stuttgart: Metzler, 2013.
Scheller, Wolf. "Wiener Walzer rechtsherum." *Jüdische Allgemeine*, March 21, 2013.
Schiefer, Karin. "'Der Film ist für mich auch ein Ausdruck einer Ratlosigkeit über den Zustand Europas und seiner Umgebung.' Ruth Beckermann über *Those Who Go Those Who Stay*," ruthbeckermann.com. October 2013. http://www.ruthbeckermann.com/aduploads/93.02.ma,austrianfilmcommission-interviews.pdf. Originally published on *austrianfilms.com*, October 2013.
Schindel, Robert. "Beginn des Romans 'Der Kalte': Erstes Kapitel (Als ob)." *Text + Kritik* 174 (2007): 52–68.
———. *Born-Where*. Translated by Michael Roloff. Riverside, CA: Ariadne Press, 1995.
———. *Der Kalte*. Frankfurt am Main: Suhrkamp, 2013.
———. "Der Kalte: Erstes Kapital (Als ob)." *manuskripte* 38, no. 141 (1998): 4.
———. *Gebürtig*. 9th ed. Frankfurt am Main: Suhrkamp, 2012.
———. Interview with Robert Schindel. Interview by Katya Krylova, August 18, 2015.
Schindel, Robert, and Martin Pollack. "'Wir kannten unsere Väter nicht.' Hat Pollacks Vater Schindels Mutter verhört? Ein Gespräch." In *Linz, Randgeschichten*, edited by Alfred Pittertschatscher, 289–313. Vienna: Picus, 2009.
Schindel, Robert, and Lukas Stepanik. *Gebürtig*. Vienna: Cult Film/Extra Film, 2002.
Schmidt, Thomas E. "Wien, die Skandalmaschine." *Die Zeit*. April 11, 2013.
Schmidt-Rahmer, Hermann, Katrin Nottrodt, and Stephan Wetzel. "Rechnitz verstehen? Der Regisseur Hermann Schmidt-Rahmer und die Bühnenbildnerin Katrin Nottrodt im Gespräch mit dem Dramaturgen Stephan Wetzel." In *Rechnitz (Der Würgeengel) von Elfriede Jelinek (theater program)*, 15–23. Düsseldorf: Düsseldorfer Schauspielhaus, 2010.
Schüttelkopf, Elke. "An der Grenze zum Vergessen." *Volksstimme*, March 23, 1995.

Shafi, Monika. "'Enteignung' und 'Behaustheit': Zu Anna Mitgutschs Roman 'Haus der Kindheit.'" *Modern Austrian Literature* 36, no. 1–2 (2003): 33–51.

Sinclair, John McHardy, ed. *Collins Concise Dictionary*. 4th ed. Glasgow: HarperCollins Publishers, 1999.

Sontag, Susan. *On Photography*. New York: Farrar, Strauss and Giroux, 2001.

Sperber, Manès. *Die Wasserträger Gottes: all das Vergangene* . . . Vienna: Europaverlag, 1983.

Staudinger, Martin. "Der Super-Gaul." In Tóth and Czernin, *1986*, 132–40.

Steindorfer, Eva. "Narrative der Erinnerung: Funktionen—Formen—Fallstricke des Erinnerns in 'Familienfest', 'Haus der Kindheit' und 'Zwei Leben und ein Tag'." In *Anna Mitgutsch*, edited by Kurt Bartsch and Günther A. Höfler, 73–86. Graz: Droschl, 2009.

Strutz, Andrea. "Split Lives: Memories and Narratives of Austrian Jewish Refugees." In *New Perspectives on Austrians and World War II*, edited by Gunter Bischof, Fritz Plasser, and Barbara Stelzl-Marx, 182–99. New Brunswick, NJ: Transaction Publishers, 2009.

Tauber, Reinhold. "Vom Wandern zwischen den Welten. Anna Mitgutschs neue Prosa ist das bisher reifste Buch der Autorin." *Oberösterreichische Nachrichten*, March 8, 2000.

Terrell, Peter, Veronika Schnorr, Wendy V. A. Morris, and Roland Breitsprecher. *Collins German Dictionary: German-English, English-German*. 4th ed. Glasgow: HarperCollins, 1999.

Teuchtmann, Kristin. "Haus der Kindheit." *Austrian Studies Newsletter* 12, no. 3 (2000): 14.

———. *Über die Faszination des Unsagbaren: Anna Mitgutsch, eine Monografie*. Frankfurt am Main, Oxford: Peter Lang, 2003.

———. "Zur Darstellbarkeit der Zeit: Erinnerung und Erfindung in Anna Mitgutschs 'Die Züchtigung' und 'Haus der Kindheit.'" *Modern Austrian Literature* 35, no. 1–2 (2002): 43–61.

Tisdall, Simon. "Victory for Van Der Bellen and the Left Is a Sigh of Relief for Europe." *Guardian*, December 4, 2016.

Tóth, Barbara, and Hubertus Czernin, eds. *1986: Das Jahr, das Österreich veränderte*. Vienna: Czernin, 2006.

———. "Vorwort der Herausgeber." In Tóth and Czernin, *1986*, 11–13.

Trenkler, Thomas. "Beckermann-Installation 'The Missing Image' in Wien abgebaut." *Kurier*, January 4, 2016.

———. "Der Fall 'Goldene Adele,' tendenziös erzählt." *Kurier*, June 2, 2015.

Uhl, Heidemarie. "Denkmäler als Symbole des Geschichtsbewußtseins in der Zweiten Republik." In *Grenzenloses Österreich. Dokumentation 5*, 109–28. Vienna: Bundesministerium für Wissenschaft und Verkehr, 1997.

———. "The Politics of Memory: Austria's Perception of the Second World War and the National Socialist Period." In *Austrian Historical Memory and National Identity*, edited by Anton Pelinka and Günter Bischof, 64–94. New Brunswick, NJ: Transaction Publishers, 1997.

———. "Renaissance des Denkmals in der Postmoderne: Kunst als Medium der neuen Erinnerungskultur." In *Denk!mal Zukunft: Der Umgang mit historischem Kulturgut im Spannungsfeld von Gesellschaft, Forschung und Praxis*, edited by Eva Klein, Rosemarie Schiestl, and Margit Stadlober, 119–26. Graz: Leykam, 2012.

———. "Die Wiederentdeckung der Orte." In *Architektur: Vergessen; Jüdische Architekten in Graz*, edited by Antje Senarclens de Grancy and Hudrun Zettelbauer, 49–54. Vienna: Böhlau, 2011.

Vloeberghs, Katrien. "Architektur der Unbehaustheit in Anna Mitgutschs Roman *Haus der Kindheit*." In *Anna Mitgutsch*, edited by Kurt Bartsch and Günther A. Höfler, 105–23. Graz: Droschl, 2009.

Vogel, Juliane. "Drama in Austria, 1945–2000." In *A History of Austrian Literature 1918–2000*, edited by Katrin Kohl and Ritchie Robertson, 201–22. Rochester, NY: Camden House, 2006.

Wantoch, Erika. "'Seit Waldheim weiß ich, wo die Grenzen sind': Erika Wantoch sprach mit der Filmautorin Ruth Beckermann." *profil* 17, no. 14 (April 6, 1987): 62–63.

Wieler, Jossi. "Hinter den Sprachmasken." Interview by Christine Diller. November 26, 2008. http://www.merkur.de/kultur/hinter-sprach-masken-22478.html.

Wiener Digital Manufaktur, "Jewish Vienna: Between the Museums," Google Play, Vers. 2.1.0 (2015). Accessed August 17, 2016. https://play.google.com/store/apps/details?id=at.jmw.betweenthemuseums.

Winestock, Geoff. "EU Countries Drop Sanctions against Austria after Report." *Wall Street Journal*, September 13, 2000.

Wörgötter, Bettina. "Ein erschütterndes Dokument gegen das Verdrängen." *Tiroler Tageszeitung*, March 23, 1995.

Wurmitzer, Michael. "Haus der Geschichte: Vorstudie präsentiert, Eröffnung doch erst 2019." *Der Standard*, May 4, 2016.

Yates, Frances A. *The Art of Memory*. London: Routledge and K. Paul, 1966.

Young, James E. *The Texture of Memory: Holocaust Memorials and Meaning in Europe, Israel, and America*. New Haven, CT: Yale University Press, 1993.

Zöchling, Christa. "Als Österreich erwachsen wurde." *profil* 47, no. 12 (March 21, 2016): 18–25.

———. "Der gewisse Jargon." In Tóth and Czernin, *1986*, 165–76.

Zweig, Stefan. *Die Welt von Gestern: Erinnerungen eines Europäers*. Frankfurt am Main: Fischer, 2001.

Index

Adorno, Theodor W., 17–18
Aichholzer, Josef, 26, 27, 28, 31
Alam, Djavad, 47
Altmann, Maria, 8
Andraschek, Iris, 23, 101, 129–33
Anschluss, 7, 11, 14, 17, 19, 22, 26, 27, 30, 32, 39–40, 91–92, 94, 95, 98, 99, 109, 110, 113, 115, 118, 124, 128, 140
Anshin, Simon, 65, 68, 70
anti-Semitism, 5, 7, 19, 26, 29, 30, 39–41, 46–47, 69, 81–82, 86, 87, 91, 93, 98, 108, 118, 124, 136, 139
archaeology, 132
archival material, use of, 27–28, 66, 85, 91, 101, 125
archival practice, 114–16
Arendt, Hannah, 76
Art, David, 91
art installations, 113, 120, 124–29, 136, 137, 138, 139; fictional depiction of, 91–93
art restitution, 8, 50
Aryanization, 8, 105, 109, 113, 115, 135
Assmann, Aleida, 15–16, 91, 139
Auböck, Maria, 130
Aufderheide, Patricia, 65–66
Augé, Marc, 131
Austrian Freedom Party, 1, 2, 5, 6, 7, 10–15, 33, 46, 50, 69, 86, 94, 127–28, 135, 136
Austrian Green Party, 1
Austrian People's Party, 1, 2, 3, 7, 10–13, 46, 81, 82

Bachmann, Ingeborg, 36, 63

Baker, Frederick, 12, 13
Barthes, Roland, 29, 38
Batthyány, Margit, 63, 64, 71, 76, 77
Batthyany, Sacha, 64
Beckermann, Ruth, 5, 6, 9–10, 19, 21, 22, 23, 25–48, 86, 91–94, 99, 101, 124–29, 133, 135, 136–37, 138–39
Beckermann, Ruth, works by: *Arena besetzt*, 33; *Auf amol a Streik*, 33; *Ein flüchtiger Zug nach dem Orient*, 25, 33; *Der Hammer steht auf der Wies'n da draussen*, 33; *Homemad(e)*, 6, 22, 25–26, 42, 43–48; *Jenseits des Krieges*, 9–10; *Die Mazzesinsel*, 28–29; *The Missing Image*, 101, 124–29, 133, 137, 138–39; *Nach Jerusalem*, 25, 26; *Die papierene Brücke*, 6, 19, 22, 25–26, 32, 34–43, 44–45, 47–48, 86, 99, 135, 137, 138; *Those Who Go Those Who Stay*, 33; *Unzugehörig*, 32, 35, 39–40, 42, 46, 91–92, 124; *Wien retour*, 22, 25–34, 35, 43, 44, 45, 47–48, 135, 137; *Zorros Bar Mizwa*, 25
Beilein, Matthias, 20–21
belatedness, 3, 16–17, 36, 54, 79, 82, 87
Beller, Steven, 13, 30, 81–82
Ben David-Hindler, Elisabeth, 108–10, 117, 133
Bernhard, Thomas, 68, 73, 83
Bismarck, Otto von, 7
Bloch-Bauer, Adele, 8
Bolt, Catrin, 23, 101, 117–23, 133, 139
Böttger, Rudolf, 102, 104–5

Boym, Svetlana, 19, 26, 28, 34, 51, 52–53, 55, 56, 58, 59, 60, 136
Breitenfellner, Kirstin, 50
Breitner, Hugo, 30
Bukovina, 34, 36, 37, 39–40, 135
Buñuel, Luis, 66, 71
Bunzl, Matti, 80
Bushell, Anthony, 50

Charim, Isolde, 12
Christandl, Jürg, 127
Cohn, Irving, 28
Cold War, 10, 70
commemoration, 8, 23, 92, 95, 96–98, 101, 109–10, 117, 122, 129–30, 132–34, 136–38, 140–41; commemorative years, 98, 140
Communism, 27, 80, 84, 118
Communist Party of Austria, 27
complicity, 7–8, 16, 24, 67, 93, 96, 98, 108, 124, 126
confronting the past, 1–24, 41, 45, 50, 53–54, 60, 65, 69–70, 73, 75, 77–83, 86–87, 89–90, 95, 124, 128–29, 135–42
contextualization of existing monuments, 23, 99, 102–8, 124–29, 133
countermonument, 100–101, 116, 131, 133
countryside, depiction of, 50, 63–64, 69–70, 78, 83
Crepaz, Alfred, 105–6
crowd funding, 111, 133
culpability, 66, 73
Curtis, Simon, 8
Czernin, Hubertus, 4, 5, 81, 87
Czernowitz (Chernivtsi), 36, 38–39, 40, 87

de Waal, Edmund, 113
Deix, Manfred, 4
Demnig, Gunter, 109
demonstrations, 4, 6, 10–13, 27, 30, 48, 86
Dichand, Hans, 87
disruption, 110, 116, 122–23, 126; of space, 100, 122–23, 131, 133

disturbance, 4, 23, 58, 67, 79, 91, 94–95, 96, 103–4, 122, 131, 140; of the past, 67, 79, 91, 94–95, 140
Doderer, Heimito von, 83
Doft, Adolf, 42–45, 47
Donnerstagsdemonstrationen, 6, 11–13
drama, 13–15, 20, 23, 51, 64–65, 70–78, 83, 88, 136, 138
Dubois, Pierre-Max, 28, 44
Dürer, Albrecht, 37

Eichmann, Adolf, 3, 113
Eliot, T. S., 72, 74
Enzensberger, Hans Magnus, 71
Erne, Eduard, 23, 64–70, 72, 77, 136, 137, 138
Erne, Eduard, works by: *Totschweigen*, 23, 63–70, 72, 74–75, 77–78, 136, 137–38
Euripides, 72, 76
Evans, Katherine Elizabeth, 50
expropriation of property, 8, 49, 51, 53, 55, 105, 109, 113, 115, 135

Faulkner, William, 16
fictional reinscription, 23, 79, 90, 95, 136, 138
Fiddler, Allyson, 13, 74, 76
Finlay, Ian Hamilton, 140
First World War, 36, 140
Fischer, Heinz, 2, 17
Franz Joseph I, Emperor, 37–38, 39
Freud, Sigmund, 16–17, 18, 19, 25, 38, 42, 56, 87
Frostig, Karen, 1, 23, 101, 110–17, 120, 132–33, 136

Gansterer, Nikolaus, 114, 117
Gauss, Karl-Markus, 49–50
Gedye, G. E. R., 92
genre, 23, 36, 41, 50, 64–65, 68, 70, 72, 73, 77–78, 83, 138
Germany, 7, 9, 15–16, 17–18, 20, 71, 75–76, 82, 91, 92, 94, 95, 100, 101, 120, 124
Gerstl, Elfriede, 43
Gestapo, 43, 64, 66, 69, 110, 112, 113; in Vienna, 43, 112, 113

Getreider, Arno, 118
Göschl, Ernst, 44
Graff, Michael, 82
Grissemann, Christoph, 14–15
Gropper, Herbert, 37
Guenther, Christina, 25–26, 27, 33, 35
guilt, 50, 73; survivor's guilt, 45

Habsburg Empire, 10, 19–20, 28, 29, 31, 36, 38, 39, 40, 140
Habsburg nostalgia, 19–20, 38–40
Haider, Jörg, 5, 7, 10–14, 21, 46, 50, 69, 86, 94, 136
Heinrich, Margareta, 23, 64–70, 72, 77, 136, 137, 138
Heinrich, Margareta, works by: *Totschweigen*, 23, 63–70, 72, 74–75, 77–78, 136, 137–38
Heller, André, 126
Helmer, Oskar, 32
Herrnstadt, Georg, 28
Herzog, Hillary Hope, 21, 41, 44, 47
Hilberg, Raul, 77
Hirsch, Marianne, 18–19, 29, 35–36, 38, 52; postmemory, 18, 35–36, 50–52
history, 4–5, 8, 9, 10, 11–12, 15, 16, 20, 22, 24, 26, 27, 28, 30, 35, 36, 37, 38, 42–43, 45, 48, 50, 51, 54, 57, 59–60, 62, 64, 65, 69, 71, 73, 74, 75, 78, 79, 81, 85, 89, 91, 94, 95, 96, 98, 99, 102, 105, 108, 109, 110, 112, 113, 115, 123, 129, 131, 133, 138, 140; historical consciousness, 96, 97, 99, 127; historical development, 20, 81, 96; historical legacy, 22, 41, 70, 89, 102, 123, 135–37, 139, 141; historical significance, places of, 11, 34, 36, 43, 91, 98, 111–13, 118–23, 140, 141; relativizing of history, 9, 23, 74, 77, 136, 138
Hitler, Adolf, 3, 5, 11, 14, 15, 30, 39, 54, 64, 87, 88, 90, 94, 99, 105, 107, 108, 115, 130, 140
Hofer, Norbert, 1–2, 7, 13–15

Holocaust, 2, 7–8, 11, 15–16, 18, 21–27, 29, 31–32, 35, 37, 39, 41, 42, 43, 45, 47, 48, 49, 54, 55, 57, 63–64, 65, 66–70, 72–77, 79, 80, 82, 83, 85, 87, 91, 92, 93, 96, 97, 98, 99, 100–101, 108–34, 135, 136, 137, 138, 139; Holocaust memorials, 8, 92, 99, 100–101, 108–34
home, idea of, 8, 19, 22, 25, 28, 29, 31, 32, 34, 38, 39, 40, 41, 47, 49–62; homecoming, 19, 22, 49, 52, 56; homeliness, 38, 41, 46, 52, 56, 60; reconstruction of, 19, 49–62
Hood, Thomas, 135, 142
Hrdlicka, Alfred, 4, 83, 90, 91–93, 95, 97, 124, 125–26, 127, 128, 129, 132–33, 134, 139
Hundstorfer, Rudolf, 7
Hungary, 23, 39–40, 63, 64, 69, 70
Hutcheon, Linda, 19

identity, 15, 16, 17, 21, 22, 25, 27, 34, 35, 41, 42, 46, 47, 49, 51, 57, 82, 86, 105
inscription of memory, 16, 37, 52, 59, 120, 130
intertextuality, 13–15, 72
Iron Curtain, 10
Israel, 37, 40, 83, 87, 89, 100

Janke, Pia, 71
Jelinek, Elfriede, 12, 13–14, 20, 21, 23, 38, 64–65, 70–78, 126, 136, 138, 139
Jelinek, Elfriede, works by: "Das Kommen," 13–14; *Das Lebewohl*, 13; *Rechnitz (Der Würgeengel)*, 64–65, 70–78, 136, 138, 139
Jewish identity, 21, 25, 34, 35, 41–42, 46
Jews, 5, 8, 9, 21, 22, 23, 25, 26, 27, 28, 29, 30, 31, 32, 33, 34, 35, 37, 38, 39, 40, 41, 42, 45, 46, 47, 49, 53, 54, 57, 58, 59, 60, 61, 62, 63, 67, 68, 73, 80, 81, 82, 84, 86, 88, 91–93, 97, 99, 100, 105, 108–10,

Jews—*(cont'd)*
    111, 113, 118, 120, 122, 124–25, 126, 128, 132, 136, 137; and Austria, 19, 20, 21, 22, 25, 26, 27, 28, 29, 30, 31, 32, 33, 34, 35, 39–42, 45, 46, 47, 48, 54, 63–64, 69, 73, 80–81, 86, 88, 89, 90, 91–92, 97, 99, 108, 109, 110, 132, 136; and Central and Eastern Europe, 26, 29, 31, 34–39, 47, 63–64, 82, 137; and Vienna, 26–32, 35, 39–42, 43–48, 80, 91–93, 97, 98, 99, 105, 108–10, 111, 112–14, 115, 117, 118, 120, 122, 124–26, 132, 133, 136
Jiranek, Johanna, 66
Judt, Tony, 82
Jung, André, 75

Kaltenbrunner, Ernst, 3
Kárász, János, 130, 131
Kecht, Maria Regina, 52
Kent, Flor, 122
Kind, Friedrich, 72
Kindertransport, 120, 122
Khol, Andreas, 7
Klimt, Gustav, 8
Koch, Magnus, 98
Kovacs, Teresa, 63–64
Kristallnacht. See November pogroms
Kunst im öffentlichen Raum Wien, 97, 129, 130, 131, 133
Kuttenberg, Eva, 91

Lachs, Minna, 118, 119
Langbein, Hermann, 84
Lässer, Bruno, 50
Lehmann, Hans-Thies, 72
Leopoldi, Hermann, 28
Lichtermeer demonstration, 6, 10, 11
Lienbacher, Ulrike, 23, 101, 102–4, 107–8, 133
Lihotzky, Margarete, 118
Litchfield, David, 64, 72, 77
Litschauer, Maria Theresia, 23, 101, 102, 104–8, 133
Lobnig, Hubert, 23, 101, 129–33
Löhr, Alexander, 81

Lorenz, Dagmar, 6, 31, 41, 46, 81, 94
Löw, Franzi, 80
Löw, Paola, 29, 30
Lübbe, Hermann, 75
Lueger, Karl, 41, 47, 98, 99; Dr.-Karl-Lueger-Platz, 41, 47, 98; Dr.-Karl-Lueger-Ring, 98; memorial church, 99; statue on Dr.-Karl-Lueger-Platz, 41, 47, 98

Mailath-Pokorny, Andreas, 126
Manoschek, Walter, 5, 9, 63, 64, 87
Markovics, Karl, 126
Massey, Doreen, 21
Mayer, Norbert, 73
melancholy, 19, 22, 23, 24, 25–30, 34, 36–37, 39, 42–43, 44, 45, 47–48, 49, 51, 66, 135, 136
memorials, 8, 21, 23–24, 43, 86, 92–93, 96–134, 136, 137, 138–39, 140–42; decentralized memorials, 8, 23, 97, 102–23, 133; memorial artists, 22, 23, 24, 99, 101, 102–32, 137, 139, 140, 142; memorial days, 8, 98; and public engagement, 23–24, 110, 113–16, 137; and social media, 111, 137; war memorials, 96–97
memory, 8, 15–16, 18–19, 20, 23–24, 25, 27, 31, 35, 36, 38, 42, 43, 45, 48, 49, 50, 51, 52, 56, 57, 70, 71, 81, 85, 90, 91, 96–134, 136, 137, 138, 139–42
memory culture in Austria, 3–10, 15–16, 17–18, 20, 23–24, 32, 75–77, 96–134, 136, 138; criticism of, 32–33, 42, 46–47, 50, 53–54, 66–70, 73–78, 89–90, 91–95, 136, 138
memory culture in Germany, 9, 15–16, 17–18, 20, 75–76, 100, 101; criticism of, 75–76
Menasse, Eva, 139
Menasse, Robert, 21, 81
Merz, Carl, 14–15
Mirren, Helen, 8
Misik, Robert, 11

Mitgutsch, Anna, 8, 19, 22, 49–62, 135, 136, 138
Mitgutsch, Anna, works by: *Abschied von Jerusalem*, 49; *Haus der Kindheit*, 8, 22, 49–62, 135, 136, 138; *In fremden Städten*, 49
Mitterlehner, Reinhold, 2
museums, 4, 8, 42, 98, 99, 101, 112–13, 115, 117, 125, 133, 137
music, 28, 44, 66, 70, 125, 137

Nabokov, Vladimir, 49
National Socialism, 3–10, 14–16, 17–18, 29, 30, 31, 39–40, 48, 49, 50, 53, 63–64, 74, 76–77, 80, 81–82, 84, 85, 86, 87, 88, 92, 93, 94, 95, 96, 97, 99, 100, 102, 104, 105–6, 107, 108, 110, 111, 114, 115, 116, 117, 118, 122, 123, 124, 126, 133, 135, 137, 139, 140, 141, 142; legacy of, 3–10, 11–12, 14–19, 21–24, 29, 48, 49, 50, 52, 53, 54, 63–78, 79, 80, 81, 82, 83, 93, 94, 95, 99, 100–101, 102–34, 135–42
Neumüller, Magdalena, 69
Neuwirth, Olga, 125
New York, 49, 52, 55, 56, 61, 62, 83, 131
Nichols, Bill, 65
Nicolai, Olaf, 140–42
Nietzsche, Friedrich, 72
Niven, Bill, 100, 101, 108, 112, 113, 116, 123, 133
Nora, Pierre, 91
nostalgia, 19–20, 22–23, 24, 25, 26, 27, 28, 29, 34, 38, 39, 40, 48, 49–60, 136
November pogroms, 29, 114, 126, 129, 130, 131, 132
Novotny, Franz, 46, 47

Omasta, Michael, 65
Österreichischer Rundfunk (ORF), 14, 99
origins, search for, 19, 22, 26, 38, 47, 49, 51, 52, 57, 60, 61, 62
Orth, Elisabeth, 126

Osthoff, Simone, 116

Pärt, Arvo, 42, 44
performance art, 110, 113–14, 117
Pirker, Peter, 97
Podezin, Franz, 64, 66, 69, 77
Ponger, Lisl, 46, 47
Ponger, Peter, 66
postdramatic theater, 65, 72
Posthofen, Renate, 30
psychoanalysis, 17, 18, 45

Qualtinger, Helmut, 14–15

Rabinovici, Doron, 11–12, 16, 21, 43, 45, 81, 96, 126, 133
Rabinowich, Julya, 139
Rathkolb, Oliver, 98, 107
Rechnitz massacre, 23, 63–78, 136, 137
reclamation of property, 22, 49, 51–57, 110
Red Army, 39, 63, 71
Red Vienna, 26, 30, 34, 105
Reisch, Walter, 28
Reiter, Andrea, 21, 37, 38, 81
remembrance, 1, 3, 15, 17–18, 20, 24, 32, 34, 36, 39, 45, 48, 50, 60, 73, 76, 77, 90, 93, 95, 96, 98, 100, 101, 102, 108, 109, 110, 111, 112, 113, 115, 117, 123, 129, 130, 133, 134, 136, 138
repression, 16–17, 23, 24, 32, 45, 63, 64, 65, 67–68, 70, 73–75, 77, 78, 82, 85, 87, 89, 91, 138
Republikanischer Club, 3–4, 81, 90, 128
restitution, 8–9, 32, 50, 53, 135, 138
roman-à-clef, 83
Romania, 34–38, 39–40, 42, 44, 47–48, 137
Rosenfeld, Sidney, 109
Russia, 71, 81
Rüter, Christiaan, 63

Salomonowitz, Anja, 139
Sandorffy, Isidor, 65, 67, 70
Scharang, Elisabeth, 139

Scheit, Gerhard, 71
Scheucher, Maria, 66
Schiele, Egon, 50
Schindel, Robert, 5, 6, 21, 23, 79–96, 124, 136, 138
Schindel, Robert, works by: *Gebürtig* (film), 79, 80–81; *Gebürtig* (novel), 6, 79, 80–81, 86, 87; *Der Kalte*, 6, 23, 79–95, 124, 136, 138
Schmidt-Rahmer, Hermann, 76
Schnitzler, Arthur, 42
Schoenberg, Arnold, 42
Schuh, Franz, 43, 47
Schulz, Julia, 23, 101, 108–9, 112, 117, 133, 139
Schüssel, Wolfgang, 11, 12, 13
Schüttelkopf, Elke, 70
sculpture, 91, 104, 105, 122, 123, 124, 128, 137
Second World War, 3–4, 5–6, 8, 9–10, 15–16, 18, 28, 31, 33, 35, 37, 39–40, 46, 54, 63–64, 69, 73, 79, 81–82, 83, 85, 86, 87, 88, 89, 91, 92, 93, 94, 97, 98, 136, 137, 140
Segal, Jérôme, 111
Segall, Senta, 45, 46
self-exculpation, strategies of, 9, 23, 65, 66–67, 73–74, 77–78
shadow, 15–16, 135, 139, 142; shadow of the past, 7, 15–16, 73, 101, 135–42
Shafi, Monika, 52, 56
silence, 23, 32, 46, 48, 53, 54, 63, 64, 90, 135, 136, 137, 142; silencing the past, 9, 23, 59, 63–78, 136, 137, 142
Silver, Frank, 28
Simonides of Ceos, 123
Sinowatz, Fred, 4, 89
Social Democratic Party of Austria, 1, 7, 10, 13, 29, 30, 105
SORA Institute for Social Research and Consulting, 1, 20
Soviet Union, 9, 36, 38, 63
Sperber, Manès, 34
Spitzer, Leo, 36
Stampf, Günter, 72

Steine der Erinnerung, 101, 108, 109–10, 117, 123, 133
Stermann, Dirk, 14, 15
Strache, Heinz-Christian, 13, 127
street names, renaming of, 98–99, 102
Switzerland, 71, 120

Tausig, Otto, 120, 121
Teuchtmann, Kristin, 50
Thessaloniki, 4, 82, 89
topography, 8, 21, 25, 27–48, 50–51, 57–59, 67–70, 83, 86, 90–93, 95, 96–134, 138–39, 140–42
Tóth, Barbara, 4
trauma, 15–17, 18, 24, 39, 41, 45, 48, 87, 108, 114, 122, 137, 138, 139
Turrini, Peter, 33

Uhl, Heidemarie, 8, 92, 96–97, 107, 116
uncanny, 38, 56, 142
unhomeliness, 38, 41, 47, 56–57, 58
United States, 37, 49, 52, 53, 57, 82, 110, 115

Van der Bellen, Alexander, 1–2
Vertlib, Vladimir, 139
victim myth, Austria, 5–6, 16, 20, 23, 30, 54, 82, 88–89, 93, 95, 109, 126, 137
Vienna, 1, 4, 6, 8, 9–10, 11–13, 14, 19–20, 21, 22, 23, 25, 26–32, 34, 35, 39–42, 43–48, 71, 80, 81, 83, 84–86, 88, 89, 90–94, 96–134, 135, 136, 138, 139, 140–42; Albertinaplatz, 91, 126; Austrian National Library, 115–16, 141–42; Austrian Parliament, 7, 30, 90, 113; Ballhausplatz, 140–42; Burgtheater, 83, 88, 90; Danube Canal, 44, 90, 118; Gestapo headquarters (historical), 43, 112, 113; *Haus der Geschichte*, 99, 140; Heldenplatz, 10, 11–12, 98, 99, 140, 141–42; Hermann-Gmeiner-Park, 118, 119, 122; Hofburg, 115, 141–42; Jewish Museum, 8, 98, 112–13, 115, 117; Judenplatz,

8, 92, 97, 110; Marc-Aurel Strasse, 35, 43–47; Marpe Lanefesh Memorial, 114; Nordbahnhof, 28, 31; Palace of Justice, 30; Palais Ephrussi (historical), 113; Palais Rothschild (historical), 113; Prater, 27, 28, 29, 118, 120; Sanatorium Fürth (historical), 113; Stephansplatz, 40–41, 47, 86; University of Vienna, 30–31, 97, 98, 99, 113, 114; Vienna City Council, 91, 97–98, 126; Vienna City Hall, 14; Vienna Regional Court, 113, 114; Vienna State Opera, 91, 113, 118, 120, 123; Westbahnhof, 118, 120, 121, 122; Wien Museum, 4; Wiener Musikverein, 99
visual art, 8, 18, 21, 22, 23–24, 42, 50, 91–94, 96–134, 136, 137, 138–42
Vogel, Juliane, 73
von Schönerer, Georg, 7
Vranitzky, Franz, 7

Waldheim, Kurt, 3–6, 11, 12, 19, 21, 33, 34, 40–41, 42, 46, 79, 81–82, 83, 86, 88, 89, 90, 93, 94, 138, 140; literary treatment of, 23, 79–95, 136, 138; and Waldheim affair, 3–7, 9, 10, 11, 12, 17, 19, 21, 22, 23, 33, 41, 42, 46, 48, 54, 79, 80–83, 84, 86, 87, 89, 90, 94–95, 96, 135, 136, 137, 138
war generation, Austria, 6, 86, 87, 88, 137
Weber, Carl Maria von, 72
Wehrmacht, 4, 5, 9–10, 33, 81–82, 87, 93, 97, 98, 124, 140–41; Wehrmacht deserters, 140–41; *Wehrmachtsausstellung*, 9–10
West, Franz, 25, 26–34, 47, 48, 137
Whiteread, Rachel, 8, 92, 97, 110
Wieler, Jossi, 70–71, 72, 73
Wiesenthal, Simon, 84
World War. *See* First World War; Second World War
Wouk, Herman, 34

Yalon, Ossi, 114
Young, James E., 91, 100, 110, 116, 130, 131; and countermonument, 100–101, 116, 131, 133

Zöchling, Christa, 6
Zweig, Stefan, 83

www.ingramcontent.com/pod-product-compliance
Lightning Source LLC
Chambersburg PA
CBHW070805230426
43665CB00017B/2493